Crisis Cycle

Crisis Cycle

CHALLENGES, EVOLUTION, AND FUTURE OF THE EURO

JOHN H. COCHRANE

LUIS GARICANO

KLAUS MASUCH

PRINCETON UNIVERSITY PRESS

PRINCETON & OXFORD

Published by Princeton University Press
41 William Street, Princeton, New Jersey 08540
99 Banbury Road, Oxford OX2 6JX

press.princeton.edu

GPSR Authorized Representative: Easy Access System Europe - Mustamäe tee 50, 10621 Tallinn, Estonia, gpsr.requests@easproject.com

All Rights Reserved

Library of Congress Cataloging-in-Publication Data

Names: Cochrane, John H. (John Howland), 1957– author. | Garicano, Luis, 1967– author. | Masuch, Klaus, 1959– author.
Title: Crisis cycle : challenges, evolution, and future of the Euro / John H. Cochrane, Luis Garicano, and Klaus Masuch.
Description: Princeton, New Jersey : Princeton University Press, 2025. | Includes bibliographical references and index.
Identifiers: LCCN 2024047849 (print) | LCCN 2024047850 (ebook) | ISBN 9780691271606 (cloth) | ISBN 9780691271613 (ebook)
Subjects: LCSH: Euro. | Europe—Economic conditions–1945– | Financial crises—Europe. | BISAC: BUSINESS & ECONOMICS / Money & Monetary Policy | POLITICAL SCIENCE / Public Policy / Economic Policy
Classification: LCC HG925 .C57 2025 (print) | LCC HG925 (ebook) | DDC 332.4/94—dc23/eng/20250206
LC record available at https://lccn.loc.gov/2024047849
LC ebook record available at https://lccn.loc.gov/2024047850

British Library Cataloging-in-Publication Data is available

Editorial: Joe Jackson, Rebecca Binnie
Production Editorial: Elizabeth Byrd
Jacket: Karl Spurzem
Production: Danielle Amatucci
Publicity: James Schneider (US), Kate Farquhar-Thomson (UK)

Copyeditor: Susan McClung

This book has been composed in Arno Pro

Printed in the United States of America

10 9 8 7 6 5 4 3 2 1

Whatever it takes.

—Mario Draghi, president of the
European Central Bank, 2011–2019

Because it is France.

—Jean-Claude Juncker, president of the
European Commission, 2014–2019

We are not here to close spreads.

—Christine Lagarde, president of the
European Central Bank, 2019–present

CONTENTS

PREFACE

In this book, we outline how monetary, fiscal, and financial policies interact; we describe how the euro was set up to control those interactions; we tell the story of how European policies and institutions evolved under the pressure of four crises; we analyze the fragility of the current moment; and we propose ways to fix the architecture of the euro.

The three of us come to this project with very different perspectives and experiences. Cochrane is a senior fellow of the Hoover Institution at Stanford and was previously a professor at the University of Chicago. He has spent his career studying monetary policy, inflation, and financial markets. He has recently published a book on the interaction between fiscal and monetary policy (Cochrane, 2023b). The analysis of the present book does not require that still-contentious fiscal theory of the price level, however. Here, we only use the basic idea that large deficits without credible plans for debt repayment threaten inflation or default, especially by tempting the central bank to print money to cover fiscal shortfalls. That idea holds in practically all theories of inflation and monetary policy. The unique setup of the euro, with a common currency, member states with independent fiscal policies, and limited centralized powers, requires interesting extensions of this standard idea. Although he is from the United States, Cochrane is the son of Eric W. Cochrane, professor of Italian history, and Lydia G. Cochrane, an academic translator and French teacher. He lived in Italy for a few years in his youth and remains an admirer of the European project. Cochrane has also previously commented on European monetary and financial affairs.[1]

Garicano has been a full professor at the University of Chicago, IE Business School, and the London School of Economics, where he has now returned. He participated in two expert groups of economists on the euro crisis, Euronomics[2] in 2011 and the INET Council on the Eurocrisis[3] in 2012. He has written extensively on eurozone crises and the institutional design of the euro. Garicano served as a member of the European Parliament from 2019 to 2022, where he was the vice president of the centrist Renew Europe parliamentary grouping in charge of economic affairs and worked as a coordinator on the Economic and Monetary Affairs Committee. He also led the parliamentary group's legislative contribution on the fiscal, financial, and political dilemmas that the Economic and Monetary Union (EMU) faced during the COVID-19 pandemic and participated as shadow rapporteur on the legislation implementing the Recovery and Resilience Facility, the Eurobond-financed program launched by the European Union (EU).

Masuch has worked at the European Central Bank (ECB) from the start of the euro, first as head of the Monetary Policy Strategy Division from 2000 to 2006, then as head of the EU Countries Division from 2007 to 2013, and as principal adviser to the Director General Economics since 2014. Before that he worked at the Deutsche Bundesbank (from 1991 to 1994) and the European Monetary Institute (from 1994 to 1998). During the sovereign debt crisis he coordinated at the staff level the ECB's position on the adjustment programs and country missions. He headed the bank's mission teams that carried out technical analyses and held discussions with the authorities of Greece (from 2010 to 2015) and Ireland (from 2010 to 2012), acting in liaison with the European Commission and in cooperation with the International Monetary Fund (IMF) mission. More recently, he has been working on EU country surveillance and convergence, on structural policies, and on monetary-fiscal interactions in the euro area. Since 2025 he is retired from the ECB. Having worked closely with many ECB and national central bank (NCB) colleagues and decision-makers during twenty-six years, Masuch is grateful for their friendship and trust, and he admires their competence, hard work, and dedication to the ECB's mandate and Europe as a whole.

We share a view that the euro and the EU are wonderful institutions. Our book is dedicated to preserving, maintaining, and improving them. We aim to help the ongoing process of European and euro-area institutional reform.

Our analysis is primarily economic. We are not legal experts. Although we briefly touch on legal issues, our comments should not be viewed as making legal judgments or critiquing the legal facets of decisions by those making policy. We do not claim that the ECB or any EU institutions violated any law or treaty.

We also touch only lightly on many interesting questions surrounding the euro and the EU. We do not say much about political economy. We say little about underlying real economic forces, especially those forces driving the central problem of growth stagnation. We do not focus on personalities and personal decisions. And we do not explore the influence of differing cultural and legal traditions.

Our purpose is not to blame people or institutions, in particular the ECB. They faced situations unimagined at the creation of the euro and an incomplete structure of the monetary union to deal with these situations. For example, in the sovereign debt crisis, the ECB could not wait for member states to legislate and implement an alternative fiscal institution to provide temporary support. Their interventions were reasonable in the heat of crises. In our view, the public servants and experts who prepared and took these decisions were honest, creative, skillful, and well-intentioned. And in the end, the crises were surmounted and the euro survived. We do not claim that we could have managed the crises better overall.

Our main theme is not actions taken in crises, but that member states and EU institutions did not clean up between crises. They did not reestablish a sustainable framework for future monetary-fiscal coordination that would unburden the ECB. They did not mitigate unwelcome incentives to ameliorate the next crisis and make further interventions less likely. These too are understandable failings, as political momentum for difficult reforms is always lacking. But the consequent problems have now built up, such that the ad hoc system that emerged from crisis interventions is in danger of a serious and chaotic failure. Now is the time to get over inertia. The EU and its member states should start a serious process of institutional reform. We aim to contribute to such a discussion.

Our perspective is, we think, underrepresented in the current economic discourse. Most of the attention goes to the immediate effects of monetary and fiscal interventions: Should the ECB raise or lower interest rates, should it buy or sell sovereign bonds, and so forth. Fewer analyses scrutinize the longer-term implications of these and other actions: how they set up precedents, create expectations for what will happen in the future, and mold behavior; and how actions unwittingly create institutions. We focus on the rules of the game and how those rules might be improved, not on specific decisions. And we focus on the often-forgotten interaction of monetary, fiscal, and financial-stability policies, where most analysis looks at each policy in isolation.

We apply modern dynamic economic theory to the historical events and institutions of the euro. Hopefully, we have explained that theory well enough in words. There are a few equations in the text, but they are present only to clarify points for technically minded, critical readers. General readers can skip the equations without detriment to their understanding.

We are grateful for many insightful discussions and comments from colleagues, in particular Oscar Arce, Pablo Balsinde, Marco Basetto, Roel Beetsma, Nicholai Benalal, Francesco Bianchi, Martin Bijsterbosch, Ulrich Bindseil, Johannes Brumm, Markus Brunnermeier, Pablo de Ramón-Laca, Cristina Checherita-Westphal, Benoît Cœuré, Xavier Debrun, Ettore Dorrucci, John Fell, Jesús Fernández-Villaverde, Mark Flanagan, Jordi Galí, Vitor Gaspar, Giorgia Giovannetti, Rishi Goyal, Daniel Gros, Sebastian Grund, Felix Hammermann, Otmar Issing, Thomas B. Jorgensen, Jarmo Kontulainen, Christian Kroppenstedt, Luc Laeven, Wolfgang Lemke, David Lodge, Christiane Nickel, Atif Mian, Edward O'Brien, Ashoka Mody, João Nogueira Martins, Lucio Pench, Beatrice Pierluigi, Huw Pill, Jesús Saa-Requejo, Isabel Schnabel, Sebastian Schmidt, Martin Schmitz, Ralph Setzer, Chris Sims, Frank

Smets, Joao Sousa, Ludwig Straub, Rolf Strauch, Mateusz Szczurek, Poul Thomsen, Vilem Valenta, Delia Velculescu, Leo von Thadden, Jens Weidmann, and seminar participants at the Barcelona School of Economics Summer Forum, Harvard Business School, and the Hoover Institution at Stanford University.

This book solely reflects our own views. No part of it should be understood or quoted as the opinions of these or other colleagues, of our current or previous employers, or of other institutions with which we are or were affiliated.

1

Introduction and Overview

Monetary, financial, and fiscal policy are always intertwined. Printing money and spending it involves both fiscal and monetary policy. Raising interest rates to stem inflation raises interest costs on government debt. It is tempting to finance government deficits or to solve sovereign debt problems by printing money to buy debt or by holding down interest rates. Bailing out banks, or lending as a last resort, uses fiscal and monetary resources to address financial instability.

Intertwined monetary, fiscal, and financial policies can create incentive problems. Knowing that a monetary rescue is available ex post, governments have an incentive to borrow too much ex ante, and bond buyers have less incentive to prepare for sovereign default risk. The problem becomes larger, the financial system is less able to bear it, and the pressure for a bailout in the next crisis is greater. Monetary and fiscal institutions are built to control these incentives.

In this book, we tell the story of how the monetary-fiscal institutions of the euro were set up, how they evolved over time, and how the current situation can be improved. Here, we give a quick overview. The following chapters tell the story in detail.

1.1 A Founding Architecture

Controlling the incentives generated by fiscal and monetary policies is even more important for a currency union with multiple member states than it is for a unitary state. It is tempting enough for a single or federal

1

government such as that of the United States to monetize deficits and pressure the central bank to buy government bonds. When member states run separate fiscal policies under a common monetary policy, the incentive is greater for each state to borrow too much, relying on the central bank to address any problems, as the costs in form of higher taxes or inflation are spread to other member states.

The euro was set up with a clear-eyed understanding of monetary-fiscal interactions. The rules separating monetary and fiscal policy in the eurozone were clearer and more restrictive than those in the United States.

The euro was founded by the 1992 Maastricht Treaty as a monetary union without a fiscal union. Each country retained authority for taxing and spending and responsibility for repaying its own debt. The Treaty included a fiscal "no-bail-out" principle, stating that member states or the European Union (EU) would not be liable for the sovereign debt of other member states or to provide transfers to this effect. The Treaty established debt and deficit limits for member states to keep them from getting in trouble in the first place.

The Treaty created the European Central Bank (ECB) and gave it great independence, but within prescribed limits. The ECB's independence was designed to help it resist pressure to interfere in fiscal affairs, not to empower it to do so. The ECB's "primary objective" or mandate was price stability, not macroeconomic stabilization, financial stability, or support for government debt markets, although many other central banks have such mandates. For the period from 1999 through 2008, the ECB held a small balance sheet and did not buy government bonds, unlike many other central banks. The ECB did not buy sovereign or private bonds. The ECB created new money by lending it to banks against collateral and counting the loan as the asset corresponding to the monetary liability, rather than by purchasing sovereign debt. The ECB conducted monetary policy by setting short-term interest rates at which it borrowed from and lent to banks. Most ECB borrowing was overnight deposits by banks at the ECB. Most ECB lending to banks had one or two week maturity. The ECB accepted long-term interest rates as determined in corporate and sovereign markets.

As with all great institutional innovations, the founding framework left a few bits unfinished. A monetary union that promises price stability either needs fiscal union or it must allow sovereigns to default while staying in the monetary union, as companies do. While the latter possibility was implicitly clear from the no-bail-out principle, neither the Treaty nor subsequent secondary EU legislation created a mechanism for sovereign default and resolution or a crisis resolution body to help avoid sovereign default. The founding framework also took no regulatory or other measures to insulate banking and financial systems from sovereign default in order to avoid banks holding a lot of sovereign debt and thus failing in a sovereign default. The architects of the euro seemed to hope that debt and deficit rules would suffice to keep countries so far from default that one could avoid spelling out those impolite eventualities, and so the ECB and fiscal authorities would be spared bailout temptations. In the context of the early 1990s, when sovereign debt troubles of advanced countries seemed to be ancient history, given the political achievement of bringing so many disparate countries into a union, and perhaps due to fear that even talking about sovereign default would make a crisis more likely, these are understandable elisions.

1.2 Erosion in Successive Crises

In 2003, however, less than five years after the founding of the euro, Germany and France violated the deficit rules and blocked the prescribed sanctions. Although the near-term effect of this violation was small—these countries did not have debt crises or require ECB financing—swift violation of the rules by the two central countries of the EU was a blow to the credibility and effectiveness of the fiscal rules, and also, plausibly, of the rest of the architecture separating monetary and fiscal policy. If this promise could be broken, how holy were the other promises and restraints?

Limitations on ECB actions weakened with each subsequent crisis: the financial crisis of 2007–2009, the sovereign debt crisis of 2010–2012, its slow-growth, zero-bound aftermath, and the events of 2020–2023. The latter include the large fiscal and monetary response to the Covid pandemic, the Russian invasion of Ukraine and consequent energy market disruption, and the inflation of 2021–2023.

The process was not intentional. The ECB clearly was pushed hard before buying bonds and interfering in markets. But in the end, the Bank felt that huge crises were brewing, and it was the only game in town capable of addressing them.

In the wake of the financial and sovereign debt crises, the ECB made major changes to its procedures to allow for a more expansionary monetary policy. These measures were designed to, and did, increase reserves and bank borrowing from the ECB. But they had fiscal side effects.

First, the ECB allowed more generous use of bonds and bank assets as collateral for loans that the ECB made to banks. Such collateral included illiquid and nonmarketable assets, such as the bank's loans to other parties.

Second, the ECB moved to fixed-rate, full-allotment allocation of reserves: banks can now borrow all they want at a stated interest rate. Previously, the ECB limited how much it would lend at the stated rate. Now the quantity of reserves and the assets that the ECB holds in collateral are strongly affected by how much banks choose to borrow and what collateral they choose to post. Third, the ECB started to purchase covered bank bonds. Fourth, and most important, in May 2010 the ECB began to buy bonds of member states in fiscal trouble (i.e., Greece, Ireland, and Portugal). In summer 2011, the ECB began to purchase Italian and Spanish sovereign debt. The ECB exposed itself to default risk, which is consequently shared by all the member states and people of the euro area.

As sovereign debt trouble continued, the ECB believed that the trouble could spark a major financial and economic crisis, potentially including the exit of member states from the euro. The ECB viewed the member states and the EU as unable or unwilling to contain events, leaving the ECB as the only game in town when addressing any crisis. To contain the turmoil, President Mario Draghi in summer 2012 uttered the famous "whatever it takes" pledge.

This pledge was widely interpreted to mean that the ECB would buy as many troubled bonds as necessary to avoid redenomination or euro exit and default, or the higher yield spreads and financial instability associated with such risks. This announcement was operationalized via the Outright Monetary Transactions (OMT) program, which allowed sovereign debt purchases. Crucially, the ECB could only make such purchases if the member state had agreed to a policy program before purchases began, a requirement called "conditionality," and had secured fiscal support from member states.

As it turned out, the euro did not break up, and the financial system did not implode. "Whatever it takes" was, this time, so powerful that the ECB did not immediately have to buy any bonds. From mid-2012 to the end of 2014, the consolidated balance sheet of the Eurosystem actually declined from € 3.1 trillion to € 2.2 trillion, mainly due to reduced lending to banks.

Most European economies returned to a slow recovery from these two crises. Desiring monetary stimulus and worried about too-low inflation, the ECB lowered interest rates. The deposit rate hit zero in 2012 and eventually became negative starting in June 2014. In 2015 the ECB also started to buy sovereign debt from all member states in a process known as "quantitative easing" (QE). Whether these measures raised inflation persistently and brought it closer to the target is still debated. In the end, inflation mostly remained a bit below 2% until 2021, and the recovery remained slow.

There are no atheists in foxholes, and nobody worries about moral hazard in a panic, as the sayings go. But ex-post insurance, bailouts, and other crisis-rescue measures lead people and governments to take more risks, expecting such help again in the next downturn. Someone has to remove those incentives.

Most observers recognized that several original explicit and implicit rules and traditions limiting ECB action and separating monetary and fiscal affairs had been weakened, if not broken. Some thought that this was a fine expansion of the central bank's power to stop crises and to provide additional stimulus, but others worried that something needed to be done to make sure that the events did not repeat on a larger scale and to restore the separation of monetary and fiscal policy.

Consequently, during and after the sovereign debt crisis, the EU and euro-area countries made several important decisions to enhance the institutional setup. An intergovernmental fiscal compact aimed to reinforce fiscal discipline. The Greek sovereign debt restructuring strengthened the credibility of the no-bail-out principle and showed that haircuts and "bail-ins" are possible. The exemption of the ECB's Greek bond holdings from haircuts, so that the ECB took no losses, strengthened the commitment against monetary financing of sovereign debts. The European Stability Mechanism (ESM) established a euro-area crisis management institution, funded by member states. Political decisions were made to set up the single (bank) supervisory mechanism (SSM). The EU Council made strong promises to address the sovereign-bank nexus—the risk that sovereign debt problems could quickly endanger the financial system.

Against this background, the ECB may have expected that Outright Monetary Transactions were a mere bridge, buying time for member states to continue individual and joint institutional and structural reforms.

But over time the implementation of these new initiatives fell short. Important reforms such as common deposit insurance and limits on banks' sovereign exposures were put off to another day. New debt reduction rules failed to significantly bring down high debts, in particular in several large member states, in spite of several years (2014–2019) with positive real growth, low or negative real interest rates, falling unemployment, and a sharp decline in oil prices in 2014 that persisted until 2021. In most member states, building sufficient fiscal buffers and implementing microeconomic reforms to boost productivity growth were left for later. Member states did little to prepare for future crises, and they did almost nothing to unburden the ECB. No clear expressions of self- or externally imposed limits on ECB actions were implemented.

Like many other central banks, the ECB's bond buying and related interventions increased massively during the huge debt-financed fiscal transfers of the pandemic, followed by Russia's Ukraine invasion and the energy market disruptions of the early 2020s. Where President Draghi calmed the waters with words in 2012, by 2022 "whatever it takes" took more and more.

The consolidated balance sheet of the Eurosystem shows that these "securities held for monetary policy purposes," mainly government bonds, increased from €0.2 trillion in 2014 to €2.6 trillion by the end of 2019, in quantitative easing, and then doubled to almost €5 trillion by mid-2022, about one-third of euro-area gross domestic product (GDP). By the end of 2023, €4.7 trillion in securities were still held by the central bank. Many other governments and central banks followed similar policies. For example, the U.S. Federal Reserve held $8.5 trillion in securities by mid-2022 and still held $7.2 trillion at the end of 2023.

It would be lovely if we could have a few quiet years to sort things out. That is unlikely to be the case, however. Fiscal stresses are compounding. Government debts have expanded sharply due to Covid and energy-related spending and subsidy programs. Higher interest rates, due to either global economic forces, ECB inflation-fighting efforts, or rising credit spreads, can quickly increase the cost of carrying those debts. Member states want to spend more on climate policies. The Russian war on Ukraine necessitates higher defense spending, and then supporting and rebuilding Ukraine. If Russia partly succeeds in its military aggression, Europe will face even larger longer-term defense costs. And member states already face rising pension, health, and other social costs.

A recession or financial downturn would provoke additional fiscal deficits. A larger war in the Middle East, a further Russian invasion in Europe, or A Chinese invasion or blockade of Taiwan would precipitate large economic and financial turmoil, and consequent fiscal stresses for EU member states. And, with government spending in many countries already at roughly half of their national income or higher, with declining and aging populations, there is no easy large source of long-run tax revenue to fund these initiatives or to back issuance of a lot more debt.

Bailouts have limits. Even the ECB's ability to put out fires without substantial inflation or direct fiscal support from member states is limited. Even member states' fiscal capacity is limited. If debts build up, if nobody prepares for losses and everybody counts on a bailout, eventually a crisis will come that the ECB and European governments are unable to contain. Such a crisis would be monumental.

Credible limits on central banks' ability to mop up after the fact are thus important so governments and financial institutions limit risks and structure a financial system that can bear risks. But accepting such limits is difficult. If the limits are credible enough so people do not expect central bank intervention, they also actually limit the central bank from taking actions that it might wish to take ex post.

Monetary and fiscal policy are also wisely separate for important reasons of political economy. Transfers of wealth from one person to another are highly politically sensitive, and usually the province of elected officials. Standard monetary policy of setting short-term interest rates does have fiscal and distributional consequences, of course. Interest rates affect the fortunes of creditors versus debtors, long-versus short-term bondholders, savers versus borrowers, and taxpayers versus bondholders. But these transfers are politically digestible to some extent as unintended consequences of politically disinterested actions. (But not always—high interest rates generated protests at the Federal Reserve in the 1970s and 1980s.) On the other hand, large-scale asset purchases aimed either at making borrowing easier or at raising bond prices, loans to banks at favorable conditions, and sovereign bailouts more directly and visibly transfer wealth among winners, losers, and taxpayers.

Should the ECB support country X's debt? If so, why not country Y's? Which spreads are justified by "fundamentals," and thus not worthy of compression, and which result from illiquidity, behavioral bias, or "dysfunctional" or "fragmented" markets, and hence get ECB support? Successful sovereign-debt interventions often require governments to launch politically difficult adjustment programs, including spending cuts, taxes, microeconomic reforms, and debt restructuring, in which a lot of people suffer.

Can an independent, apolitical organization stay independent and apolitical while involved in such deeply political decisions, hurting or benefiting the pocketbooks of so many people and powerful constituencies? Can the central bank of a monetary union stay independent if it passes judgment on the quality and credibility of a sovereign country's economic policies and of its elected political bodies, and based on this judgment, decides whether to rescue bondholders, and likely the incumbent government, with public money?

The ECB in 2015 initially structured its quantitative easing purchase programs to be neutral across countries for just this reason. But as more and more of the ECB's bond buying, lending, and other interventions move toward fiscal, economic, and transfer policies that benefit or hurt countries differentially, its independence will become fragile.

Independence is not an absolute virtue. It serves practical purposes. Governments set up independent central banks to help the government to pre-commit against using monetary policy and central bank powers for short-term political purposes, and to avoid political battles over using central bank powers for such purposes. Losing independence loses this valuable pre-commitment.

The heart of our economic analysis describes this erosion of institutional limits as a result of crisis interventions. We recommend reforms to restore a separation between monetary, fiscal, and financial policies; control disincentives; and lead to a stable and vital euro for the foreseeable future—one that can weather the shocks that are sure to hit.

A beautiful ship was constructed. Out at sea, it ran into severe storms. Its captain and crew patched the holes as best they could. Now, though, it is time to return to dry dock and fix the ship properly.

1.3 Reform

How should the monetary-fiscal arrangements of the euro be reformed to control the perverse incentives that have emerged from crisis-management expedients?

The original architects of the euro, while amazingly prescient, turned out to be too optimistic. They hoped that debt and deficit rules plus an independent ECB with a limited mandate would keep debt crises from ever occurring. They included limits on ECB intervention and the no-bail-out fiscal rule, but they did not include mechanisms for dealing with sovereign default. To avoid the ECB stepping in again and again, we must complete the structures for which they laid the foundations.

Governments, which are responsible for fiscal policy, not the ECB, must decide whether a country in fiscal trouble and its bondholders will receive support, which kind of support, and the conditions of such support. Governments must finance that support. Governments must assess the sustainability of a country's debts, impose any fiscal or economic policy conditionality of support, and decide when an orderly sovereign debt restructuring should be a precondition for such support.

Yes, orderly restructuring. In a monetary union without fiscal union, the holders of sovereign debt must occasionally bear risks. If that is unthinkable, we have a fiscal union in which taxpayers of the whole union guarantee member states' debt. Fiscal union is fiscal union, whether achieved directly or via the printing press, whether constructed thoughtfully, or whether patched together during a crisis.

Speed being of the essence in a crisis, institutions to make such decisions must be in place ahead of time, and be ready and able to act quickly. Making it up on the fly, a default of inaction, and a requirement for unanimous decisions by all governments will not work. Decisions made on the fly, rather than via well-constructed and limited institutions, also lead to crisis-inducing uncertainty and bad economic and political incentives. Intervention should be operationalized and financed via a European fiscal crisis-management institution, which may be a new EU institution or a substantially enhanced European Stability Mechanism (ESM). Approval or disapproval of interventions should at least require only a qualified majority, not unanimity.

Banks whose deposits and lending are concentrated in their own country and that hold large quantities of that country's sovereign debt, with deposits de facto insured by the same sovereign, which may also be expected to recapitalize the same banks in a crisis, are a recipe for sovereign problems to cause financial problems. The financial system then becomes a hostage to sovereign debt. This fear of financial meltdown invites ECB intervention or fiscal bailouts. European financial regulation must be reformed to remove this blatant fragility.

Sovereign debt in a monetary union without fiscal union cannot be risk free, yet it is still treated as such in banking regulation. Regulators must assign sovereign debt appropriate risk or concentration weights. Sovereign risk must be in the hands of investors and well-diversified financial institutions that can bear risk, but not necessarily banks. Banks that do hold significant domestic sovereign debt must hold higher capital buffers or be required to diversify their sovereign holdings.

Banks must be delinked from influence and protection by national governments. Banks must not be subject to conflicting national regulators, or to pressure from national authorities to buy that nation's bonds or subsidize its favorite industries. Banks should access a common European deposit insurance and a single European regulatory mechanism. Lender-of-last resort loans to specific banks with liquidity problem, such as Emergency Liquidity Assistance (ELA), should become a responsibility of the ECB. The ECB then also needs to be able to require recapitalization, in which banks issue new common equity to private investors or resolution by the Single Resolution Board (SRB). Banks must be able to compete and operate across the union, thereby isolating a country's economy financial system from its fiscal problems. Completing banking union as Europe has completed the single market in most other industries would be beneficial.

More generally, Europe suffers from financial disunion and fragmentation. If sovereign debt were held in well-diversified mutual funds, directly by people, and by long-term investors such as insurance companies and pension funds rather than by highly leveraged banks funded by deposits, that step alone would cure much financial fragility. With a strong European fiscal institution that can guide orderly restructuring where needed and provide fiscal transition help with conditionality, and with sovereign default no longer threatening financial meltdown, the ECB can stop buying sovereign bonds in crises. By doing so, the ECB will no longer decide whether to rescue bondholders of a country in trouble, it will no longer take on default and price risk, and it will have much less reason to manage bond market volatility. The ECB should then move on, first to purchasing only a diversified portfolio of debts and then to purchasing only European debt issued by or guaranteed by EU institutions, such as the European Commission, euro-area intergovernmental organizations, such as the ESM, or member states collectively. The Eurosystem balance sheet should no longer carry default risks of member states. If the ECB again purchases national debts in a deep crisis, that should only happen under the authority of the European fiscal crisis-management institution, which would indemnify the ECB in case of any losses, and the debt should quickly flow off the ECB balance sheet.

Outside a deep systemic banking crisis, the ECB should no longer provide loans to banks at favorable interests rate that imply subsidization of banks relative to market conditions. In particular, the ECB should no longer accept nonmarketable claims as collateral for its main refinancing operations and longer-term loans to banks. Doing so subsidizes the issuance of risky debts. Subsidization of banks and of bank lending, as well as recapitalization of banks with public funds, are government tasks.

The rather convoluted architecture of the Eurosystem, which retains many historical functions of national central banks, should also be reformed. National central banks, which can purchase and hold their nations' sovereign bonds, are a weak point. So are large Target2 balances and ECB loans at risk-free interest rates to and from national central banks. These loans can finance national balance of payment deficits in place of private cross-border capital flows.

Finally, the ECB alone should be in charge of money creation. National central banks may continue to implement monetary policy, but they should no longer be able to create or withdraw euros via "national, non-monetary tasks" such as purchasing or selling securities or foreign reserves.

Each element of these reforms supports the others, and each provides greater incentives to accomplish the others. Bank reform makes it easier to avoid sovereign debt intervention and to allow restructuring; less intervention makes it more urgent to reform banks; and so forth.

Thus, rather than set a trap where each reform must wait for the others, a virtuous feedback loop emerges in which each reform helps on its own and increases incentives to accomplish the others.

This set of reforms is consistent with the philosophy of a monetary union without fiscal union and with the ECB's treaty obligation to "act in accordance with the principle of an open market economy." It updates the original design to reflect the lesson that fiscal troubles can occur, and the union needs a plan and institutions to manage fiscal troubles.

Many observers advocate a more comprehensive fiscal and political union to complement and reform the monetary union. This is, of course, a much larger structural and political change. We think that these monetary-fiscal reforms are urgent. The next crisis is coming sooner than you think. Reform should not await a much larger, more comprehensive, and more contentious unification project. That project requires a treaty change, which can be vetoed by any of the twenty-seven EU member states. Thus, we focus on what can be done within the current union. Our reform proposals would not hinder the development of a comprehensive fiscal union, and indeed they are likely to support such a move.

Pressures exist in the other direction as well. We have confined our analysis to economics, and our fears to the economic consequences of continuing down the present path. The political danger is real as well. Further European integration, shifting sovereignty from the national to the EU level, does not enjoy the widespread optimism and support among national governments that prevailed in the 1990s. The euro and its management by the ECB do not enjoy unqualified political support by the people or governments of the euro area. The United Kingdom stayed out of the euro and then left the EU altogether. Euroskpetic voices continue in other countries. Trust in EU institutions is declining, trust in technocrats is declining, and euroskepticism is a rising political force. Each large intervention by the ECB has produced substantial wealth transfers to member states, banks, and bondholders. The ECB explains its interventions in a mysterious language that most people, and many professional economists, including the authors, often cannot decode. Each intervention thus breeds more resentment, rightly or wrongly. The euro and EU have held together so far. But the next great crisis and the next great bailout threaten the euro as a political institution as well as an economic one.

As much as any authors are proud of their work, however, we admit that monetary and fiscal reforms are not the most important economic problem facing the euro area. As the Draghi (2024) report persuasively argues, Europe's problems are structural: "Europe largely missed out on the digital revolution led by the internet and the productivity gains it brought: in fact, the productivity gap between the EU and the US is largely explained by the tech sector. The EU is weak in the emerging technologies that will drive future growth. Only four of the world's top 50 tech companies are European." Indeed, stagnant long-term growth is Europe's largest economic problem. Long-term growth comes from increased productivity, increased efficiency, microeconomic reform, a business environment that fosters innovation and investment, and increased productive capacity, not, centrally, anything having to do with monetary policy and central banks.[1] Monetary and fiscal polices can encourage, and fail to discourage, "an open market economy with free competition, favouring an efficient allocation of resources," as stated in the ECB's mandate. Fiscal policy is intertwined with growth as well. Long-run growth has suffered from the microeconomic effects of fiscal policy, such as the disincentives of high marginal tax rates, insufficiently targeted transfers, and misallocations of fiscal subsidies. Excessive regulation has also stifled innovation, investment, and productivity growth.[2] Growth stagnation has also contributed to debt problems, and faster growth would lower deficits and make debt much easier to repay.

But as much as past events such as the Great Depression have monetary and fiscal roots, Europe's current growth weakness does not stem from the monetary-fiscal troubles that we describe here. In the end, monetary, fiscal, and financial stability arrangements are part of the fundamental framework of good institutions that allow growth to emerge. They can help to avoid future crises, which would drag growth down further. They can remove existing disincentives for national governments to pursue pro-growth agendas. But monetary-fiscal reform is not the fundamental spark needed to revitalize Europe's once fast-growing innovative economies.

We fix what we can. The European pro-growth agenda is a topic for another book entirely.

1.4 Other Voices

We are hardly the first to write about the eroding fiscal foundations of the euro, nor are all our points individually novel. That's a feature. Hopefully, the reader will find integration of points made by many other authors more convincing than claims that nobody else noticed big flaws in the quarter century of the euro's operation. We point to other views as much as we can in context, but here we acknowledge a small portion of the massive amount of related analysis and commentary on the structure of the euro.

Corsetti et al. (2015, xiii) deal with some of our issues, though with a focus on overall EU debt sustainability. They call for reforms to European Stability Mechanism lending, including "incentives to avoid excessive debt levels" and measures to "make future debt restructuring . . . less painful than is currently the case." They propose regulatory changes to eliminate the "diabolic loop between banks and sovereigns." They advocate European Safe Assets, in particular for the ECB to buy in quantitative easing operations. They note how bailout expectations led to excessive debt: "The existing rules did not prevent countries from issuing too much debt, nor providing liberally excessive lending, as both private agents and the governments correctly anticipated that the Treaty was too weak to make the no-bailout clause credible." They also add useful detail on the Greek crisis beyond our summary. However, their primary focus is a debt-swap proposal for dealing with existing sovereign debt.

Brunnermeier, James, and Landau (2016) analyze how the differing economic philosophies, historical roots, traditions, and institutions of France and Germany shaped the design of the euro and the response to financial crises, leaving the ECB and other institutions struggling in between. Our complementary approach is focused on standard economic incentives.

Mody (2018) provides an exciting, blow-by-blow account of discussions between the key decision makers during the financial and sovereign crises. He argues that the creation of the euro was a flawed political project, unworkable because of economic differences between countries that led to significant economic difficulties and divisions within Europe. He is critical of the handling of the 2008–2012 crisis. We focus less on the decision-making process, centering our analysis instead on the institutional setup and incentives and how decisions created new institutions and incentives. Most of all, we think that different countries can share a currency without fiscal union, and the euro is a few simple reforms away from being highly beneficial to Europe.

Rostagno et al. (2021) is an excellent and insightful discussion by ECB experts on the evolution of the monetary policy design, analysis, and decisions of the ECB. It describes how the ECB came to innovative, unconventional tools in the financial crisis and the persistent zero bound era. This book is complementary to ours in that it focuses on monetary policy rather than monetary-fiscal interactions and incentives. It includes a lot of sophisticated quantitative model-based analyses.

Sinn (2014, 2018) also analyze an erosion of fiscal and monetary boundaries in the euro. He focuses on the possible political consequence that support for the euro could weaken, and offers different reform proposals.

Bénassy-Quéré et al. (2018), a joint article by fourteen prominent European economists, includes several of our key diagnoses and proposals. In current institutions, they note the "doom loop between banks and sovereigns," and "incomplete banking union and fragmented capital markets," which prevent "better risk sharing through market mechanisms." They agree that "Fiscal rules are non-transparent, procyclical, and divisive, and have not been very effective in reducing public debts." As a result, "the flaws in the euro areas fiscal architecture have overburdened the ECB," and "The resulting loss of trust may eventually threaten not just the euro, but the entire European project."

They advocate six reforms that are largely congruent with ours:

First, breaking the vicious circle between banks and sovereigns through the coordinated introduction of sovereign concentration charges for banks and a common deposit insurance . . . mechanisms to bail in creditors of failing banks need to be strengthened, . . .

Second, replacing the current system of fiscal rules focused on the "structural deficit" by a simple expenditure rule guided by a long-term debt reduction target. . . .

Third, creating the economic, legal and institutional underpinnings for orderly sovereign-debt restructuring of countries whose solvency cannot be restored through conditional crisis lending. . . .

Fourth, creating a euro area fund, financed by national contributions, that helps participating member countries absorb large economic disruptions. . . .

Fifth, an initiative to create a synthetic euro area safe asset that would offer investors an alternative to national sovereign bonds. . . .

Sixth, reforming the euro area institutional architecture . . . the policy responsibility for conditional crisis lending should be fully assigned to a reformed ESM, . . . The latter should include a layer of political accountability

This book is part of an emerging strand of academic literature that uses modern dynamic economic theory to understand historical events and institutions, and it uses historical analysis to learn about theory. This literature is a stylistic and methodological inspiration, as well as an economic foundation.

Sargent (2012) is a readable and insightful analysis of fiscal and monetary affairs in the early years of the United States, and the lessons that it does and does not offer for Europe today. Hamilton's bailout of foreign bondholders set a reputation that stood the United States in good favor for subsequent borrowing. Too good, actually—investors assumed that state debts incurred for infrastructure would be covered by federal bailouts. When the federal government allowed states to default, that hurt overall borrowing ability. But it also induced states to balanced-budget policies, which largely put an end to sovereign bailouts or defaults.

Fiscal-monetary interactions are clear in war finance. Hall and Sargent (2022) puts the Covid spending and inflation in the context of World War I and World War II experience, and more generally by Hall and Sargent (2014), Hall and Sargent (2021) for eight wars and two insurrections. Sargent and Velde (1995) applies a wide variety of economic analysis to the fiscal and monetary crisis that precipitated the French Revolution. Kehoe and Nicolini (2021) surveys the rich and instructive monetary-fiscal history of Latin America.

Bordo and Jonung (2000) and Bordo, Jonung, and Markiewicz (2013) summarize the lessons for the euro of many historical experiences with fiscal and monetary unions.

2

Key Economic Ideas

Most policy analysis looks at *actions* and their short-term effects: Should the ECB raise or lower interest rates or buy bonds? But monetary, fiscal, and financial policies revolve around what people expect to happen, how they expect governments to behave in the future, and how governments' current actions shape those expectations. Governments can borrow only if people expect them to repay debt rather than default or inflate it away. People take or avoid risks and governments borrow and spend depending in part on how much support they expect from the ECB and other authorities in the next downturn.

Thus, we analyze policy as being encoded in expectations, rules, regimes, institutions, commitments, norms, and traditions; written but also unwritten; reinforced or undermined by repeated past behavior of fiscal and monetary authorities; and by an implicit list of how the policymaker will act in many different circumstances.

Three central ideas from contemporary economics underlie that analysis: monetary-fiscal interaction, time consistency and pre-commitment, and tax smoothing with state-contingent default.

2.1 Monetary-Fiscal Interaction

Monetary and fiscal policy are always intertwined. Governments are always tempted to print money to finance deficits or pay off debts.[1] From the founding of the euro, the incentive for member states to borrow too much and then count on a fiscal or monetary bailout was obvious. As we will see, the euro was set up to try to control this incentive.[2]

19

Additional, more subtle fiscal-monetary interactions pervade the structure and institutions of the euro. Everyday interest-rate policy, bank lending rules, the cross-country payment system, the devolution of some authority to national central banks, and other elements have important fiscal effects and constraints.

The concern by monetary policymakers over financial stability also pervades the operation of the euro. These concerns also lead to interactions between monetary and fiscal policy. Central bankers are reluctant to tighten if banks will fail. Banking crises lead to bank bailouts and debt guarantees, benefiting bank shareholders and creditors. Banking crises also lead the central bank to prop up the value of bank assets.

Asset Purchases

As with other central banks, the ECB's central policy levers are asset purchases, lending to banks, and interest rates. Each has fiscal as well as monetary implications.

With bond purchases, central banks usually aim to lower long-term yields, thereby raising aggregate demand and inflation. Unlike private banks or regular people, the central bank simply creates new money to buy assets. A bank sells a bond to the ECB, and the ECB adds newly created euros to the bank's account at the ECB.

Bond purchases have fiscal as well as monetary effects. They are often called "monetization" of government debt. Modern governments don't directly print money to finance deficits; they issue bonds, and central banks can buy the bonds in return for money.

Asset purchases help government finances because money usually pays a lower interest rate than government debt, and central banks rebate the difference to the government. Asset purchases can also directly lower interest rate in government bond markets, especially in times of market turmoil. Asset purchases can help governments to forestall default, avoid rollover difficulty, and lower market pressures for fiscal and economic reform. By propping up the market value of government bonds, asset purchases transfer resources to individuals, banks, or other financial institutions that hold the bonds as assets.

In the euro area, asset purchases can imply transfers between countries. The debt of member states of the euro area carries default risks, which can differ significantly across countries. Since in the end euros created by the central bank are liabilities of all member states, the ECB's purchase of risky member-state debt in return for reserves can spread default risk through the whole eurozone. That risk can materializes either through central bank losses or via inflation. We describe each mechanism in detail here.

Expected future purchases can have fiscal effects. When the ECB announces that it intends to buy a country's debt, or it puts in place a new program to do so, the risk premiums and thus the yield spreads on that debt can fall quickly. The "ECB put option" is valuable; it represents a valuable contingent transfer from the rest of the eurozone to the country and its debt holders. Purchases can have a secondary effect as well: The more debt of a country that the ECB holds, the less likely it may be that the ECB will allow that country to default.

Lowering long-term yields or yield spreads seems the ECB's frequent intent, as part of monetary policy. Fiscal effects are unintended or unavoidable consequences, but consequences nonetheless.

Asset Purchases and Inflation

Again, in asset purchases, central banks trade newly created money for an asset. Extra money does not invariably cause inflation. If the money (reserves) pays the same interest as the asset (risk-free short-term government bonds of a single state such as the United States), then there really is no effect at all. Banks are just as willing to hold one as the other, the central bank makes no profits, and there are no implied transfers from one state to another. That huge quantitative easing of this sort had so little effect on inflation is not immediately surprising.

If extra money created by asset purchases threatens inflation, the central bank can mop up extra money by selling assets. Knowing that, people are happier to hold money, especially now that money in the form of reserves pays interest. But if the central bank is unwilling to sell assets, as doing so will mean lower bond prices and higher interest rates, or if the central bank runs out of assets to sell because some assets have defaulted or lost market value, the central bank can no longer soak up all the extra money. Then, inflation breaks out. Similarly, if the central bank stops paying full interest on reserves, people will want to get rid of the reserves and inflation will break out. A central bank with insufficient assets can try to pay interest on reserves by creating new reserves with no corresponding assets, but eventually that tactic fails. And if people expect that the central bank will be unable to stop inflation in the future, they raise prices and try to spend cash today, so inflation breaks out right away.

If the central bank cannot stop inflation with asset sales, member states must raise tax revenue or cut spending to soak up money and there-by stop inflation. There are many mechanisms for such fiscal support.

Most prominently, the fiscal support comes through a reduction in the ECB's profit rebate. The ECB (including the national central banks) normally makes a profit since it pays less interest on its liabilities—cash and reserves—than it earns on its assets. It rebates these profits to member states after deducting its expenses. When the ECB loses money, it reduces the profit rebates. Member states must then raise tax revenue or cut spending to make up the difference.

Normally, after a loss, the ECB would wait for profits to accumulate internally, rebuilding the value of its assets. But if the ECB needed to soak up cash immediately and cannot or does not wish to sell assets, it may request recapitalization from member states, essentially a negative rebate. A recapitalization would also be useful if inflation is breaking out because people see that the ECB's assets are much less than its liabilities, and they are trying to get rid of euros quickly, just as recapitalization can stop any private bank run. In a recapitalization, member states provide the ECB with new assets via the national central banks. Those resources must come from taxation in excess of spending. If governments borrow to provide the ECB with new government debt to sell, those governments must credibly promise future fiscal surpluses to sell new debt. By this means, taxes soak up extra money.

Central bank recapitalizations have happened in other countries. For example, in the fall of 2022 the U.K. Treasury indemnified the Bank of

England for realized losses on its large portfolio of long-term bonds. (The indemnity was not a surprise decision. In the United Kingdom, central bank income goes straight to the government, rather than paid to the government as a dividend as in the United States and the EU. Swifter booking of profits requires swifter indemnification of losses.)

Governments might also exchange the central bank's troubled or unsaleable assets for more valuable assets. Such schemes are common when central banks bail out private banks in crises. The difference in value ultimately comes from taxpayers.

The euro is thus fundamentally backed by the fiscal policies of the euro-area member states. Loss or doubt of that fiscal backing can cause inflation and devaluation. ECB-issued money and reserves (i.e., deposits held by commercial banks at the ECB) are effectively Europe-wide sovereign debt, and claims on Europe-wide taxes. Eurobonds, or more precisely eurobills, already exist: they are euros and euro accounts at the ECB.

Asset Purchases by the ECB

The ECB purchases debt through two types of programs, with two sets of intentions. First, the ECB may feel pressure to support the debt of an individual country if an individual member state may default, it has trouble borrowing at low rates, it has trouble rolling over debt, or if its yields rise, imperiling leveraged financial institutions that hold its debt. The point of such purchases is to allow governments to borrow at lower interest rates or to borrow more money. The ECB also supports the debt of such states indirectly through lending programs, described next.

Such purchases are not painless. Much of our history in the next few chapters describes the long process by which the ECB began to buy sovereign debt in a sequence of programs reluctantly, and under pressure of events. The ECB describes such purchases, and announcements of purchase programs, as maintaining "depth and liquidity" of "malfunctioning" or "fragmented" markets, and above all to maintain the "transmission" of monetary policy whose only aim is "price stability"—malfunctions that coincidentally seem to happen only to countries with fiscal problems.[3] But those objectives mean lower spreads, the point of the purchases and announcments is to lower spreads, and lower spreads and purchases have clear and large fiscal implications.

Second, the ECB purchases debt from all euro member states in proportion to their size (via the ECB's "capital key"). The ECB first undertook such purchases in Quantitative Easing (QE) programs that began in 2015, and later to support fiscal expansion in the Covid-19 pandemic. QE aimed to lower long-term yields of all euro countries in order to boost aggregate demand in the whole euro area and increase inflation toward the target, a clear monetary policy motivation. These bond purchases can also have fiscal effects. They make it easier for all governments to borrow, and they insulate them from higher credit spreads or rollover risks. These programs tend disproportionately to help countries with weaker fiscal positions and higher spreads.

Some ECB bond purchases aimed at individual countries are "sterilized," meaning that the ECB sells other assets so the total volume of euros is the same. The implied fiscal transfers, taking on default risk and lowering a country's yield spreads, remain.

Even if the ECB buys bonds, lowers yields and stems a crisis, the bonds recover, and the ECB can soak up the created money, the ECB exposes its balance sheet to default and interest rate risks. If the rescue had not worked out, it would have cost a lot. There is a tendency in all government finance and the associated accounting rules to regard backstopping debts or writing options as free, and congratulating oneself when it works out ex post. But luck eventually run out, and the cost of these policies comes due.

ECB purchases of public debt can also directly allow a government to reduce its funding costs, potentially at the expense of the rest of the union. In the Eurosystem, sovereign bonds are mostly held by the national central banks, financed at risk-free rates via bank reserves or Target2 liabilities to the ECB. Income and risks on these holdings are not shared among national central banks, which therefore return profits to their national treasuries, not to member states as a whole. Thus, the national treasury earns back the spread between the market yield on its bonds and the risk-free central bank rate. The treasury essentially gets to borrow at the latter rate. These are not small effects. In 2022, Eurosystem holdings on average amounted to about one third of outstanding public debt in 2022.[4]

In this arrangement, national central banks apparently keep the default risk of their domestic sovereign debt holdings. But what happens in such a default is a completely unanswered (and largely unasked!) question. Governments might partly exempt national central bank holdings from haircuts. Or they might not. The national central bank might be recapitalized by its treasury. Or, given that the treasury is in default, maybe not. The other euro member states might recapitalize the national central bank, in which case the default risk is in their hands.

Lending to Banks

In addition to asset purchases, the ECB lends newly created money to banks, taking eligible asset including bonds as collateral against the loan. The bank can use the loan from the ECB to buy the bond in the first place. In this situation, the ECB still creates money that helps to finance sovereign or private borrowing. The interest rate the bank pays on such loans to the ECB is the same for all collateral, and typically lower than the interest rate the bank receives on sovereign bonds. In the absence of default, the banks rather than the ECB get the profits.

Central bank loans to banks, which use them to buy or hold sovereign debt, seems to separate the ECB from implicit fiscal transfers, since the bank bears the default and price risk of the bond. But for that to be the case, the ECB and euro-area governments would have to countenance sovereign or bond issuer default, and then countenance that bank equity holders, depositors, and other creditors lose money. Otherwise, default risk stays with the ECB and other members of the euro area. Indeed, fear of financial "contagion" is one of the reasons why the ECB interferes in sovereign markets in the first place. Fear of bank failures following the collapse of the interbank market spurred the ECB's first big interventions in 2008–2009. In these cases, the ECB effectively took on private, not sovereign credit risk. If the sovereign or bank bailout comes from direct fiscal transfers from other member states rather than the ECB, then they bear the fiscal risk directly rather than via the ECB.

Protecting the Balance Sheet

However, the seeds of an important idea lie in this structure. The more the Eurosystem's assets are protected from default, from loss of value due to higher interest rates, or from inflation, the more the ECB's ability to mop up money and defend the price level can be insulated from member-state fiscal problems or other problems stemming from losses on the ECB's assets. *Separating* the value of central banks assets backing the euro from fluctuations in general fiscal surpluses of the member states is the central art of good monetary-fiscal institutional design.

The treatment of ECB holdings of Greek debt in 2012 offer an instructive example. In the Greek sovereign debt restructuring, private bondholders received a haircut. They received new bonds worth much less than the face value of their initial claims. But the ECB was exempted. Its holdings of Greek bonds paid full value. This exception from an economic perspective is similar to a transfer from taxpayers and bondholders to the ECB to protect the value of the ECB's assets from the Greek default.

By exempting the ECB from Greek haircuts, the EU maintained the euro's backing while other bondholders took large losses. It is an example of how a separate central bank balance sheet is useful to distinguish surpluses that back currency and reserves from general government surpluses. If governments could restructure and default more generally, and it was clear that the ECB would never bear losses, the ECB could hold sovereign debt without compromising the ability of its balance sheet to back the euro.

On the other hand, if the ECB does not take on default risk with asset purchases, it can fail to raise bond prices. Bond prices could even decline as a result of the ECB's purchases, as a given restructuring must fall more heavily on bonds in private hands, raising their default spread! Nothing is free in life. Since the Greek exemption, ECB purchases have been announced to be "pari passu," sharing losses in any restructuring.

Similarly, if the ECB holds more foreign or indexed debt that does not fall in value with euro-area inflation or higher interest rates, its power to control inflation is greater. Many reform proposals include the creation of Eurobonds, guaranteed by EU taxes or collectively by member states. If the ECB were to hold such Eurobonds, its balance sheet would be more secure as well. If those were short-term and indexed, and the ECB was legally prioritized in any restructuring, the ECB's assets would be safer still.

Interest Rate Targets

Monetary and fiscal policies are also intertwined in the regular business of raising and lowering short-term interest rates.

When the ECB raises interest rates to fight inflation, it also raises the interest costs that governments pay as they roll over outstanding debt and on their new borrowing. Governments must then cut spending, raise tax revenue, issue new debt against credible promises of future surpluses to pay the higher interest costs, or default. This effect is substantial. At a 100% debt-to-GDP ratio, each increase of one percentage point in the real interest rate eventually raises the annual deficit by one percent of GDP.

There is an interaction between the ECB balance sheet and interest rate policy. Large quantitative easing purchases essentially shorten the maturity structure of government debt, and thereby increase the speed with which governments roll over debt and with which higher interest rates raise government deficits. This subtle mechanism flows through the profit rebate channel. When the ECB raises the interest rate on reserves above the rate that it earns on its assets, it must reduce transfers to member states. The net effect on government finances is just as if the government had issued shorter-term debt to begin with and had to roll it over more quickly. The loss appears on government accounts as a lower transfer from the ECB rather than greater interest cost of the debt, but the quantity is the same.

The ECB bought lots of long-term government debt in quantitative easing and Covid stimulus programs. As interest rates rise, the value of those bonds fall, which leads to reduced fiscal transfers back to countries. This mechanism also has distributional implications across countries. The ECB bought longer-term debt from some countries than others, some countries had issued longer-term debt than others in the first place, and some countries had lower bond prices and higher interest rate spreads than others. With a small balance sheet and low spreads, these are small effects, but as the ECB's balance sheet grows, so do these distributional effects.

When monetary policy produces inflation or deflation, that has a direct fiscal effect. Unexpected inflation lowers the real value of nominal government debt. The government raises more money in taxes but pays the same amount to bondholders. Contrariwise, unexpected disinflation raises the real value of nominal debt. Nominal tax revenues fall, but interest payments do not change. Governments must tighten fiscal policy to pay this windfall to bondholders. For example, if a government has sold 100% of GDP debt in a 5% inflation environment at a 7% nominal or 2% real yield with 10-year maturity, and the central bank afterward successfully lowers inflation to 2%, then the government must run 5% of GDP surpluses for ten years to pay off the debt rather than 2% of GDP.

Higher central bank interest rates also increase real financing costs for private households and firms, thereby pushing the economy toward lower growth and possibly a recession. Via the Phillips curve, less economic activity is thought to reduce inflation. That is not an unwanted side effect; rather, it is the central mechanism in the standard economic analysis of how central banks reduce inflation by interest rate rises. But in recessions, governments lose tax revenue and spend more for anti-recession stimulus and for social programs such as unemployment insurance. Financial troubles in recessions may lead to bailouts, which also raise deficits.

In all these ways, higher interest rates have fiscal consequences, almost all of them negative. Fiscal policy must tighten to support monetary policy; current or expected future surpluses must rise to pay all these costs. If they do not, the unfunded deficits are an inflationary fiscal force that partially or completely offsets the intended disinflationary effect of interest rate rises. In a wide variety of contemporary models, including new-Keynesian, old-Keynesian, and fiscal theory, an interest rate rise that is *not* accompanied by fiscal tightening now or in the future, at least to pay for higher interest costs on the debt, *raises* inflation (Cochrane, 2023a). Successful disinflation, including during the 1980s, has included fiscal and microeconomic reforms that produce larger primary surpluses.

Monetary-fiscal interactions are often glossed over in the analysis of monetary policy. They are less important if there is plenty of fiscal space. If governments have small debts, live far from the threat of sovereign default, and have built a track record of sound fiscal policy, they can easily raise tax revenue, cut expenditures, and borrow by promising to do so in the future. Then governments can easily offset these fiscal effects of monetary policy such as higher interest costs. As debts are larger, as the central bank balance sheet has more government debt, as governments run larger persistent deficits, as governments near the boundaries of their borrowing capacity, as tax rates reach the limit at which they generate less long-run revenue, as growth slows, and in moments of sovereign stress, all these monetary-fiscal interactions are more important. The latter situation is more typical of the present moment than it was at the founding of the euro, the development of our standard monetary theories that ignore fiscal interactions, or the previous large inflation in the 1970s and 1980s.

2.2 Time Consistency and Commitment

Why do governments repay debts at all? Once debt has been issued and the proceeds spent, why not default or inflate debt away rather than raise economically distorting and politically unpopular taxes or enact politically difficult spending cuts and growth-oriented reforms? The answer, of course, is that without assurance that debt will be repaid, people won't lend to the government in the first place or they will only lend at higher yields to compensate for the higher probability of default. Governments are tempted to a "just this once" default, which hits only past investments and still promises repayment to new investors, but investors are naturally suspicious that "just this once" quickly will become a habit.

This is a general problem in economics. The purest tax is a "capital levy": Grab wealth once, unexpectedly, and promise never to do it again. Unlike an ongoing capital tax on profits and rates of return, an unexpected capital levy does not discourage investment decisions going forward. But if people see that possibility ahead of time, they don't invest in the first place and there is less capital to tax. And if a government attempts a one-time tax, it is hard to convince people that a second time is not right around the corner.

Kydland and Prescott (1977) famously inaugurated the modern analytical understanding of this "time-consistency" problem in the context of monetary policy.[5] A benevolent central bank wishes for a small output gap. The bank wishes people to expect little inflation in the future, so the inflation-output trade-off today will be more favorable. But when that future comes, the bank will wish to inflate in order to boost the economy. People know that, however, so they expect inflation, worsening the Phillips-curve trade-off today, no matter what promises central bankers make.

Formally, write the Phillips curve as

$$\pi_t = E_t \pi_{t+1} + \kappa x_t,$$

where π denotes inflation and x denotes the output gap. Then lower expected inflation $E_t \pi_{t+1}$ lowers current inflation or raises current output. But the same equation at time $t + 1$,

$$\pi_{t+1} = E_{t+1} \pi_{t+2} + \kappa x_{t+1},$$

means that the central bank will wish more left-hand-side inflation to boost output at time $t + 1$. People foresee that, so $E_t \pi_{t+1}$ in the time-t equation rises as well.

In a sovereign debt crisis, the central bank would like to do a "just this once" bailout, and promise never to do it again so as to restore incentives. But people understand that if the situation recurs, the central bank will bail out "just this once" again, and people take actions expecting a bailout.

The answer to time-consistency problems is intuitively clear: Governments and central banks must find ways to *precommit*, to set things up ex ante in a way that raises the costs *to them* of taking actions that they will prefer ex post, but whose anticipation leads to bad incentives for other actors. Like Odysseus facing the sirens, they must tie themselves to the mast.

Legal and constitutional limitations, the institutional separation of central bank from fiscal authorities, restricted mandates, separated balance sheets, policy rules (Friedman's money growth rule or Taylor's interest-rate rule), and other formal or informal rules, reputations, norms, and traditions all help to enforce such precommitments.

Many institutions of society can be understood as solutions to precommitment problems. Property rights exist to protect the returns to investment against ex-post majoritarian expropriation. They allow the capital in capitalism to exist.

If a government wishes to borrow, default—either direct or via inflation—must be costly to the government. By taking steps to make default more costly, the government constrains its future self to take on the economic and political costs of higher tax revenues, lower spending, or growth-oriented reform so it can and will repay debt. Only in this way will investors lend the government money to begin with.

Promises alone are not precommitments. Precommitments must be *costly* to break.

Reputation is a precommitment mechanism, frequently considered in the context of sovereign debt. Governments repay debt this time to burnish a reputation for repayment, so they can borrow in the future. Governments abstain from wealth confiscation today so that people will invest and create new wealth tomorrow. Teachers give and grade (ugh) tests so next year's class will study. But such signaling and reputation-building are fragile. Absent explicit costs, there is always the temptation to declare an event a once-in-a-century crisis, default, inflate, grab capital, and promise never to do it again. But once-in-a-century crises then seem to happen every few years.

Pure reputation is also a weak mechanism because multiple lenders have an incentive to forgive too quickly. Once debt has been defaulted or inflated away, after all, the government is a better lending prospect for new investors. Pure reputation works only if governments really are of two immutable types, thrifty or spendthrift, and not defaulting convinces investors of the governments' type. But governments are not immutably anything, and voters change them if they are. Thus, for reputation to be effective, investors and money holders must agree to punish a government ex post for defaulting by refusing new loans. But each individual lender has an incentive to cheat on collective punishment, which they tend to do. Some countries default over and over again, yet new investors seem to line up quickly afterward to buy new bonds. Institutions that incur direct and unavoidable costs for breaking promises are thus more effective precommitments. (Eaton and Gersovitz, 1981; Aguiar and Amador, 2021 summarize and apply the large literature on sovereign default including the reputation mechanism.)

The ECB originally envisioned that it would not intervene in sovereign debt markets. Sovereigns, knowing this, would borrow soberly and pay their debts in all but the most extreme cases. Investors, knowing this, would provision for losses in those cases and not expect ECB intervention. Money holders, knowing this, would not fear inflation.

The trouble is that if a sovereign or financial crisis emerges, internal and external pressure on the ECB to intervene is immense. If the ECB can intervene, the ECB likely will intervene. But everyone knows that, so an imperfect pre-commitment is not credible, and incentives are distorted anyway. Thus, to be effective, a pre-commitment must ensure that the ECB *cannot* intervene ex post. The most effective precommitments are formal and legal, including mechanisms that enforce laws.

The architects of the euro did not write such stringent limitations, and they were likely wise not to do so. They likely did not intend ironclad rules that could never be broken, no matter how severe the crisis. They likely intended a strong tradition of restraint, but an escape clause, offering a sort of strategic ambiguity: Rules and traditions against intervention that are tough enough to provide good incentives, but leaving enough residual flexibility so the ECB can intervene in rare but extreme circumstances. As it did. One can tie oneself too tightly to the mast. Don't join the sirens, but leave enough slack in case the ship starts to sink.

But strategic ambiguity has now been lost. Frequent and routine intervention is now widely expected. The architects of the euro did not, naturally, think several steps ahead how to restore strategic ambiguity in the wake of large and unexpected crises. This is, properly, a job for their successors—us.

We are not lawyers, and we offer no opinion whether some crisis interventions were counter to the Maastricht Treaty, or violate formal rules governing the ECB, member states, and the EU. The European Court of Justice has ruled for the ECB in cases that challenged the Outright Monetary Transactions program.

We can see these forces at work in the history of interventions. Interventions came bit by bit, under an acronym-laden proliferation of special programs, often initially explicitly announced as temporary, and using a complex and novel terminology, with terms such as "contagion," "fragmentation," "dysfunction," or "dislocation" in sovereign debt markets. In part, by this approach the ECB tries to communicate that sovereign debt intervention is consistent with treaty mandates, and informal rules and traditions against bailing out sovereign debt. In part, however, the ECB depicts each new program or intervention as a special and temporary exception to the rules, just this once. The ECB also depicts its interventions as directed at malfunctioning markets, not to save sovereigns and bondholders who fell prey to bad incentives. Doing so tries to put moral hazard back in the box and convince people that interventions won't happen again, and especially not in response to trouble brought on by irresponsible borrowing or investing.

But actions speak louder than words. As we can see by the increasing size of interventions, the dismantling of previous external and self-imposed limits, and the accumulation of large sovereign debts in the ECB's asset portfolio, verbal efforts to restore a regime in which people do not expect interventions have not worked. Instead, the emergency patchwork has evolved into a new set of implicit institutions and expectations that bond purchases and targeted lending are now part of the standard toolbox.

Moreover, this effort to contain moral hazard after taking exceptional action was limited. The ECB has not vowed, "Never again." It has not said, "We will not intervene in the next crisis to prevent sovereign default. Get ready to handle bond losses and sudden stops." It has not announced limits to what the next program may do. Most public statements of the ECB suggest pride in having staved off disaster and readiness to do so again.

The end result blurs the distinction between monetary and fiscal policy. It runs counter to the original expectations created by the Treaty, the strong promises by the leading politicians at the time of the introduction of the euro, and the initial design of the ECB's strategy and operational framework. And it risks setting us up for chaos when a next, larger crisis erupts, and the ECB's powder runs dry. So the effort to precommit against arbitrary intervention and to contain the consequent moral hazard must be reinvigorated.

However, since the ECB cannot and should not completely precommit not to intervene no matter how extreme the next crisis, the pre-commitments that it can offer will be more effective if the pressure to act and the costs of not acting are lower. That means fiscal and economic reform in member states, so that they are not in perpetual trouble. That means financial reform, so that insolvent sovereigns can default or restructure debts without a financial crisis. And that requires the construction of crisis-management tools outside the ECB so that the ECB is no longer the only game in town.

2.3 Self-Fulfilling Crises

Sovereign debt is potentially vulnerable to a multiple-equilibrium scenario: A country has a lot of debt. If the interest rate on its debt is low, the country can run enough primary surpluses to service the debt. However, if the interest rate on its debt rises, then the country can no longer service the debt and a default or rollover crisis breaks out. If investors believe that there will be no default, they charge a low rate and no default happens. If investors start to worry about default, the interest rate rises and the default breaks out. Expectations of default can be self-confirming. Like a bank run, either equilibrium can emerge, quickly, and in response to what seems like trivial news or no news at all.[6]

The mechanism can also exist in subdued form. A one-percentage-point rise in interest rate, perhaps from a one-percentage-point rise in fundamental default probability, might lead to a half-percentage-point rise in default premium since the country must pay higher interest costs on its debt. The half percent rise in interest costs leads to another quarter percent rise in risk premium, and so forth. The initial one-percentage-point rise in default premium results in a two-percentage-point rise in the yield spread. The multiple equilibrium results when the feedback exceeds one.

Short-term debt is a particular gasoline on this fire. The more the government relies on short-term financing, which must be rolled over frequently, the more quickly higher interest rates feed into the budget and the more quickly the feedback loop takes off. Long-term debt offers insurance against interest rate increases for governments, just as it does for businesses and mortgage borrowers. But, as all insurance requires a premium, long-term debt typically must pay a slightly higher rate.

It feels unfair. The country does not plan to default. It issues debt when rates are low and government and private forecasts soothingly assure low rates in the future. The government feels that it can repay that debt. When credit spreads rise, if the government does not default, the higher interest rates appear to be just a transfer from taxpayers to bondholders who are suddenly raising prices for no reason. The country and advocates for intervention complain about dysfunctional, irrational, or fragmented markets, illiquidity, contagion, market power, speculative attack, or collusion. That the country could have insured against the event by locking in low interest rates via slightly more expensive long-term debt gets forgotten in this morality play.

These issues pervade discussion of ECB management of sovereign debt problems. A "whatever it takes" commitment such as the one that ECB president Mario Draghi issued in 2012 is an attempt to cut off a perceived self-fulfilling debt crisis equilibrium. If successful, the ECB doesn't actually have to buy any bonds.

Whether and under what conditions such multiple equilibria are real, and, if so, whether that possibility applies to countries such as Greece in its crisis is contentious, however. Self-fulfilling equilibria are possible, but it is also possible that a country simply becomes unable to pay its debts. Investors, seeing trouble ahead, run now. In an uncertain world, higher yields reflecting actual risks, but not certainty, of default are *fundamentally* justified. It is difficult for a central bank to distinguish multiple-equilibrium-driven yields from fundamentally driven yields in real time. Insolvency is poorly defined anyway. Almost all governments can pay their debts if they wish to do so. We're betting on future policy, not external cicumstances. Illiquidity is hard to tell from insolvency in sovereigns as much as in bank runs. And proclaiming multiple equilibria and dysfunctional markets is always tempting to justify intervention and the hope that intervention will be costless. Borrowing less, maintaining spare fiscal capacity, borrowing long term, not playing with fire in the first place, spending more effectively, and adopting growth-oriented microeconomic reforms remains a robust but often politically unattractive solution.

Draghi's success is unusual in the long history of governments trying to diagnose and select multiple equilibria with words. Governments defending overvalued exchange rates have over and over again said "whatever it takes" until speculators called their bluff and made the governments actually spend precious resources defending their exchange rates. One must have the means and the will to really do *whatever* it takes.

Whether doom loop or fundamentally driven, however, sovereign crises are primarily rollover crises, not funding crises. The government cannot find new lenders to pay old ones, or it cannot pay sharply higher interest costs on its debts. Thus, much more long-term debt, even perpetuities, are an important part of an architecture to reduce sovereign debt problems in the eurozone. Clever financial engineering such as floating-rate debt with options to temporarily fix may also be useful.

2.4   Central Bank Independence and Mandates

Modern central banks enjoy a great deal of independence from the governments that set them up, have specific mandates from their governments, and follow rules limiting the tools they may use. The ECB's mandate is price stability. The U.S. Federal Reserve has explicit mandates for price stability, employment, and legal authority for financial stability. Both follow a short-term interest rate target and face legal and self-imposed limits on the assets they may buy and sell.

Central banks are created by governments. Independence, mandates, and tool limitations are mechanisms for the governments to pre-commit, to avoid time-consistency problems, and to avoid some moral hazards. Independence is a means to an end, not an intrinsically worthy characteristic.

At the simplest level, governments know that they will be tempted to stimulate the economy, especially ahead of elections. By creating an independent central bank to control monetary policy, the government tries to pre-commit itself to forswear this temptation. An independent bank, plus a rule that the treasury may not issue money, is also a pre-commitment against monetizing debts and deficits. It helps fiscal authorities to pre-commit to repay debts, and thereby to be able to borrow in the first place. An independent central bank with rules limiting asset purchases also pre-commits the government against lending to favored industries or constituencies or printing money for subsidies.[7]

Independence must come with limited authority, a limited mandate, and a limited set of tools. For example, independent central banks are prohibited the one tool that is most surely effective in combating inflation or deflation: They may not print money and send it to people or businesses, and they may not confiscate money from people or businesses. The former is a fiscal transfer, the latter a tax. To create money, central banks must either buy an asset, or lend money against collateral, counting the loan as a corresponding asset. Yes, such central bank operations have fiscal consequences, but nothing as clear as monetary gifts or seizures. Why? Taxes and transfers are the most political of decisions. They must be reserved for politically accountable representatives. So if central banks are to be a valuable precommitment, they must be independent. But if they are to be independent, they must forswear the most effective tool for controlling inflation.

Central banks are often asked to stabilize business cycles. This is formalized in the U.S. Federal Reserve's "maximum employment" mandate, and the ECB's secondary mandate "to support the general economic policies in the EU." But central banks may not set wages or prices, modify labor laws and regulations, transfer incomes, subsidize industries, modify tax rates and social program incentives, offer Keynesian fiscal stimulus, or pursue any of the hundreds of other government interventions that are plausibly more effective for employment, growth, and other economic goals than setting the overnight interest rate or exchanging bonds for reserves. Moving interest rates has political and distributional consequences, but far less than those of direct interventions.

There are often limits on what financial transactions central banks may pursue and what assets they may hold. Central banks can typically set interest rates, lend to banks, and take bank deposits. But they are often forbidden to buy stocks or to buy corporate bonds, or they must buy an index rather than favor one issuer over another. They may be restricted to setting short-term interest rates, not long-term rates. They are typically restricted to dealing with banks, not other financial institutions or individuals.

These restrictions differ by circumstance, and circumstances change over time. The dangers of inflationary finance and cross-country subsidies in the EU led the founders of the euro to forbid the ECB from buying government debt in the primary market. The ECB was only allowed to lend newly created money to banks against adequate collateral. In the modern era, the U.S. Federal Reserve has been restricted, outside emergencies, to *only* buying government or government-guaranteed securities, lest it take on credit risk or lest it subsidize particular issuers. But as buying Treasury debt leads to the temptation to finance deficits, the Fed may not buy debt directly from the Treasury and must buy debt at market prices. Yet in and after World War II, the Fed was required to buy government debt and to hold down the rate on that debt, with the explicit fiscal goal of holding down debt service costs. Other central banks have had hard rules against buying government debt as a bulwark or direct pre-commitment against inflationary finance. Such central banks "rediscounted" private bills (i.e. lent money only against short-term *private* securities) or held only foreign debt or gold.

Many restrictions are not enshrined in law, but rather self-imposed and enshrined in traditions. Central banks know to limit themselves in order to preserve their independence.

A mandate such as price stability (or exchange rate, employment, and so forth) offers guidance on what the government wants the central banker to do. But the same mandate thereby includes an implicit, and sometimes explicit, statement of what the central bank may *not* do. No matter how important a social, economic, environmental, or political problem may seem, no matter how much a printing press, subsidized lending, or bond buying might solve that problem, the limited mandate says that in return for independence, the central bank may not act on its own to address that problem.

The limits described by the mandate and limited tools must not just be empty promises; they must include mechanisms to back up their limits. If central bankers violate mandates, either in technical legal terms or in the wider spirit and norms, there must be judicial, executive, legislative, reputational, or other consequences.

Central banks can be too powerful and too independent. Not all central bankers dislike inflation. Some central bankers may be too friendly to the financial industry. Others may indulge their own policy preferences, subsidizing industries or constituencies with low-interest loans or directing bank lending via central bank regulatory authority. Many of the limitations on central banks flow from this simple fact.

Simply devolving power to an independent central bank, immune from political pressure, does not automatically give the government a pre-commitment to follow the government's desired long-run policies. Independence is thus not absolute. In addition to mandates and legal limits, central bank officials are appointed by governments, must report to governments, and are either periodically reappointed or face term limits. And politically accountable bodies should from time to time consider if the central bank mandate, tool set, limited independence, and oversight are working well. Does "price stability" really mean 2% inflation forever? What limits on asset purchases should be enshrined in law?

2.5 Tax Smoothing and State-Contingent Default

Well-managed government debt confers great advantages. It is not optimal for governments always to run balanced budgets. Governments should borrow in times of recession, pandemic, war, or other shocks. In good times, they should slowly repay debt and build the capacity to borrow again. Governments should borrow to finance productive public investment as private companies borrow to build factories. (We emphasize truly productive, and investments that are actually investments. Both words are frequently misused.) Debt allows "tax-smoothing" (Barro, 1979): It is inefficient to finance a war or other crisis with very high taxes that return to normal lower tax rates after the crisis is over. It is better to partially finance the crisis with debt, which is repaid by a long period of slightly higher taxes. The economic distortions of taxation rise approximately with the square of the marginal tax rate. A long period of low tax rates thus damages the economy much less than a short period of very high tax rates. Countries win wars, or better survive major crises, if they are able to borrow more, credibly repay, and not destroy their economies via taxation.

It is also not optimal for governments to forswear all inflation or default. In a rare and severe crisis, a government *should* default on part of its debt or inflate it away, even though that policy will raise the interest rate that the government pays in good times. A very rare capital tax can have some of the same benefits as a just-this-once capital tax, since it gives only a small disincentive to investment. Lucas and Stokey (1983) explain that by engaging in "state-contingent default" in bad states of nature, the government smooths distorting taxes across *states of nature*, as well as over time.

This result has important lessons for the euro. It is not optimal to structure the euro so that it *never* inflates, the ECB *never* intervenes, or sovereigns *never* default. If the probabilities of such events are small enough, then the moral hazards that they produce are also small, and utter catastrophes can be avoided in the rare events.

The trouble with this lovely theory, of course, is that crises now recur often. Moreover, just how much spending each event really requires is not obvious. Lucas-Stokey state-contingent default can be a fig leaf for habitual inflation and default. Rare state-contingent default works best if it is limited to observable states and clearly necessary spending in those states. It works best when people clearly do not expect default in most circumstances and are arranging their affairs to weather default. We are clearly past that point.

If a government chooses partial default over higher distorting taxes or painful spending cuts, whether that default should come from explicit default or inflation represents another interesting trade-off. Explicit default has important financial costs. It can fall on a narrow class of investors, and in particular banks, which may then have a hard time intermediating new credit to other parts of the economy. Inflation hurts a wide class of people and implements a transfer from all savers to borrowers, as well as from bondholders to governments. Inflation also distorts the economy, given that prices and wages are somewhat sticky and some prices are stickier than others. Examining the sticky-price case, Schmitt-Grohé and Uribe (2004) find that an optimal fiscal policy results in minimal state-contingent default via inflation. The non-distorting inflation tax on capital ends up distorting the economy a great deal though sticky prices. Inflation also has redistributive effects, including via lowering real wages, that the concept of painless default through inflation usually ignores.

One may argue the particular quantitative result, but our point is that there is a trade-off. It is not obvious that inflation is less harmful than explicit default, especially orderly default under a well-oiled debt-restructuring mechanism with appropriate conditionality and a financial system that is not hostage to sovereign restructuring.

If countries never explicitly default, then there must be occasional bursts of high inflation. Beyond the concerns of nominal bondholders, beyond transfers between savers, borrowers, workers, and employers, and beyond financial troubles of explicit asset write-downs, bursts of high inflation reduce trust in and utility of the euro and the ECB. All these theories presume that the events are widely understood, and there is merely a technocratic decision of how to devalue nominal bonds. But that is not at all how inflation versus restructuring operates. In a default or restructuring, it is clear that those who lose are those who took risks in pursuit of rewards, and it is clear what events motivate the losses. If the cost is spread through inflation, whose cause is always nebulous to the general public and misdirected by much spin, it feels like institutions—the ECB, as well as the euro itself—are failing, rather than executing a technocratically managed optimal state-contingent default.

2.6 Lender of Last Resort and Financial Crises

Bank failures and financial crises pose a challenge to central banks that is similar to those posed by sovereign debts. Central banks are tempted to keep banks from defaulting on debts, just as they are tempted to keep governments from defaulting. And it's not just a temptation: Historically, support such as lender-of-last resort authority, along with financial or banking regulation, have been explicit tasks of central banks. The ECB was unusual in being set up without an explicit financial stability mandate, although it has evolved to take on financial stability functions over time, especially after the 2008 financial crisis and in fears that sovereign problems might spill over into the financial system.

Banks are prone to runs, which is why central banks and financial regulators often intervene. But as with sovereigns, insurance ex post leads to moral hazard ex ante. Knowing that rescues will come, depositors, especially those with explicit insurance, pay no heed to bank risk, and banks take on too much risk. Regulators try to contain risk, banks try to find ways around the regulations, and new institutions try to take on the functions of banks. But the size of the risks, the size of the consequent bailouts, and the number of regulations tends to get bigger with each crisis. This cycle has been going on for centuries.

In our view, this cycle now accepts too much moral hazard of expected financial rescues, regulations and regulators have shown themselves ineffective, and this cycle is also primed for a yet bigger crisis. The simple answer, that banks should issue equity and long-term debt rather than short-term debt to fund risky lending, just as other companies do, is waiting to be deployed once our political system gets through trying everything else one last time, as banks, their shareholders, regulators, creditors, and incumbent governments all profit from the bailout cycle at the expense of taxpayers.

Runs

A bank run breaks out when depositors and holders of similar assets run to get cash simultaneously. Since the bank doesn't have enough cash on hand to satisfy everyone, the bank can fail. Runs can happen when the bank is *insolvent*, when its assets are not valuable enough to satisfy creditors. Runs can also happen when banks are just *illiquid*, unable to sell assets quickly enough to raise the necessary cash. Bank runs can represent a multiple-equilibrium phenomenon. If nobody else runs, you don't run. If everyone else is going to run, you should run too (Diamond and Dybvig, 1983). More likely, banking crises involve both fundamental issues and panic components (Rochet and Vives, 2004). The role of the lender of last resort, then, is to eliminate or control the panic component.

Bank runs are not that easy to get going. The bank must fund itself with large amounts of run-prone liabilities, such as uninsured deposits: These liabilities promise that depositors can always get the full value of their investment instantly rather than in a few days or weeks, payable in cash or bank reserves not bank assets; creditors are paid first come first served, incentivizing a run; and failure to pay shuts down the bank. The bank must also face difficulty in getting cash to satisfy its running depositors: It must be unable to borrow from other banks, to sell assets, or to sell additional equity, including selling the whole bank to another bank or new investors.

Prohibitions on interstate and branch banking in the United States made runs worse. If a small-town bank in Nebraska failed, Chase, based in New York, could not buy the assets and keep it running. Such limitations are past in the United States. Full banking union in the EU and the easing of regulations limiting bank ownership would be useful for this reason, allowing easier private recapitalization of troubled banks.

Since the Great Depression, individual bank deposits have been insured, limiting this source of runs. However, large deposits are uninsured and can and do run. Recently, the Silicon Valley Bank (SVB) in the United States suffered a run of large uninsured deposits, when depositors learned that the bank lost money on its long-term bond portfolio. More important, the financial system features large amounts of uninsured deposits and deposit-like and run-prone short-term debt, including commercial paper, repurchase agreements, and derivatives contracts. Duffie (2011) describes how modern dealer banks fail.

The list of requirements for a run is a useful reminder that we do not have to live with recurrent crises. Financial crises are centrally driven by the run-prone nature of bank *liabilities*. Bank assets—diversified portfolios of loans and bonds—are far safer than those of industrial corporations. Just why, then, do we have volumes of regulations, armies of regulators and supervisors, and an alphabet soup of organizations promulgating more regulation of the safest asset books of any group of companies? Why regulate the risks of portfolios of loans and bonds, and not, say, the risks of Google's moonshot software projects, or SpaceX's literal moonshots? Because the latter are funded by equity, which can absorb losses without consequence to the financial system, and the former are funded by 9 euros of borrowing for every 1 (or fewer) euros of investors' equity.

Capital—equity issued by the bank to raise investment funds—is supposed to be the first risk buffer. If the value of assets falls, the price of equity falls rather than a default on debt. Unlike creditors, stockholders can't demand their money back and bankrupt the company if they don't get paid. Equity earns a good return when assets rise to compensate for this risk-bearing function. But banks can evade having equity take losses by reducing equity buffers. They use profits to pay dividends or buy back shares, or simply abstain from issuing new equity as the business expands. Then, when the crisis hits the bank is more fragile, and the lender of last resort will come to the rescue. Contra Modigliani and Miller, leveraged banks are more valuable than unleveregad ones because leverage unlocks bailouts. Bank shareholders then profit from high leverage, at the expense of taxpayers, and creditors don't demand higher interest rates.

If banks funded their investments with equity (stock), which offers no right to get your money back, or long-term debt, which does not promise money until a later date, they would not suffer runs or ever require central bank support. Bank regulation is slowly and painfully moving to greater amounts of such capital for this reason. But the evident possibility of a financial system that ends private-sector crises forever is a long way away (Admati and Hellwig, 2024, Cochrane, 2014).

Systemic Runs

An individual or local bank run is not a macroeconomic problem, however. A macroeconomic problem occurs only when a run spreads to multiple banks and similar financial institutions. A financial crisis is really by definition a simultaneous run on many banks. Terms such as "systemically important," "risk to the financial system," and "contagion" are widely overused. It's important to understand and to state what the issue is—and isn't.

Gorton and Metrick (2012) describe the mechanism of a modern systemic run in detail, emphasizing the run on repurchase agreements that broke out in 2008. Debt, and especially short-term debt, is "information-insensitive." When the issuer is far from insolvency, the value of debt does not vary with the issuer's health, unlike equity, whose value goes up and down constantly. As a result, short-term debt holders like bank depositors do not do much monitoring of a bank's health. Consequently, deposits and short-term debts are very liquid and trade as money. If someone offers you bank deposits in a check or sell you a short-term bond from a bank, you don't worry that he or she knows something you don't know and is trying to pass off a shady security. But if there is even a rumor that a bank may be in trouble, people start to worry that someone trying to sell them the bank's short-term debt knows something, and the debt suddenly becomes illiquid. Short-term debt holders do not specialize in monitoring bank health, so when they worry, they just dump the debt.

And when they hear news that one bank is in trouble, they don't look carefully at another similar bank's books—they just dump that bank's debt too. A systemic run on all banks develops. This is one concrete meaning of "contagion."

In a systemic crisis, people want to hold cash, not uninsured bank deposits and similar short-term debt. But there isn't enough cash to go around. The financial system as a whole does not have enough cash to make good on all the short-term promises to deliver cash.

Macroeconomic Consequences

Systemic bank runs can be socially costly as well as unpleasant to bank creditors. Widespread runs are associated with economic depression, as in 2008 and going back historically, including the Great Depression and the banking panics of the 19th century and before.

There are several mechanisms for this economic damage. In a monetarist analysis, the surge in money demand against a fixed or insufficiently elastic supply leads to deflation and depression, as argued by Friedman and Schwartz (1963) about the Great Depression.

If a bank fails and a new bank or other set of equity investors is not able or willing to quickly buy up the assets, infuse cash, honor its debts, and keep its operations going, then the bank is no longer able to make new loans and its individual and institutional knowledge is lost. Bernanke (1983) and Bernanke and James (1991) argue that the depth and persistence of the Great Depression was due in part to the failure of banks, leaving nobody around who could take deposits and make loans.

In the financial accelerator model (Bernanke, Gertler, and Gilchrist, 1996), the financial system relies on investors who swoop in and buy assets at low prices in bad times. But if investors are themselves borrowing, then they can be constrained when the value of their assets falls in a downturn, unable to provide cash just when it is most important—and profitable—for them to do so. Prices fall more.

Central Banks

For over a century, governments have responded to the threat of systemic runs with an expanding set of policies, usually located in the central bank: lender of last resort support to banks, deposit insurance and related short-term debt guarantees, extensive bank risk regulation, monetary expansion including low (now zero) interest rates, easy lending to banks against looser collateral, and now asset purchases designed to raise the value and liquidity of bank assets. Each of these measures produces ex-ante moral hazards.

The Bank of England evolved the lender of last resort function in the 19th century. The U.S. Federal Reserve was founded to be the lender of last resort and to "provide an elastic currency" following the 1907 crash. Setting interest rates and worrying about inflation came much later.

A lender of last resort stops a bank run by providing cash, against collateral, to banks that are having runs. The central bank takes collateral that private lenders are not willing to take during a crisis. Central banks also lend to financial institutions that take even worse collateral and encourage such lending via low interest rates.

The central bank has a key advantage as the lender of last resort— it can print money. It thus has what it takes, in potentially unlimited quantities, to stem nominal defaults. Even the largest private bank, clearinghouse, or bailout fund eventually runs out of cash and thus invites a run or "speculative attack."

The lender of last resort naturally risks becoming the lender of first resort, funding risky investments. Anticipating lender of last resort support, banks may not invest in adequately high-quality and liquid assets that they can sell or borrow against in bad times; investors may too quickly invest in bank debt at too low rates; banks may issue insufficient equity and raise funds instead from too much short-term debt and deposits. Historically, banks operated with equity as high as 40% of assets, and unregulated and presumably small-enough-to-fail shadow banks voluntarily operate today with 20% or more equity, double the 10% that regulations require of protected banks, over the latter's loud protests (Jiang et al., 2020).

Famously, Bagehot (1873) proposed that during financial panics, the central bank should lend freely, but at high interest rates, and only against good collateral. In practice, central bankers have followed only the first of Bagehot's rules, "lend freely." They quickly lower interest rates and lend at low or even subsidized rates. They expand collateral criteria to include riskier and illiquid assets, and they offer more money against the same collateral. Following the SVB run, the U.S. Fed even allowed banks to borrow against the face value of assets, not their lower market value. The ECB did not do that. In crises, the ECB lowered collateral requirements and provided large amounts of loans to banks at favorable rates. Following the pandemic, the ECB even lent at rates below the deposit rate at which the ECB borrows from banks. Lending to banks at subsidized rates amounts to recapitalization, a gift to shareholders. This is not criticism. Bagehot's rules are not written in stone, and the central bank is not maximizing profits.

In the financial crisis and in 2020, governments and central banks went beyond anything Bagehot imagined, including large-scale asset purchases and direct recapitalization of big banks. In place of good collateral and a penalty rate, central banks try to offset moral hazard instead with bank regulation and self- or legally imposed limitations on crisis interventions.

Central banks today also aggressively address the macroeconomic facets of systemic runs. Greater money demand does not meet a fixed supply. Central banks promptly lower interest rates and "inject liquidity." Monetarist scarcity of the means of payment is not likely an important economic problem.

Central banks clearly feel that the crisis-stopping value of these measures is worth the moral hazards. But as each crisis has been larger than the last, financial moral hazard has evidently grown. As with sovereigns, that induced fragility makes intervention more likely in the next crisis.

Farhi and Tirole (2012) is a contemporary theoretical analysis of the moral hazard posed by lender of last resort operations. Brunnermeier (2015) calls the result "financial dominance," paralleling the concept of "fiscal dominance." Monetary policy can be subservient to financial fragility as it can be subservient to sovereign default. Farhi and Tirole advocate an analog of central bank independence as a precommitment against excessive intervention, "independence with respect to the financial industry."

Summary

Bank rescues, like sovereign bailouts, can help to stem financial crises after they break out, but rescues induce additional fragility when people expect that rescues will come. Large financial bailouts can create fiscal risks and costs. If the risks materialize, the extra money so created either causes fiscal transfers or inflation.

Limitations on the ability of central banks to bail out ex post, both external and self-imposed, and a juggernaut of regulators and supervisors attempt to control moral hazards. But in banking today, everybody expects a bailout. While the interventions of 2008 at least led to attempts to stiffen regulation and precommit against interventions, the banking crises and bailouts of 2023 in the United States and Switzerland show that effort failed. Banks took on large and simple risks, regulators failed to see them, runs developed, and bailouts promptly followed. This time, there is not even an apology or promise to reform (Cochrane and Seru, 2024). Financial system participants expect interventions in any crisis. The definition of "crisis" has become so nebulous as to almost mean "somebody somewhere might lose money." And even the tiny two-percentage-point increases in bank equity demanded by the latest addition to regulations provoked a firestorm from banks.

Yet, as with sovereign debt, it is not evident that even the ECB has the resources to stop the next larger crisis, at least not without inflation. An ideal bailout is one that comes but nobody expects. The worst possible bailout is one that everyone expects but does not come.

2.7 Monetary Union

In a monetary and trade union without political, fiscal, and banking union, the above-mentioned considerations on fiscal and monetary policy interactions, revolving around credibility, time consistency, default, and inflation, become complicated by the division of decision-making authority.

In such a union, a benevolent monetary authority has an incentive to inflate away nominal debt when there is fiscal trouble. This temptation leads to a "free rider" or "moral hazard in teams" problem (Holmstrom, 1982; Chari and Kehoe, 2007). The fiscal authority in each country recognizes that debt monetization will lead to higher inflation for all. But it alone enjoys the full benefit of its own higher debt, while the inflation cost is diluted to everyone. A race to the bottom can result. When fiscal transfers are on the table, there is a similar incentive for each country to take on too high debt or delay reforms, and when getting in trouble, calling on its neighbors to help.

These problems can also be solved, in principle, with precommitments: If the central bank is not *able* to help ex post, if other countries are not *able* to offer fiscal transfers ex post, countries have the incentive not to get in to trouble ex ante. This idea underlies the founding commitments of the euro, including restrictions on ECB authority and the no-bailout clause. Aguiar et al. (2015) study this situation, showing how debt ceilings and other precommitments help to avoid moral hazard.

But governments and central banks do not like to bind themselves so they really *cannot* act. There is always some crisis so severe that governments *should* break the rules. Even countries immune from moral hazard can suffer horrible shocks. Not helping them just to maintain moral hazard incentives seems heartless. So despite the beauty of iron-clad and inviolable precommitments, we will always be in a fuzzy middle where the precommitment makes intervention costly to contain moral hazard, but not make it impossible; where precommitments allow "just this once" exceptions but somehow limit them, and quickly reestablish faith that it won't happen routinely. The hard task, then, is to sort of precommit, without inducing a slippery slope that every shower is treated like a biblical flood. We see attempts to institute such a regime throughout our history of interventions. So far they have not been successful.

Sovereign member states might also exit the monetary union. This event is called "redenomination risk." (See Constâncio, 2018.) A government with an unsustainable fiscal position faces an unpalatable menu of options: explicit default on its bonds, cutting spending, increasing tax revenue, or growth-enhancing reforms that offend powerful constituencies. A country in a union cannot choose implicit default via inflation. But it can introduce a new national currency, exit the union, and default by redenominating its debt in national currency and afterward devalue.

Debt promised euros, so this substitution of currencies likely constitutes legal default. But it may be legally easier. Default via redenomination, like default via inflation, also carries over to private debts, which the government may have backstopped. For example, if a country's banks are stuffed with sovereign debt, then a sovereign default means that the banks cannot repay the euros that those banks have promised to depositors. Redenomination can, and historically does, therefore extend to bank accounts and private debts in the country. Redenomination and devaluation can cut the real value of government worker salaries, pensions, and subsidies without the politically explosive steps of nominal cuts. Greece and Italy were urged by some people to exit and devalue during the euro crisis, and such an exit was one of the greatest fears at the ECB and among other defenders of the euro. That exit would likely have collapsed the whole project.

Abandonment of the gold standard in the 1930s is a legal and economic precedent for sovereign redenomination, though also in a quite different economic environment. Countries including the United States and the United Kingdom left the gold standard, abrogating both private and sovereign promises that bondholders could demand repayment in gold. Again in the 1970s, the United States abandoned the remaining Bretton Woods gold clauses, breaking the right of foreign central banks to receive gold in place of dollars.

The effect of redenomination hinges on the legal question of whether and which public and private debts that promise euros can be repaid in new local currency, and what court has power to do anything about a sovereign's decision to do so. An attempt to redenominate debt is likely to lead to legal chaos.

Redenomination also creates financial instability: The moment people start to anticipate such an event, all debtors in the country, not just of the sovereign, face a significant risk premium, causing the country's growth to drop, impeding new lending or rolling over loans, and aggravating the initial situation (De Grauwe and Ji, 2013). Short-term debts will not be rolled over, people will pull money out of banks, and so a crisis will break out in anticipation of redenomination. Despite the pundits who see redenomination and exit as a low-cost way to escape debts, in fact an orderly restructuring of sovereign debt inside the monetary union may well be less costly and chaotic than an exit, and a preannounced or anticipated exit most of all.

Thus, a good monetary union adds benefits for remaining in the euro, as well as costs to exit and redenomination. It is in the country's interest to accede to exit costs, as that precommits to repayment and thereby lets the country borrow more easily. When Greece or Portugal joined the euro, their borrowing costs plummeted. They had renounced, or at least made much more costly, the previous habit of inflating away debt and devaluing the currency in bad times. They had made inflation and redenomination more costly ex post, and reaped the ex-ante benefits of ample new borrowing at low rates. They overdid the borrowing, and the ex-post costs came to bite, but how costly their crises were proves the point that it was valuable to sign up for such costs as an ex-ante precommitment.

3

The Design of the Economic and Monetary Union

The initial design of the Economic and Monetary Union (EMU) was set out in the 1992 Treaty on the European Union, known as the Maastricht Treaty. The Treaty reflected many of these economic issues.

With the monetary union, eleven (now twenty) European Union (EU) member states gave up their separate currencies in favor of a common currency managed by a new European institution, the European Central Bank (ECB). However, fiscal and many economic and financial and banking policies are still made by independent member states. The EU has almost no taxing rights and does relatively little spending. It has some centralized powers, particularly in trade, single-market, competition, and agriculture policies, but it is far from a full political union or a federal state such as the United States.

The architects of the euro well understood the potential for moral hazards and disincentives. A country might spend and borrow too much and then pressure the ECB or other member states to bail it out. If each person orders their own wine at a dinner where the guests split the bill, the bill can mount quickly. If banks are loaded with government debt, default becomes more costly, raising pressure for monetization or bailouts. If bondholders expect fiscal or monetary bailouts, they have little incentive to assess and manage sovereign risk. And if countries expect fiscal or monetary bailouts, they are shielded from market incentives for fiscal and microeconomic reform.

To address these risks, the architects of the EMU envisioned a separation of monetary and fiscal policies. The ECB was in charge of monetary policy. Member states were in charge of their fiscal policies. Member states foreswore inflation and devaluation. They were supposed to borrow moderately, to repay their debts, and to ensure sufficient fiscal space for bad times.

The ECB was thus set up as an independent central bank, given a primary mandate to focus on price stability. The Treaty explicitly prohibited monetary financing of government budgets, including sovereign bond purchases in the primary market. In its first decade, the ECB did not buy or otherwise support sovereign debts. A fiscal no-bail-out principle that member states would not intervene directly accompanied this monetary no-bail-out principle. Member states agreed to debt and deficit limits in order to join the euro. Many rules, traditions, norms, and writing built the founding philosophy on these structures. Well-run national banking regulation would keep banks out of trouble and remove the troublesome question of ECB intervention.

But suppose that these guides are insufficient, and a member state cannot borrow, roll over, or repay its debts? While that eventuality was implicitly clear from the no bail-out principle and the prohibition of monetary financing, it was glossed over in the design of the EMU. Would sovereigns really default, haircut, or restructure debts, just as corporations and sovereigns borrowing in foreign currency do? In joining the EMU, did member states really and fully give up the privilege of avoiding nominal default via the printing of money? Should banks and bank regulators really think of sovereign debts of European countries as having default and rollover risks? The regulatory answer to the latter, in practice, is no: Bank regulation still treats sovereign debt as uniquely risk free.

Clearly, it was hoped that debt and deficit limits and the apparent pre-commitment not to intervene, together with a revived fiscal and economic responsibility, would make such impolite questions irrelevant.

The clarity and depth of the EMU founders' vision are impressive. But like all founding documents, they could not write rules for every eventuality of a new system. The EMU would have to evolve, fill in the cracks via secondary legislation or treaty changes, and adapt the founders' vision to new eventualities. Alas, the implementation of such a founding vision was not completed, the unfinished parts remained unfinished and caused trouble, and the structure weakened as it evolved over the years. This process, its consequences, and how to reestablish a more functional and resilient EMU constitute our central story.

3.1 The Triple Lock

Three central provisions separated monetary and fiscal policy in the EMU design: A prohibition on monetary financing of sovereign debts, limits on debt and deficits, and a no-bail-out principle that member states shall not support others' debts by fiscal means. Together, these form a "triple lock."

The EU treaties restricted the ECB's ability to buy government debt or conduct similar quasi-fiscal operations. Article 123 of the Treaty on the Functioning of the European Union (EU Treaty, or the Treaty for short) says: "Overdraft facilities or any other type of credit facility with the European Central Bank or with the central banks of the member states (hereinafter referred to as 'national central banks') in favour of Union institutions, bodies, offices or agencies, central governments, regional, local or other public authorities, . . . shall be prohibited, as shall the purchase directly from them by the European Central Bank or national central banks of debt instruments."[1]

The article prohibits the direct (i.e. primary market) *purchase* of sovereign debt by the European Central Bank (and by national central banks) from the issuing country. The article also prohibits the ECB from *lending* to member states' governments. With these two prohibitions, the Treaty was taken to forbid monetary financing of sovereign debt.

In addition to these formal and legal restrictions, the ECB initially elaborated internal policies against sovereign purchases, described below.

Article 125 of the Treaty, sometimes called the "no bail-out clause," specifies that member states and their creditors will not be bailed out by the union or by other member states: "The Union [or] . . . A Member State shall not be liable for or assume the commitments of central governments, regional, local or other public authorities, other bodies governed by public law, or public undertakings of another Member State, without prejudice to mutual financial guarantees for the joint execution of a specific project."

The architects of the EMU recognized that there would still be a temptation to bail out governments and monetize debts if sovereign default loomed. They also included limits on debts and deficits so that countries would be less likely to get in fiscal trouble in the first place.

The 1992 Maastricht Treaty set "reference values" for fiscal deficits, equal to 3% of gross domestic product (GDP), and debt, equal to 60% of GDP. These reference values were not hard limits to be met every year. The deficit ratio could be exceeded if "the excess over the reference value is only exceptional and temporary and the ratio remains close to the reference value." The debt ratio could be exceeded if it "is sufficiently diminishing and approaching the reference value at a satisfactory pace."

The 1997 Stability and Growth Pact (SGP; Regulation (EC) N° 1466/97) added detailed procedures to ensure that countries stay within debt and deficit limits. All EU members are subject to the SGP, although non-euro-area members cannot be fined under its provisions. The SGP consists of two main procedures, or "arms." Under the "preventative arm," member states must submit their stability program each year to the European Commission, in which member states set out their budgetary policies and objectives. These programs are examined by the Commission, which may issue recommendations to countries that risk excessive debt or deficits. Under the "corrective arm," countries that do not comply are subject to a procedure that may lead to sanctions and fines. (See article 126 of the Treaty on the "Excessive Deficit Procedure.") Both recommendations and decisions were to be taken by the Council of the EU (composed of the economic and finance ministers of the member states), hence preserving a lot of political discretion. Undefined "exceptional circumstances" and "other relevant facts," the latter in the case of the preventative arm, may also apply, and the deadline for closing the deficits may be prolonged in "special" circumstances. So these were far from automatic rules.

The original 1997 Pact was amended many times, first to give it more flexibility and then to make it more binding. As the SGP is not part of the Maastricht Treaty but secondary legislation, such changes were not as politically difficult as a Treaty amendment would have been, since Treaty amendment requires unanimity, as well as a referendum in some member states. But it likewise does not enjoy as much force.

The debt and deficit limits, designed to reduce pressure on the ECB and member states for bailouts, also embed a clever implicit fiscal-monetary coordination. The 3% deficit limit was defined for the overall budget balance, including interest payments on the debt, not just primary deficits. This feature means that governments with larger debts and higher interest rates must automatically reduce spending or increase tax revenue. Moreover, such a definition of the deficit limit forces member states to provide fiscal support for monetary policy. If the ECB raises interest rates, countries are supposed to pay the consequent higher interest costs on their debt via higher tax revenue or less spending.

We apparently have a triple commitment: The ECB shall not print money to finance deficits or bail out debt; member states shall never borrow enough money to get in trouble in the first place; and member states shall not be obliged to bail each other out directly.

However, one may also regard the need for three prongs as an admission that none of them is adequately strong on its own. If debt and deficit limits are sufficient to keep a country out of fiscal trouble, then we don't need rules against fiscal or monetary bailouts. If the precommitment against bailouts and monetization is firm, and if countries in trouble default just as companies do, then there is no need to limit borrowing. Borrow what you want and can, and default when you can't repay—caveat emptor. Placing limits on debts and deficits recognizes that EU institutions and countries will be tempted and able to ignore rules ex post.

The rules are also not ironclad, and wisely so. There is always a large enough shock for which one must bend rules and worry about moral hazard later.

3.2   A Missing Piece

A missing piece, in our view, was a fourth prong: The Maastricht Treaty did not include any mechanisms to address fiscal trouble should it actually arise despite the first three prongs. There was no procedure for orderly restructuring of sovereign debts and no mechanism for temporary fiscal help for a country facing a crisis to get its affairs in order and reassure markets. By contrast, the Bretton Woods fixed exchange rate regime included the creation of the International Monetary Fund (IMF), designed to manage debt and balance of payments problems.

By this silence, the Treaty left an impression that sovereign default is somehow specially unthinkable. It is implicitly a catastrophe, necessarily causing a financial calamity or ending the currency union. At least, that attitude pervaded when sovereign default loomed.

Silence also left the impression that sovereign default is impossible. Bank regulation does not require banks to hold any capital buffers against their government bonds. Even high-yielding sovereign debt is treated as risk free. No wonder that banks hold a lot of undiversified sovereign debt and prefer that debt to comparable corporate debt. A sovereign restructuring then spills into financial turmoil.

When default loomed in the sovereign debt crisis, the consequences of the omission became real. Policy discussion were dominated by the presumption that default might lead to euro exit, or even the dissolution of the euro, as well as fears of "contagion" or financial calamity, rather than execution of a plan for restructuring and reform within the euro.

We do not blame the euro's architects for these omissions. The Treaty included an impressive and far-sighted structure. It was natural for its architects to assume that additional fail-safe mechanisms would be implemented later. One cannot pre-plan all contingencies in founding documents. The architects of the euro surely felt that if the unthinkable happened and a debt crisis did break out, European institutions, including the ECB, would muddle through somehow, perhaps breaking some rules or promises along the way, as they did. But then they would sit down and create mechanisms to prevent a recurrence. Procedures would evolve over time with experience, as did those of the IMF. As we will describe below, that process started during the European sovereign debt crisis, but then it was abandoned. This is a crucial elaboration and reform step that we urge.

Including a resolution mechanism would also have been politically awkward. Bretton Woods was not created in a union of equals. The EMU is. "Just whose default are you planning for here anyway?" some countries were sure to ask. Conditionality was sure to be seen as some countries planning to tell others how to run their affairs. When setting up a union, premised in great part on a spirit of cooperation rather than punitive rules, it would have been natural to think that even talking about defaults, rescues, and conditionalities would undermine that spirit of cooperation. Of *course* we're all going to be good partners. Nobody here is going to default, so why are we talking about it so much?

They may have feared, correctly, that creating a resolution and temporary help mechanism would raise the chance that it would be used. It would be better for us all to agree that default is unthinkable, so of course we're all going to behave responsibly.

Finally, recall that the late 1980s and early 1990s, when the institutions of the euro were discussed and decided, enjoyed a benign macroeconomic and fiscal environment. Few people other than economic historians thought about monetary-fiscal interactions, advanced-country sovereign defaults, or large-scale bank failures at all. Crises such as those in Latin America were on the other side of the world, in smaller emerging markets. Nobody imagined the financial crisis, which is part of why it happened. Even after the financial crisis, nobody imagined the sovereign debt crisis, which is part of why it happened. The fact that the architects of the euro didn't spell out what to do in such apparently unlikely circumstances is understandable.

The lessons of the subsequent crises seem clear today, however. The EMU needs institutions that can manage sovereign restructuring. Regular bankruptcy law and procedures are not well suited to sovereign restructuring. Such an institution should also be able to promptly offer temporary fiscal support, and any ECB participation must leave out implicit fiscal support. The institution must be able to require "conditionality," that the country enact a program of structural adjustment in order to receive support: more effective taxes, restrained spending, and pro-growth microeconomic policies. It must also be able to impose debt restructuring, bondholder haircuts, as part of the support package or if conditionality fails. If default is unthinkable, then the country can more easily refuse or renege on conditionality terms. The European banking and financial regulatory system must be insulated from such restructuring by recognizing that sovereign debt is risky and planning accordingly. Such a mechanism could also have eased pressure on the ECB to buy stressed country bonds.

Conditionality is admittedly a blunt instrument. Countries get in trouble from bad microeconomic and fiscal policies. The prospect of fiscal or monetary help blunts the market incentive to pursue better policies. As Otmar Issing explained (Issing, 2015, 6): "Ultimately, if the costs of poor national policies are increasingly borne by other European states, there is little reason for one to expect that certain governments will finally fight tax evasion, stem corruption and overcome the vested interests that are blocking reforms. . . . It remains in the first place a national responsibility to implement badly needed structural reforms." Just what policies a country needs to follow is always a difficult and controversial issue. Countries need higher tax revenue to fill the fiscal gap, but lower tax rates to spur growth. Transfers can help people weather an economic downturn, but they add to the fiscal problem. Still, if other states are going to offer help, then some even blunt conditionality is necessary to offset the disincentive for doing anything.

Some might view the Treaty's omissions as features rather than bugs. The more costly a default, the greater incentive to avoid default ex ante. If there is no mechanism to restructure debts or to provide temporary fiscal support, parties will work harder to avoid the need to use them. If sovereign default blows up a country's banks, perhaps that country will be more careful to avoid debt that threatens default. This incentive view of deliberate financial fragility is common in the academic literature.

However, many financial costs of default, as well as of alternative "solutions" such as high inflation and ad hoc cross-country transfers, are also external to the indebted country, so such incentives are not well aligned. If German and French banks are stuffed with Greek debt, the Greek government may care less about avoiding default. Moreover, there is no evidence that the architects of the euro deliberately set up a fragile fiscal foundation in order to make sovereign debt trouble more painful. Therefore, given the history of fiscal and sovereign debt crises before and outside the EU, our judgment lies on the side of having multiple layers of safety. Seat belts are, after all, better than spikes on the dashboard (Peltzman, 1975) for enhancing automotive safety. Mechanisms that make orderly default practical and isolate the financial system from an induced crisis can also strengthen the commitment to allow defaults instead of fiscal or monetary bailouts.

3.3 Monetary Union without Banking Union

Economic and monetary union was conceived and introduced without a comprehensive banking union. There was no common banking regulation, no common supervision, and no common deposit insurance. Each remained functions of national supervisors, which in many cases are the national central banks (NCBs) and national regulators.

Hence, dealing with a banking crisis and failing banks was left to national fiscal authorities, NCBs, and national regulators. Even the lender-of-last resort function (Emergency Liquidity Assistance, or ELA) was assigned to *national* central banks, which would decide as part of their national, nonmonetary tasks how to offer such support.

Although significant steps toward banking union were set in motion in 2012, to this day, the common market and free trade provisions that are the backbone of the European Union do not extend fully to banking. Formal and informal control of national banking systems remains politically attractive. Member country regulators and politicians have placed obstacles in the way of European-wide consolidation. National regulators demand "ring-fencing" of liquidity and capital at the national level, limiting banks' ability to use resources in one country to address problems in another.

As a result, the banking market remains fragmented across countries, with little cross-border banking integration. This limits banks' ability to diversify risks and achieve economies of scale. Two particularly notable risks are banks' excessive exposure to the debt of their own sovereign and their vulnerability to local political influence.

An alternative word with integrated, euro-area-wide banks would allow for effective private cross-border risk sharing (Maragopoulos, 2021). Imagine how much less disruption would follow the failure of a Spanish bank, for example, if it were just a branch of a European-wide bank, whose assets were a diversified portfolio of private and sovereign debt throughout the union, which could draw on resources throughout the union, which could easily issue widely traded equity and debt and which could rely on a well-developed ECB lender of last resort.

The Treaty also did not include concrete cooperative rules and procedures to address a banking crisis that occurs simultaneously in several countries, or spills from one to another. It is difficult for national fiscal authorities, banking regulators, and supervisors to act jointly to stabilize, recapitalize, or wind down banks in trouble, avoiding beggar-my-neighbor behavior.

In the resulting system, sovereign crises spill over into national banking systems.

This oversight may simply have resulted from the general lack of interest in advanced-country financial stability and sovereign debt issues in global central banking circles before the financial and European debt crises. If you think that bank failures are isolated to individual banks and result from country-specific and local conditions, such as local real estate or industry shocks; if you think that sovereign debt problems are ancient history and won't infect banks, then a purely national system of regulation, with the sovereign's fiscal resources standing behind banks, makes sense. The oversight also may have resulted from a political desire to keep bank regulation and supervision at a national level, as fiscal policy was kept at a national level. It may have seemed sensible to the architects of the euro that countries, which were not going to get in sovereign trouble due to debt and deficit limits, could easily handle the troubles of their individual banks. It was natural for them not to envision that banking crises could engulf a country or spill from country to country, and that the same sovereign that is supporting banks could be in trouble.

Now we know otherwise. As it turned out, banks were exposed to European and global shocks, and the very states that were supposed to stand behind them sometimes were the source of trouble.

The lesson of the 2008 financial crisis and the sovereign debt crisis is that such national compartmentalization is harmful. Individual states can try to give a competitive advantage to their banks with lax regulation or try to use national banks to support national businesses. Individual states can run out of resources to support national banks that are even partly open to union-wide business, as Ireland found out. A state that might have fiscal trouble cannot be the lender of last resort to banks that will be in trouble during a debt crisis. Commingling sovereign and banking risks in individual countries makes crises much worse.

3.4 Monetary Union without Fiscal Union Is Feasible

Contrary to the popular proverb, a currency union without fiscal union union is perfectly possible, so long as it is clearly understood that member states default if they cannot repay their debts, just as private firms and individuals do. If sovereigns cannot be allowed to default, it's a fiscal union.

Companies, even large ones, may participate in the euro area. If they get in trouble, they default. Bond holders lose money. The world does not end. The companies are not kicked out of the currency zone or forced to create their own new currency. (Admittedly, large companies are increasingly bailed out by fiscal authorities and by central banks, but the point is that default is possible.) In the previous centuries-long, continent-wide monetary union, based on gold coins, sovereigns defaulted. It was not pleasant, but it was possible, and nobody had to leave the currency zone. That sovereigns must in the end be allowed to default occasionally is an inescapable conclusion of a monetary union without fiscal union. The Treaty's flaw is being silent on the issue, allowing an expedient ambiguity. But that ambiguity proved costly.

The proverbs also suggest that monetary union with fiscal and banking union would be a panacea. But fiscal union has its own problems.

3.5 The European Central Bank

The ECB was designed to manage the common currency. Its primary mandate is price stability, which since 2021 it defines as an inflation target of 2%. Its main instrument is the short-term interest rate. It was designed to stay away from sovereign debt support and, largely, banking regulation. It was granted great political independence to help it resist pressure for action outside its mandate.

A politically independent central bank with a limited mandate is a classic institution by which a government or union of governments precommits against the temptation to use monetary policy to inflate away debt, to finance fiscal deficits, to bail out a government in fiscal trouble, to direct credit to politically popular constituencies, to transfer resources among member states, or to temporarily goose the economy with low interest rates or a bit of inflation. The ECB was set up exactly in this way and to these ends.

The Price Stability Mandate

Article 127 (1) of the Treaty on the Functioning of the European Union sets forth the ECB's official legal mandate:

1. The primary objective of the European System of Central Banks (hereinafter referred to as 'the ESCB') shall be to maintain price stability. Without prejudice to the objective of price stability, the ESCB shall support the general economic policies in the Union with a view to contributing to the achievement of the objectives of the Union as laid down in Article 3 of the Treaty on European Union. The ESCB shall act in accordance with the principle of an open market economy with free competition, favouring an efficient allocation of resources, and in compliance with the principles set out in Article 119.

2. The basic tasks to be carried out through the ESCB shall be:
—to define and implement the monetary policy of the Union.[2]

The mandate is as important for what it omits, and thereby precludes, as for what it includes. The ECB's primary mandate does *not* include employment, macroeconomic stability, cross-country variation in economic conditions, a primary role in financial stability, support for sovereign debt, or industrial-policy credit subsidies and allocation, except as these might be incidentally important to price stability.

This mandate has had a powerful effect, also on ECB communications. The ECB has been careful to phrase all of its innovations and interventions as necessary in the pursuit of price stability, or of "monetary policy transmission" necessary for it to stabilize prices.

The ECB's price-stability mandate contrasts, for example, with the U.S. Federal Reserve mandate, which explicitly includes "maximum employment" as a separate objective. Employment varies across member states, so emphasis on employment might have led to policies that help some states at the expense of others. The ECB's narrow mandate was also a part of the general consensus on the superiority of pure inflation targets that emerged in the early 1990s. Economists and central bankers recognized that monetary fine tuning of the real economy is not generally successful, and employment is maximized within the constraints of what monetary policy can do by simply controlling inflation. Inflation-targeting reforms in New Zealand, Canada, and Israel proved remarkably successful in stabilizing inflation with little macroeconomic pain.

To an Inflation Target

A mandate is not carved in stone, and its brief words leave plenty of room for interpretation. The mandate evolves by the continual dialogue between the ECB, the EU, and the public, as well as by precedent and experience. The ECB itself was central to the founding of the monetary union by interpreting, elaborating, and implementing its mandates and legal foundations; by announcing its monetary policy strategy and operational framework; and by setting precedents, publishing its legal opinions and assessments, and explaining and propounding this founding philosophy.

In particular, the ECB was left to interpret just what "price stability" means. In October 1998, the ECB provided a quantitative definition of its objective as follows: "Price stability shall be defined as a year-on-year increase in the Harmonised Index of Consumer Prices (HICP) for the euro area of below 2%. Price stability is to be maintained over the medium term."

The ECB also stated that monetary policy would have a "forward-looking, medium-term orientation," given that there exists "short-term volatility in prices which cannot be controlled by monetary policy."[3]

To understand what this means, consider two alternatives. The ECB might have chosen to target average inflation over some medium term, say four years, without the "forward-looking" qualification. Then, if inflation were 3% in years one and two, the ECB would try to bring inflation down to 1% in years three and four, so that inflation averaged 2% over the full four-year period. The ECB's "forward-looking" objective means the opposite: It will ignore the 3% overshoot and just try to keep inflation at 2% going forward.

As a second and deeper alternative, the ECB might have interpreted "price stability" to mean just that—stability in the level of prices. Or the ECB might have interpreted it as a target for the level of prices that grows 2% per year. In either case, periods of excess inflation would be followed by periods of low inflation or slight deflation to restore the price level to its target path. The ECB does not interpret "price stability" to mean stability of the price level.

Few complain, as few complain about the Federal Reserve's (and most other central banks') similar interpretation of its "price stability" mandate. An *inflation* target that forgets about past errors was the standard interpretation of such targets in the 1990s in academia and central banks. Still, the Treaty authors, like the authors of the Humphrey–Hawkins Full Employment Act of 1978 in the United States, presumably chose the words "*price* stability," not "*inflation* stability," for a reason.

In the following years, the ECB's inflation objective has drifted upward from "below 2%." Most recently, in 2021, the ECB announced a symmetric 2% inflation target, with inflation below 2% also seen as undesirable. This drift came in several steps and different motivations.

Following the 2003 evaluation of its monetary policy strategy, the ECB clarified that it would aim at inflation rates "below, but close to" 2%.[4] This new aim was broadly understood to be in the range of about 1.7–1.9%.

There were three motivations for this slight rise in the effective inflation target. First, the ECB worried that since interest rates cannot easily go below zero, any deflation might spiral out of control. Aim higher. This worry about inflation below 2% was to dominate ECB monetary policy in the 2010s. Second, an inflation target biased upward toward 2% addresses measurement bias in the price level. Like all price indices, the HICP does not perfectly adjust for better-quality goods. Getting a better-quality good at the same price is an increase in purchasing power, so zero measured inflation is actually a bit of deflation. Third, a Europe-wide HICP ignores inflation differentials within the euro area. The ECB views that deflation is a worse problem than inflation. Prices and wages may be more sticky in the downward direction than the upward direction, and downward price adjustments may carry larger short-term economic costs. If prices are going to grow, say, 3% more in Italy than in Spain, the ECB would prefer 0% inflation in Spain and 3% inflation in Italy to −1% inflation in Spain and 2% inflation in Italy.

Following the ECB's second strategy review, in mid-2021 the ECB announced a new symmetric inflation target of 2%, implying slightly higher inflation than the previous aim of below but close to 2%. This review followed 10 years of mostly below-target inflation, zero or negative interest rates, and persistent fear of too low inflation or a deflationary spiral. The ECB felt that the asymmetry of a 2% upper bound in the original definition of "price stability" made it more difficult to move inflation upward toward 2%. Inflation is driven in part by expected inflation. If people believe that inflation can never be higher than 2% but can be lower than 2%, their inflation expectations will be systematically lower than 2%. The ECB's move was thus part of a larger strategy to increase inflation back up to the 2% upper bound, without the ability to move interest rates down any more, by managing expectations. This strategy, like the Fed's move to "flexible average inflation targeting" in the same period, suffered in retrospect from bad timing, as the problem of the day soon turned to inflation well above target, not deflation.

The ECB was clear from the outset that its monetary policy must focus on price stability in the euro area as a whole, and thus it would not try to address cross-country inflation differentials or support specific individual countries' economies, sovereign debt, or banking systems. Following the 2003 evaluation of its monetary policy strategy, the ECB (European Central Bank, 2003a) stressed: "In any currency area—be it a currency union or a single country—monetary policy cannot and should not try to reduce inflation differentials across regions or cities. Instead, depending on the sources and causes of the inflation differentials, regional remedies may be needed."

The ECB on Economic Policy and Monetary-Fiscal Separation

The ECB stressed that its narrow functions require that member states take up other functions; that sound national fiscal and economic policies, including structural reforms, were crucial for member states to prosper and reap the benefits of monetary union. This separation of responsibilities was expressed in speeches from ECB board members and articles in the ECB's Monthly Bulletin and also enshrined the ECB's design of the monetary strategy and operational framework. In this way the ECB attempted to pre-commit against intervention, and to guide expectations of people, governments, and markets consistent with the original intent.

Wim Duisenberg, who became the first president of the ECB in June 1998, stressed already in early 1998:

> The option of using monetary and exchange rate policy in the event of country-specific problems . . . with the aim of reducing the burden of financing a high level of government debt will no longer be available. . . . The absence of a monetary policy oriented to the economic situation in individual member countries

puts even greater premium on removing rigidities, particularly in product and labour markets. These markets should be flexible enough to allow wages and prices to be adjusted quickly. Such flexibility would be needed to avoid increased unemployment should local economic conditions worsen—due, for example, to an asymmetric shock or a relatively weak local productivity increase.[5]

Duisenberg's plea for microeconomic flexibility was not heeded.

In an important ECB Bulletin article (European Central Bank, 2003b), the ECB also wrote about the relationship between monetary policy and fiscal policies in the euro area. Here, the ECB explicitly stressed the importance of both monetary and fiscal no-bail-out principles:

> The "no bail-out" clause, which stipulates that neither the Community nor any Member State is liable for or can assume the debts incurred by any other Member State (Article 103), . . . imposes further incentives on the part of national fiscal authorities to preserve budgetary discipline. In this respect, high government debt cannot be inflated away, nor can a government that does not stick to the rules rely on being eventually bailed out by other governments. Thus, in the current institutional framework, individual governments cannot shift part of the burden of high government debt to other parts of the euro area. In this way, it also ensures that unsound fiscal policies in one country will tend to lead to higher risk premia for the debt of that country and not for the debt of other countries. This in turn increases the incentives for fiscal discipline at the national level.

The last sentences are particularly important: Well before the 2008 financial crisis, the ECB anticipated in public that countries could have sovereign debt problems, that such problems would lead to higher yield spreads, that those derive from "fundamentals," not "fragmentation" or "dislocation," and that fiscal or monetary intervention to stop rising yield spreads would lead to moral hazard, silencing important market signals and pressures on governments to follow better policies. The ECB made clear that it should not be expected to prop up the debt of individual member states by buying such debt, either to forestall restructuring or to hold down yield spreads.

Beyond Price Stability

The ECB's mandate is not solely focused on price stability. Additional roles for the ECB have evolved over time.

As quoted previously, the mandate also includes that the ECB shall "support the general economic policies in the EU." That clause includes the proviso "without prejudice to the objective of price stability," indicating that price stability comes first. The ECB should not trade inflation for any other policy goal. Still, this language allows the ECB a role in general economic policy, including fiscal policy or policy with fiscal characteristics, which is unusual for independent central banks.

The mandate also adds that "The ESCB shall act in accordance with the principle of an open market economy with free competition, favouring an efficient allocation of resources." This "market economy principle" is an interesting proviso, as it may also reflect the fear that the "general economic policies in the EU" might someday contravene that principle, and it also constrains the ECB not to support such policies. For example, it seemingly rules out increasingly popular industrial policies, credit-allocation policies, protectionist, or place-based policies, should the EU itself move in those directions. It also refers to policies *in* the EU, not just *of* the EU, thus referring to member-state policies as well as EU policies.

Before the financial crisis, sovereign debt crisis, and large-scale asset purchases, including corporate bond purchases, these provisions may have seemed like harmless boilerplate, but now they matter.

With the 2003 strategy review, the ECB also announced a concern for employment stabilization (European Central Bank, 2003b): "In the case of some . . . economic shocks (e.g. of a cost-push nature) . . . it is widely recognised that a gradual response of monetary policy is appropriate to avoid unnecessarily high volatility in real activity. Thus, the medium-term orientation . . . helps to avoid introducing unnecessary volatility into the economy and embodies a concern for and a contribution to the stabilisation of output and employment."

This move too might fall under a concern for general economic policies, although the ECB did not make that claim.

By and large, however, the ECB justifies its actions as necessary for maintaining price stability, and to preserve the "monetary transmission mechanism" in the pursuit of price stability, even when its actions seem to support economic policies in the EU or other goals. For example, explaining its climate initiatives, the ECB writes: "Higher temperatures, storms or droughts—but also deforestation, soil erosion or pollinator losses—can push up prices and ultimately inflation. Price and financial stability can only be preserved if climate and nature are stable."[6] Even at the cost of confusing the price level with relative prices, the ECB prefers to motivate its climate initiatives in terms of "price and financial stability" mandates rather than support for economic policies in the EU. (See also section 3.1 of the 2021 policy review,[7] which frames climate policy as deriving from price and financial stability mandates.)

Similarly, announcing the €750 billion Pandemic Emergency Purchase Program (PEPP) in spring 2020, the ECB said that the purpose of the program was "to counter the serious risks to the monetary policy transmission mechanism and the outlook for the euro area posed by the outbreak and escalating diffusion of the coronavirus, COVID-19."[8]

The ECB's mandate evolves over time, in part as the ECB announces and interprets its mandate, and others accept that reinterpretation. Currently, the ECB justifies its actions predominantly through a relatively narrow view of its mandate: price stability, monetary transmission, and—to a lesser extent—financial stability; rather than support for general economic policies. This narrow justification comes with a rather expansive view of what forces impinge on monetary transmission and price stability.

The Balance Sheet and Tools

As a reminder, central banks issue currency and reserves, accounts that banks hold at the central bank. (We often use the term "reserves" to refer to all accounts that banks hold at the central bank.) Banks may freely exchange reserves for cash, so together those form the stock of government-provided money. Central banks balance those liabilities with assets.

The ECB initially did not buy and sell government or other debt to create or extinguish new money. Instead, the ECB created new money and lent it to banks. The loan counts as the asset against the liability of newly created money. Like the universe, central bank money can indeed spring from nothing. ECB loans to banks are called "refinancing" or "repurchase operations," since the ECB lends against collateral.

As Bindseil et al. (2017) explain:

> The ECB decided before 1999 that the Eurosystem would initially not have holdings of securities for monetary policy purposes, which it referred to as "permanent operations", because securities once purchased may be held for a long period until they mature, and because permanent operations were considered less neutral towards capital markets. Hence, it decided that it would use credit operations, which it also referred to as "temporary operations" because they would have relatively short terms of usually one day (marginal lending facility), one week (main refinancing operations) and three months (longer-term refinancing operations).

This structure is unusual for contemporary central banks. The structure seems to reflect the Article 123 prohibition on monetary financing and the Article 127 (1) obligation to respect the market economy principle (both quoted earlier in this chapter). It represents a good case in which the ECB interpreted, implemented, and elaborated on the founding principles.

The ECB's primary tool of monetary policy was to raise and lower the interest rates that it offers on such credit operations. The ECB established a "corridor" for short-term rates. The upper bound of the corridor is the marginal lending rate at which banks can borrow from the ECB. The lower bound is defined by the deposit facility rate at which banks can deposit funds at the ECB. The corridor was wide, 2 percentage points, in the early 2000s, but has narrowed over time, reaching 0.40 percentage points in September 2024.

The ECB initially also adopted a reference value for monetary aggregate M3. This "monetary pillar" was not a conventional monetary target. It signaled that monetary aggregates would play an important role as indicators, together with the economic analysis, including inflation forecasts. These indicators informed the ECB's interest rate decisions. Quantitative easing, forward guidance, and unconventional policy tools came later.

In the initial decade, the Eurosystem consolidated balance sheet remained small. Excess reserves, beyond those necessary by regulatory reserve requirements, were negligible. Since the deposit rate was below the lending rate, with market rates in between, banks had an incentive to minimize borrowing and holding reserves.

Table 3.1 presents the main balance sheet items on selected dates, and figures 3.1 and 3.2 plot trends in the major Eurosystem balance sheet assets and liabilities, respectively.[9]

In mid-2001, the total balance sheet was only €863 billion. Assets included €128 billion in gold and €302 billion in foreign currency assets. Most of these assets were inherited from national central bank (NCB) assets before the euro. Loans to banks added another €236 billion. Liabilities included €350 billion in currency (banknotes in circulation), and €118 billion in reserves, almost all required by regulation.

In mid-2008, shortly before the collapse of Lehman Brothers, the balance sheet had not grown much (apart from banknotes), and it retained its character. The Eurosystem's total assets and liabilities were €1463 billion, which included €227 billion in bank reserves and €677 billion in cash. Loans to banks had grown to €483 billion. Securities were still only €115 billion, which included government debts purchased by NCBs under nonmonetary policy tasks.

Fourteen years later, at the peak of its expansion in mid-2022, the balance sheet had grown to €8,789 billion. The bulk of that expansion came from government securities purchases. Securities were €5,129 billion.

	2024-W26	2022-W26	2008-W26	2001-W26
Assets				
Total assets	6,522,003	8,788,761	1,462,710	862,767
Gold and gold receivables	757,478	604,274	209,353	128,512
Claims on non-euro-area residents in foreign currency	510,227	519,276	135,270	279,018
Claims on euro-area residents in foreign currency	14,130	26,911	56,283	22,540
Claims on non-euro-area residents in euros	17,029	11,562	14,686	5,654
Lending to euro-area credit institutions denominated in euros	94,988	2,126,085	483,006	236,201
Other claims on euro-area credit institutions denominated in euros	32,514	34,469	31,723	538
Securities of euro-area residents denominated in euros	4,714,734	5,129,109	114,708	27,665
General government debt denominated in euros	20,832	21,677	38,002	70,168
Other assets	360,071	315,399	379,679	92,471
Liabilities				
Total liabilities	6,522,003	8,788,761	1,462,710	862,767
Banknotes in circulation	1,559,914	1,603,570	677,441	350,199
Liabilities to euro-area credit institutions related to monetary policy operations denominated in euros	3,237,486	4,591.783	227,208	117,841
Other liabilities to euro-area credit institutions in euros	36,134	71,008	206	6,097
Debt certificates issued	0	0	0	3,784
Liabilities to other euro-area residents in euros	205,137	835,002	81,404	69,722
Liabilities to non-euro-area residents in euros	221,837	433,962	77,470	10,226
Liabilities to euro-area residents in foreign currency	15,018	11,531	2,998	3,902
Liabilities to non-euro-area residents in foreign currency	5,343	6,195	15,575	16,977
Counterpart of special drawing rights allocated to IMF	178,966	184,896	5,148	7,183
Other liabilities	212,075	327,456	147,357	75,031
Revaluation accounts	750,441	608,538	156,231	141,340
Capital and reserves	99,651	114,820	71,672	60,465

TABLE 3.1. Eurosystem Consolidated Balance Sheet (in millions of euros). Source: ECB, https://data.ecb.europa.eu/publications/ecbeurosystem-policy-and-exchange-rates/3030616.

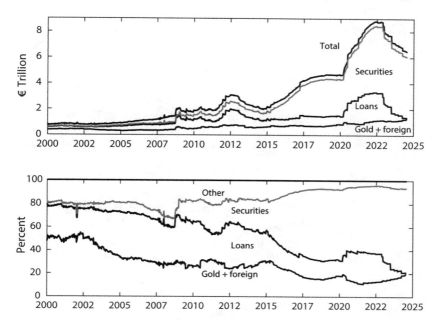

FIGURE 3.1. ECB Balance Sheet: Selected Assets. Top: € trillion. "Total" refers to the highest line while "Securities," "Loans," and "Gold + foreign" refer to the space or distance between two lines. Bottom: percent of total. "Securities" are securities of euro-area residents denominated in euros. "Loans" refers to lending to euro-area credit institutions related to monetary policy operations denominated in euros. "Gold + foreign" refers to gold and gold receivables plus claims on non-euro-area residents denominated in foreign currency plus claims on euro-area residents denominated in foreign currency. All four items show the distance between the lines.

These were mainly government debt, but also corporate bonds. Lending to banks also increased, to €2,126 billion. Most of this lending was "long-term refinancing operations," in which the ECB lends new euros to financial institutions against collateral for several years. These new assets mostly created €4,591 "liabilities to euro area credit institutions related to monetary policy operations," essentially bank deposits at the ECB. Currency also rose to €1,603 billion. By mid-2024, the balance sheet had contracted, mostly via a sharp reduction in ECB loans to banks.

The actions underlying this balance sheet expansion capture much of the monetary policy side of our story. As figure 3.1 shows, loans to banks increased sharply in the 2008 financial crisis, around 2011–2012

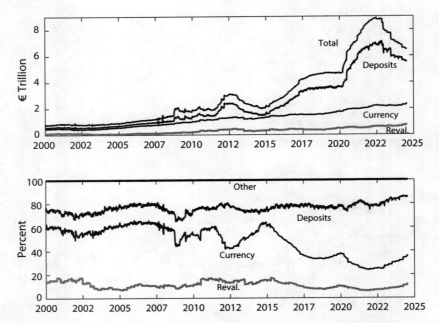

FIGURE 3.2. ECB Balance Sheet: Selected Liabilities. Top: € trillion, bottom: percent of total. "Deposits" refers to liabilities to euro-area credit institutions related to MPOs denominated in euros. "Currency" refers to banknotes in circulation. "Reval." means revaluation accounts.

in the sovereign debt crisis, and in 2020–2021 during the pandemic. Each time, however, lending to banks receded quickly, again reducing the balance sheet. By mid-2024, central bank loans to banks had declined to €95 billion, well below even the pre-2008 levels. By contrast, securities purchases are the main force behind the more persistent rise in the balance sheet, during the quantitative easing period of 2015–2017 and 2019 (Asset Purchase Programme, APP) and the Covid era (Pandemic Emergency Purchase Programme, PEPP). As figure 3.2 shows, the extra money thus created wound up mostly redeposited at the ECB in form of bank reserves. Securities held for monetary policy purposes did decline by about 10% from mid-2022 (when the ECB started to raise policy rates) to €4,715 billion by mid-2024, but they remain at a high level.

Capital plus reserves of the Eurosystem have been small throughout (currently about €100 billion). The capital has little financial meaning.

The revaluation accounts of €750 billion can be seen as capital buffers that belong to national central banks. They capture unrealized gains on gold and foreign currency investments. In the event of mark-to-market losses on these assets, the revaluation accounts absorb those losses. By contrast, security holdings are booked at amortized costs, not market values. Therefore, unrealized losses on bond holdings—for example, those stemming from the increase in market yields since the end of 2021—are not immediately visible from the published balance sheet. The accounting rules imply that such losses are recognized only after a delay.

Originally, the ECB controlled the size of its balance sheet closely. The ECB specified an interest rate and offered a fixed amount of funds to lend at that rate. Banks wishing to borrow from the ECB received only a partial allotment of the funds they requested. This system discouraged banks from borrowing from the ECB in order to finance other investments.

Shortly after the collapse of Lehman Brothers in September 2008, the ECB switched to "full-allotment" procedure, lending any amount that banks wish to borrow at a fixed rate against a significantly broadened list of eligible collateral.[10] The reserve supply curve became completely flat. This encouraged balance sheet expansion and encouraged banks to borrow from the ECB and to lend or buy assets. The ECB also thereby encouraged banks to invest in sovereign debt.

This policy differs from that of the U.S. Federal Reserve, which since 2008 targets the interest paid on overnight reserves, but also fixes the supply of reserves and the size of the balance sheet. (The more recent policy of offering reverse repo contracts, whereby money market funds may lend to the Fed up to a limit, allows some endogeneity to the Fed balance sheet.) The Federal Reserve does comparatively little lending to banks, and its lending rate is not a main instrument of policy. Also unlike the Fed, the ECB has moved to longer-term lending.

We do not mean these comparisons as critical of the ECB, but simply to point out that other regimes are possible. In fact, the Fed has by some analyses erred in letting the balance sheet shrink too much on occasion, causing Treasury market volatility. The simplicity of the ECB's procedures and the fact that it automatically avoids such trouble are facts in favor of its fully horizontal supply of reserves. The ECB shows to the world that a central bank does not have to control the size of its balance sheet in order to control the price level.

Financial Responsibilities

The ECB was not tasked with a primary role in financial stability, banking supervision, or to be the lender of last resort backed by the printing press. These tasks are common to many central banks. At the founding, bank regulation and supervision remained a national responsibility. A kind of financial stability mandate emerged later, largely through the ECB's interpretation of its role.

Article 127 (1) of the Consolidated version of the Treaty on the Functioning of the European Union, quoted earlier in this chapter, continues,

> 5. The ESCB shall contribute to the smooth conduct of policies pursued by the competent authorities relating to the prudential supervision of credit institutions and the stability of the financial system.
>
> 6. The Council, acting by means of regulations in accordance with a special legislative procedure, may unanimously, and after consulting the European Parliament and the European Central Bank, confer specific tasks upon the European Central Bank concerning policies relating to the prudential supervision of credit institutions and other financial institutions with the exception of insurance undertakings.[11]

Thus, the ECB was not completely insulated from bank supervision. The Treaty foresees that the ECB "shall contribute to the smooth conduct of policies pursued by the competent authorities," which means supervisors (often national central banks) and regulators. Just what the phrases "contribute to" and "smooth conduct" mean is obviously and deliberately elastic—just the sort of invitation to later elaboration that one expects of a founding document. The Treaty furthermore included an option that "prudential supervision" of the banking system could be assigned to the ECB at some point.

The issue of how much bank and financial supervision the ECB could pursue was controversial. During the negotiations of the Maastricht Treaty, Germany opposed the inclusion of banking supervision as a task of the ESCB. Article 127(6) was a compromise (see chapter 10 in Lastra, 2015).

Over time, the ECB's financial stability and supervisory role expanded both formally and by precedent. In 2012, in the wake of the financial and sovereign debt crises, the Single Supervisory Mechanism (SSM) was agreed to as a new arm of the ECB, based on this Article 127 (6) process. It began operations in November 2014. The ECB's larger and larger interventions in markets rather obviously also had an aim of financial stability, sometimes labeled as such and sometimes described as supporting or easing "monetary policy transmission."

3.6   The Institutional Structure of the ECB

The full monetary authority is the European System of Central Banks (ESCB), or Eurosystem, consisting of the ECB and National Central Banks (NCBs). The latter still operate. Following common usage, but with some imprecision, we use the word "ECB" to refer to the entire Eurosystem unless a distinction is important. The ECB is owned by the NCBs, not by the EU, and the NCBs are in turn largely owned by member states.

Decision-Making Bodies and Independence

The Governing Council of the ECB decides monetary policy. The Council consists of the six members of the Executive Board of ECB, including the president, the vice president, and the governors of the NCBs of euro member states. The board prepares the meetings of the Governing Council. More than 3,500 staff from all over Europe work for the ECB in Frankfurt am Main, supporting the work of the board.

Board members are appointed by the European Union Council after consulting the European Parliament, which holds hearings with the candidates.[12] Board members serve for 8 years and cannot be reappointed. The governors of the NCBs are appointed by the respective national governments, without consultation of the European Parliament. Board members and national bank governors can be removed from office only in the event of incapacity or serious misconduct. Only the European Court of Justice can force an executive board member to retire.[13]

The board members consequently have great independence once appointed. The Statutes of the ECB (European Central Bank, 2011) also formalize its independence:

> In accordance with Article 130 of the Treaty on the Functioning of the European Union, when exercising the powers and carrying out the tasks and duties conferred upon them by the Treaties and this Statute, neither the ECB, nor a national central bank, nor any member of their decision-making bodies shall seek or take instructions from Union institutions, bodies, offices or agencies, from any government of a Member State or from any other body. The Union institutions, bodies, offices or agencies and the governments of the Member States undertake to respect this principle and not to seek to influence the members of the decision-making bodies of the ECB or of the national central banks in the performance of their tasks.

Independence is a means to an end, a pre-commitment, and not an absolute value. Some argue that the ECB has too much independence and not enough accountability. Whether the ECB should have more independence or more accountability is an important issue for the political-economic side of EMU structural reconsideration.

National Central Banks

National central banks (NCBs) did not disappear with the creation of the euro. They implement monetary policy tasks decided by the

Governing Council of the ECB, as many operations are decentralized. Only tasks and functions of NCBs regarded as essential to the single monetary policy were shifted to the EU level. NCBs remain "financially independent" institutions. They also continue to carry out "national tasks" under national legislation. Article 14.4 of the Statute of the ESCB and of the ECB (European Central Bank, 2011) states: "National central banks may perform functions other than those specified in this Statute unless the Governing Council finds, by a majority of two thirds of the votes cast, that these interfere with the objectives and tasks of the ESCB. Such functions shall be performed on the responsibility and liability of national central banks and shall not be regarded as being part of the functions of the ESCB."

Specific "financial assets" and liabilities and related transactions are defined as national tasks, "not related to monetary policy." These can include, for example, foreign reserves, Emergency Liquidity Assistance (ELA; see Xanthoulis, 2019), or the purchase of securities for general investment purposes. Financial liabilities related to national tasks include the acceptance of government deposits or deposits from other central banks and international institutions or the capital and revaluation accounts of national central banks.

"National task" activities can also create euros or reserves. The Bundesbank explains: "Ultimately, setting up such portfolios provides central bank money to the banking system (ie creates liquidity) as much as conducting monetary policy operations does."[14] In this sense, "monetary policy" and "national tasks" are separated by intent, not by effect. National banks can, effectively, print euros too. The Bundesbank notes that the ECB can, if it wishes, offset the increased money by raising interest rates, selling other assets, or constricting its bank lending under the partial allotment regime.

The December 2002 Agreement on Net Financial Assets (ANFA) between the national central banks and the ECB set an overall limit to the total net amount of financial assets resulting from such national, nonmonetary policy tasks. The aim of the limit was to prevent "national task" operations from producing so many euros that they interfere with the single monetary policy.[15]

The ECB is formally owned by the national central banks, which contribute capital. The term "capital key" describes the shares of each NCB in the overall capital of the ECB. This share is proportional to the share of population and GDP, equally weighted. The capital, about €10 billion, is per se financially insignificant (see table 3.1), but it has important consequences. Profits resulting from the Eurosystem's monetary policy—resulting primarily from the higher interest received on securities and loans to banks than that paid on deposits and cash—are distributed to the NCBs according to the capital key. Some sovereign debt purchase programs are made in proportion to the capital key. So the capital of the ECB has nothing to do with the present value of payments that a share in the ECB generates. It is largely an accounting device to apportion the fiscal consequences of ECB monetary policy across NCBs, and thus member states.

Distribution by capital key is part of many EU economic policy provisions. Capital key determines the capital share and voting rights of each member state in the European Stability Mechanism. It has been crucial in many discussions on the establishment of an EU safe asset, including the Commission's proposal for sovereign bond-backed securities. It has featured in many proposals around the regulatory treatment of sovereign exposures.

The bulk of Eurosystem purchases of sovereign debts are held by the respective national central banks. Profits or losses from those and other assets held by NCBs, even if for monetary policy purposes, are not shared (da Costa and Silva, 2023).

Thus, national central banks basically derive their income from three sources: (1) their share in the overall pooled income deriving from ECB monetary policy operations, (2) monetary policy assets on their own balance sheet, and (3) net financial assets that are "not related to monetary policy." From this overall income, they cover their operational costs. National laws prescribe when an NCB should use profits to increase its capital. The remaining profits are distributed as dividends to the national treasury. This is the final step by which Eurosystem operations end up as fiscal resources to member state governments.

National Central Banks and Recapitalization

Again, sovereign debt and Emergency Liquidity Assistance (ELA) loans, are mostly held by national central banks, not the central ECB, and resulting profits or losses remain at the national level and are not shared. Thus, in the event of default of the sovereign or of a bank with large ELA debt, or other problems, NCBs would first eliminate profit rebates to their treasuries. But then, what happens if an NCB has substantial negative capital, how and when it should be recapitalized and by whom, are unsettled questions.

One might have thought that the Eurosystem would include recapitalization of one NCB from the others. But that is incompatible with quite so much independent profit and loss under "national tasks."

One might have thought then that an NCB would receive a needed recapitalization from its member state. Then, the member states would have to raise tax revenues or cut spending, now or in the future, in order to plug the hole in the balance sheet of their central banks. However, as with many other presumably rare scenarios, the Treaty is silent about when and how NCBs should be recapitalized, or by whom. There are no other established relevant euro-area-wide laws or regulations. Recapitalization of NCBs depends on specific national laws and policy decisions by national governments.

The ECB provided a legal assessment of this issue in its convergence reports. It makes clear that the capital of individual NCBs is crucial for the financial independence of the Eurosystem as a whole, and also to enable NCBs to absorb losses and to contribute further to the ECB's capital in case this is requested by the ECB, not the other way around. The ECB concludes that member states are indeed expected to recapitalize their central banks, from fiscal resources:

> An NCB should always be sufficiently capitalised. In particular, any situation should be avoided whereby for a prolonged period of time an NCB's net equity is below the level of its statutory capital or is even negative. . . . Any such situation may negatively impact on the NCB's ability to perform its ESCB-related tasks but also its

national tasks. Moreover, such a situation may affect the credibility of the Eurosystem's monetary policy. Therefore, the event of an NCB's net equity becoming less than its statutory capital or even negative would require that the respective Member State provides the NCB with an appropriate amount of capital at least up to the level of the statutory capital within a reasonable period of time so as to comply with the principle of financial independence.[16]

How that opinion will work out in reality is a good question. What happens when a member state is going through a debt crisis and simultaneously needs to recapitalize its national central bank, which may have experienced big losses on the same sovereign debt or emergency lending to its banks? The pressure for the ECB to at least provide bridge financing to the NCB will be strong. The political and institutional repercussions of recapitalization, especially in times of fiscal and financial stress, can only be imagined. Such uncertainties suggest that the ECB and NCBs should build financial buffers and not take too large duration or default risks onto their books. Our overall set of reforms would make such crisis events a good deal less likely.

3.7   Balance of Payments and the ECB

The ECB has ended up, unwittingly, playing a major role in financing large and persistent trade deficits and surpluses across the countries of the eurozone, as well as facilitating capital movements.

Adjustment without Nominal Devaluation

Capital and current accounts must balance. When a country imports more goods and services than it exports, the country must pay for the imports. It must transfer abroad financial assets including money, stocks, or bonds. When investors on net wish to move their wealth abroad, they wish to import stocks, bonds, or other financial assets that are claims to wealth abroad. To do that, the country must export more than it imports to receive those financial claims. What if a country wants to import goods but other countries do not want to buy its assets? What if investors want to move capital, on net, out of a country, but nobody wants to buy its goods? Then local prices and wages must decline relative to foreign ones until the desire to import goes away and foreigners' desire to buy exports rises.

With floating exchange rates, a devaluation or revaluation of the currency can create this relative price movement. But with a common currency, price adjustments to a change in desired trade or financial flows must come from changes in actual prices, wages, and interest rates instead.

Or the ECB can be the counterparty, providing the money needed for imports or exchanging common money for a country's assets. In the eurozone, national central banks and the ECB can play a central role in trade and financial adjustments across countries.

Internal devaluation via falling prices and wages, or increasing interest rates to attract capital, is usually thought to be more painful and to take longer than nominal devaluation by an exchange rate depreciation. This causes many economists to prescribe relatively small currency areas and reliance on devaluation to address adverse balance of payment shocks.

However, nominal devaluation via exchange rate depreciation has the same effect on all wages and prices, all industries, and all areas of a country, where internal devaluation adapts to the differences between traded and nontraded goods and services, and differences across sectors and areas within a country. Country borders are not the same as economic borders. Adjustments within a country have always come from changes in prices and wages. Nominal devaluation is followed by such relative price changes. Historically, repeated devaluations have not been economic panaceas either.

Country Fundamentals and Balance of Payments

In a monetary and economic union without fiscal and full political union, the balance of payments of individual member states still plays a major role. Indeed, a free market in goods and services should allow *more* cases of prolonged trade deficits and capital surpluses, and vice versa, as less developed parts of Europe catch up due to demographic differences or other natural economic forces. For example, an advanced country with many middle-aged workers naturally desires to save. A less advanced country that needs investment naturally wants to borrow and give the former country's savers a good return on their retirement savings to do so. And the point of that borrowing is to import the capital goods necessary for the economy to invest.

Adverse economic shocks, bad policies, or fiscal problems also lead to capital flight from a country and its sovereign debt, which would put pressure on the exchange rate if there were one. Investors will demand higher interest rates to compensate for increased risks of default or euro exit.

Absent devaluation, the latter sources of balance of payment problems normally require difficult but rapid and durable policy adjustments by the national government. If fiscal, structural, and financial-sector policies are not credibly improved, capital will continue to leave the country and net imports will have to decline. People will have to reduce consumption. Wages and prices will have to fall. Unemployment will increase. Interest rates will rise to induce investors to stay. In turn, these events provide a powerful incentive for the government to adjust and improve its policies. Banks and prescient regulators, knowing that deposit outflows may happen, have an incentive to ex ante limit banks' risks by reducing maturity mismatch, by reducing the share of short-term run-prone financing, by reducing their sovereign exposure, and by increasing their capital buffers.

The ECB and Cross-Border Credit Flows

But this process is difficult, and many officials wish to smooth such market forces. In a fiscal union, authorities may use fiscal transfers to substitute for capital flows to finance trade deficits across areas. In the eurozone, the Eurosystem can finance trade deficits.

When a national central bank buys a country's bonds, it issues reserves that the country can use to finance trade deficits. The reserves are then held by the exporting country's banks. Thus, the country sending goods holds an ECB liability, and the ECB rather than the exporting country's investors holds the bonds.

When the ECB buys sovereign bonds, it may thereby hold down interest rate spreads. Doing so can silence the incentive for private investors to hold bonds or provide capital to the country, it can silence signals to banks that sovereign debt is risky, and it can silence the signal to the country to get its policies in order.

The ECB not only buys debt, it lends money to banks that can post debt as collateral. This has much the same effect of financing trade and capital flows.

In the eurozone, a great deal of balance of payments financing can come from the ECB via Target2 (now just called "Target") balances, rather than from the private accumulation of assets. Target2 balances are cross-border loans provided from one NCB (creditor) via the ECB to another NCB (debtor).

Suppose that Italians buy more German goods than vice versa. One would think that Italian purchasers ask their banks to send euros to the Italian central bank, which sends them to the German central bank, which in turn credits the bank account of the German seller. Then, German investors (which could include the German bank) would use those euros to buy Italian securities. The securities going to Germany finance the goods going to Italy. But instead, the Italian central bank does not send euros. It simply owes the German central bank those euros, and the German central bank creates new euros to pay the German seller. The Target2 debt of the Italian central bank to the German central bank is the security matching the trade flow.

To avoid having such bilateral balances, each day the ECB nets them out so each central bank only has a debt or asset claim on the ECB itself.[17] Thus, the Central Bank of Italy perpetually owes the ECB money, and the ECB perpetually owes money to the German central bank.

Persistent flows turn into stocks. Target2 claims increase steadily in response to persistent trade and capital flows. In spring 2024, Germany held about €1,050 billion Target2 claims, Luxembourg about €250 billion, and the Netherlands about €90 billion. For their part, Italy had about €500 billion liabilities, Spain about €425 billion and Greece about €110 billion.[18]

Target2 loans all pay the same ECB policy rate. They do not pay additional premiums to compensate for risk, they are not collateralized, and they have no maturity. This treatment implies that the ECB and national central banks consider Target2 claims to be fully risk free.

Target2 balances can reach significant amounts only if the ECB creates significant reserves. Indeed, notable Target2 balances emerged only once the ECB moved to ample excess reserves. ("Excess" means over regulatory reserve requirements.) At its simplest, before the ample reserves era, German depositors would not have simply held larger domestic bank accounts, funding larger reserves.

Suppose that an Italian buys a German car. The Italian purchaser's bank sends euros to the seller's German bank. Without any excess reserves in the banking system, the Italian bank would now be short of reserves—it would not have enough in its account with the Italian central bank. The bank would have to borrow euros in the interbank market or by issuing bonds with sufficiently attractive yields. The only place with excess euro reserves to lend is the seller's bank in Germany. Those reserves would have found their way back to the Italian bank, with securities moving in the other direction. The German bank does not want to hold on to excess reserves, yielding no or little interest. The German bank could make an investment in the Italian bank's bonds, or it could provide a loan to that bank. The German bank could lend the reserves to a German investor, who buys shares in an Italian company, which makes a deposit in an Italian bank, which then lends them back to the original Italian bank. One way or another, the trade deficit ends up being financed by private cross-border lending or securities transfer at market rates.

(Why is the Italian bank short of reserves after the car has been paid? Imagine that the reserve requirement states that banks must hold 10% of any deposits as reserves. The Italian bank sends €100 in reserves to the German bank. Yes, the Italian bank has €100 less deposits requiring reserves, but that only absolves it of the need to hold €10 in reserves. By sending reserves to the German bank, the Italian bank has lost the reserves that it needs for the reserve requirement of €900 of its other deposits.)

Now move to the situation since the early 2010s, with ample excess reserves in the trillions of euros, which pay the same interest as private risk-free securities. In addition, banks can get any loans they need from the ECB in fixed-rate full-allotment tenders, which has been the ECB's operating procedure since the Lehman collapse in 2008. Now, the Italian bank likely is holding enough excess reserves that it doesn't need to borrow reserves in the first place. It can just run down its reserve account with the Italian central bank, and the German bank just lets its interest-paying reserve account grow. If the Italian bank does need or chooses to borrow reserves to replenish its account, it can borrow the funds it needs from the ECB at lower costs than from the private market. ECB loans are all at the same low rate, no matter the borrower and no matter the collateral. Indeed, the unsecured interbank lending market has essentially died. In either case, Italy's Target2 deficit and Germany's Target2 surplus just sit there.

Target2 loans are not just an accounting phenomenon. They are real cross-border loans provided by one national central bank via the ECB to another NCB. They finance cross-border purchases of goods or assets. The creditor central bank, and thus indirectly the respective member state as owner of the capital of the NCB, holds a valuable claim on the ECB, and the debtor central bank owes a valuable debt to the ECB. The ECB transforms a risky claim in to a risk-free claim by taking on the risk, which ultimately is borne by the taxpayer.

The risk became palpable in the sovereign debt crisis, which we describe in detail below. If a country leaves the euro, that country may well default on its Target2 debt, as well as its sovereign debts. It is not clear how the ECB would react, as there is no rule book for such defaults. But like sovereign default, it would blow a hole in the ECB's balance sheet, which eventually is covered by the remaining member states.

Target2 balances did not finance the entirety of the balance of payments. Plenty of cross-border lending and purchases of private and sovereign debt also helped finance the large and persistent trade deficits of some countries.

The large accumulation of Target2 balances and their use to help finance persistent trade deficits or private capital outflows is another unfinished and unreformed part of the euro structure. It is almost certainly completely unintended and unforeseen. The architects of the euro likely did not foresee large and persistent trade deficits among member states, and they did not foresee country risks or sovereign debt crises that would prompt capital outflows. They certainly did not foresee that if these should occur, and if the ECB were to change to an ample reserve regime—which was largely uncontemplated by anybody at the time—that Target2 balances could unwittingly become an important means of financing trade deficits or private capital outflows. When the ECB changed to ample reserves and easy lending to banks, it was thinking about how to stimulate the euro-area economy as a whole by easing financial conditions for banks as a whole. That such aid would go to banks in more troubled countries may have been a short-term side benefit. That it would end up financing trade deficits or capital outflows in place of private cross-border asset purchases was surely an unintended and unforeseen consequence. When the ECB declared "whatever it takes" and announced purchases to support sovereign debt, it likely intended to avoid an even more painful internal devaluation or the risk of an exit of troubled countries from the euro area.

Even if national central banks and Target2 balances cease to exist and the central ECB issues all reserves and holds all assets, the ECB's balance-of-payment support could easily continue. Such support within the euro area is not regulated or prohibited. It is not mentioned in the Treaty or in secondary regulation, either as a function of the ECB or as a task of the EU Commission or member states. This is another missing element of the framework underpinning the euro. It is related to the lack of an IMF-style European fiscal crisis management institution, which provides balance of payment support in a crisis.

It is, however, one of the unfinished pieces that should be reformed. In the end, there will and should be persistent trade deficits and capital flows, reflecting different economies. Those should be financed by the private accumulation of securities.

3.8 Summary

In sum, the initial EMU design aspired to separate monetary and fiscal policies in order to contain the disincentives posed by a monetary union without a fiscal or banking union. Fiscal policies, in line with fiscal rules, would stabilize debt at low levels. Monetary policy would ensure price stability unhindered by fiscal, political, or other pressures. Bank regulation and lender of last resort or other banking crisis management were left largely to member countries in a still-fragmented banking system.

The initial architecture of the euro erected walls between fiscal and monetary policy to buttress their separation in the face of inevitable pressures. Those included debt and deficit limits, a prohibition against ECB monetary financing of sovereign debts, and the fiscal no-bail-out principle.

Left out was just what would happen if despite all these admirable structures a sovereign default did loom. The initial architecture was silent on that point.

In one view, in a monetary union without fiscal union, in extremis, countries that get in deep enough trouble must default, just as companies and banks do. In the initial architecture, that event was apparently regarded as so unlikely, and also so politically impolite, that no explicit provision needed to be made. Writing default processes during the formation of the euro is a bit like negotiating a prenuptial agreement while walking to the altar. But sovereign default was implicit in the rules against monetary financing and fiscal bailouts. Don't worry, thought the architects—they'll figure it out when the time comes.

There is also a contrary view: One cannot have sovereign default in any monetary union. It is an unthinkable, union-ending event that must be prevented at all costs. That view tends to go hand in hand with the view that large bank failures are also inherently systemic catastrophes that cannot be allowed. Creditors cannot lose. Alas, the silence in the euro's founding let both views survive, and their battle accounted for a lot of chaos in the subsequent crises.

In what follows, we describe what happened as this admirable but necessarily incomplete structure faced a sequence of crises. The monetary-fiscal innovations taken in response to crises overturned the separation of monetary, fiscal, and financial policy that existed at the outset of the euro, and with that its attempt to contain the disincentives that make the euro more fragile.

4

Prelude to Financial Crisis

4.1 Debt and Deficits

The introduction of the euro and the transition to the single monetary policy went smoothly. The first years of the euro and the ECB were economically and financially calm, especially compared to the following years, with low inflation and only a mild recession in the early 2000s. Yet it was also a time in which stresses and weaknesses in the euro's design started to build up.

Contrary to the founding vision, governments ran large deficits. Portugal, Germany, France, the Netherlands, Greece and Italy breached deficit limits in the first five years of the decade (Morris, Ongena, and Schuknecht, 2006).

In 2002, only three years after the introduction of the euro, the European Commission recommended that the Council of Economic and Finance Ministers from all member states (official name: Economic and Financial Affairs Council, ECOFIN) issue a warning to Portugal and Germany about their deficits. On February 12, 2002, the Council rejected the Commission's recommendation on the basis that the countries had taken corrective measures (Morris, Ongena, and Schuknecht, 2006). A few months later, however, on November 2002, the Commission started a procedure against Portugal, whose deficit in 2001 reached 4.1% of GDP.

During 2003, the Commission tried to start a procedure against Germany and France. This effort did not succeed. Germany and France had been given until 2004 to correct their deviations, but "it became clear by Autumn 2003 that the measures taken by both countries would not be sufficient to comply with the Council's recommendations"(Morris, Ongena, and Schuknecht, 2006). The Commission recommended that the Council issue "notices." In November 2003, the Council of Economic and Finance Ministers decided to ignore the Commission's recommendation and to suspend the procedure, directly contravening the relevant fiscal rules (Chang, 2006). Indeed, the process was annulled later by the European Court of Justice on the basis that the Council "could not, by itself, take initiatives in the absence of an appropriate recommendation by the Commission" (Morris, Ongena, and Schuknecht, 2006).

The credibility of the fiscal rules was in tatters. The European Commission tried to revise the rules. But both French president Jacques Chirac and German prime minister Gerhard Schröder argued in favor of a softening of the rules.

The final compromise, reached in March 2005, did not touch the key elements of the fiscal framework specified in the Maastricht Treaty, 3% deficit and 60% debt to GDP reference values. But it added more flexibility to the Stability and Growth Pact. Among other provisions, countries could exceed the 3% deficit during recessions, with slow repayment in normal times. The regulations also created country-specific cyclically adjusted medium-term objectives.[1]

Looking at structural or cyclically adjusted deficits is reasonable in principle, as countries should borrow in recessions and repay in good times. But it suffers the obvious pitfall that potential output, the output gap, and thus structural balances are hard to estimate in real time and easy to be optimistic about. Recessionary falls in GDP often have a permanent as well as a transitory component. For example, neither Europe nor the United States recovered to the previous trend line or contemporary potential GDP forecasts after the 2008 financial crisis.

The ECB criticized changes to the corrective arm of debt and deficit rules for placing "greater emphasis on flexibility and discretion in subjecting countries to the excessive deficit procedure and in requiring prompt corrective action." In rather strong terms by central banking standards, the ECB stated: "In the view of the Governing Council of the ECB, changes to the corrective arm entail risks of weakening the SGP [Stability and Growth Pact]. That is why it had recommended not to modify the corrective arm and expressed its serious concern about these changes in its statement of 21 March 2005."[2] The Bundesbank was even more outspoken: "The outcome of these decisions [of the European Council] will jeopardise the aim of achieving sustainable public finances in all EU member states participating in monetary union. A particular worry from the perspective of a central bank is that public finances which are not lastingly sound make a stability-oriented monetary policy difficult."[3]

One may object that 3% of GDP is a tight deficit limit, and countries fighting crises have borrowed and repaid more than that. But the promise was made, and at the first occasion when the rules became inconvenient for the two largest members of the euro area, the promises were broken, suggesting what new promises might be worth.

4.2   Peripheral Debt and Trade Flows

In the meantime, the peripheral countries in the euro area were reaping, and to some extent squandering, the benefits of monetary union. By joining the euro, they had effectively precommitted to no longer inflate or devalue their way out of the next crisis but instead face the politically costly alternatives of adjustment or default. Therefore, they would stay out of such crises to begin with. Bond investors did not need to fear inflation and devaluation. Capital and goods could flow freely out as well as in, and firms did not have to fear nationalization or export and capital controls. Investors and banks became willing to lend across borders, without requiring a hefty interest-rate premium to guard against these possibilities, to governments, to companies, and to individuals.

The Greek state, which adopted the euro in 2001, for instance, saw the interest of its 10-year bond drop from 22% to 3.6% between 1994 and 2003. Facing much lower interest rates and an abundant credit supply, people, businesses, and governments borrowed heavily. Not all borrowing went to capital investment; it also went to support consumption. That is not necessarily bad: a country that has become suddenly a good place to do business will borrow to finance capital investment for that business, but it can also borrow to consume today a bit of tomorrow's bounty—if the bounty arrives.

In the event, borrowing to finance consumption, consumer durables, and residential housing (also a consumer durable, really) in several countries was, at least in retrospect, overdone relative to productive investments and microeconomic reforms that would eventually repay loans. During 2004–2007, bank credit to households in Greece and Ireland grew 20 to 30% each year, and in Spain it grew about 20%. (See International Monetary Fund, 2017.) Current account deficits increased. Porsches went south, and paper promises went north.

The ability to borrow at low rates, in combination with institutional weaknesses, seems to have set off a soft budget constraint mentality in some governments. Countries abandoned efforts to reduce future primary deficits or to introduce growth-enhancing but politically costly reforms (Fernández-Villaverde, Garicano, and Santos, 2013). Greece, for example, abandoned in 2001 a plan to reform the public pension scheme to make it sustainable. Portugal saw public debt grow from 55% of GDP in 1999 to 74% in 2006, and 114% in 2011.

In Spain, foreign investment flowed into the semi-public savings banks (*Cajas*), which financed real estate projects, often run by developers and local politicians that sat on the boards of the *Cajas* (Cuñat and Garicano, 2010). Irish banks financed a huge real estate boom. In Portugal and Greece the government itself channeled large amounts of new debts.

Some political-economy researchers suggest that low interest rates and capital inflows led in part to the failure to reform. (See Fernández-Villaverde, Garicano, and Santos, 2013 and Gopinath et al., 2017.) Who wants to take difficult fiscal, structural, and microeconomic reforms when money is flowing in? Challe, Lopez, and Mengus (2019) find that those countries that were net recipients of capital over the decade experienced a relative decline in the quality of their institutions. As they argue, governments with easy access to credit cannot commit to not bailing out their domestic residents. If the government can borrow and not worry about repayment, why shouldn't its citizens do so?

In sum, even in the relatively quiet period before the financial crisis, some of the institutions or safeguards intended to ensure the separation between fiscal and monetary policy deteriorated. Fiscal rules were being ignored by the largest member states. And if France and Germany won't obey the rules, why should Greece and Portugal do so? France and Germany certainly lost any right to complain.

The national central banks of the Eurosystem also increased their holdings of euro-area government debt securities by about €190 billion between the end of 2004 and the end of 2009.[4] These purchases likely were not part of the ECB's monetary policy. The ECB only started purchasing government debt as part of its monetary policy in May 2010. They were thus likely falling under "national non-monetary tasks" of national central banks, as set out in the agreement on net financial assets (ANFA).

Increasing government and private debts, held abroad, financed larger current account deficits. The net foreign asset positions of Greece, Portugal, and Spain declined from −30 to −40% of GDP in 1999 to around −100% of GDP in 2010. Ireland's fall from +50% of GDP to the same level was even sharper. Meanwhile, Germany accumulated nearly 40% of GDP in foreign assets.[5] Net assets are sent abroad to pay for net imports.

Inflation rates diverged across the euro area, and with them effective real exchange rates. With a common currency, the nominal exchange rate is 1. But if prices are twice as high in one country as another, one can think of that as a real exchange rate of 2:1. These economic developments, together with high debt-financed private and government consumption, are often called macroeconomic "imbalances."

The imbalances did not go unnoticed. But in spite of repeated warnings from the ECB—not least from ECB president Jean-Claude Trichet in hearings at the European Parliament and meetings of the finance ministers of the euro-area member states or "Eurogroup"—these trends were largely ignored by governments of euro-area countries. For example, in November 2005, President Trichet told the European Parliament: "No significant progress has been made in fiscal consolidation, and the outlook for countries with excessive deficits is a matter of great concern, as there is a high risk of commitments for this year and the next not being met.... In some euro area countries, wage developments have substantially and persistently exceeded labour productivity growth, leading to relatively strong and sustained increases in unit labour costs, higher inflationary pressures and losses in competitiveness."[6]

4.3 Fragile Banks

Bank regulation contributed to the buildup of stress by treating sovereign debts as completely risk free, and thus encouraging banks to hold more sovereign debt. Bank regulators evidently took the silence on the subject of sovereign default in the foundation of the euro to mean that it would never happen. Or they just not have thought about how a transition from national currencies to a common currency, with explicit rules against fiscal and monetary bailouts, changed the situation. They ignored centuries of history replete with sovereign defaults when countries could not print money to repay debt.

Zero risk weights, and zero concern by regulators, distorted banks' incentives. It also likely influenced banks' internal risk management. If the regulators treat sovereign exposure as risk free, why should banks worry? If it's risk free, even a small interest rate spread seems an arbitrage. If it's risk free, there is no worry about correlated or concentrated risks, so loading up on one country's bonds can't be a problem. It was easy to increase leverage and raise share prices by buying risky public bonds without any need to issue or retain more capital. Moreover, if it's risk free, why resist pressure to buy sovereign debt? Why not even help the government and win political favor by buying its bonds, no matter how highly indebted the country?

In all these ways, bank regulation gave another green light to governments to borrow and helped to reduce the interest rates at which they could do so.

4.4 Banking Crises

Despite these growing stresses, European inflation during the first decade of the euro fluctuated in a narrow rage around the ECB's 2% target bound, while economies grew steadily.

The global financial crisis that started in the United States in the spring of 2007 began to be felt in Europe shortly afterward. The first ones to suffer were European (particularly German) banks exposed to losses in the U.S. mortgage and asset-backed security markets. IKB, a German lender, had set up and guaranteed a special-purpose vehicle to invest in U.S. mortgage-backed securities. On July 29, 2007, KfW, a large state-owned bank that held a substantial equity stake in IKB, recapitalized IKB—in effect a bailout with taxpayer money.[7] Other German banks, including WestLB and Sachsen LB, both owned by regional governments, found themselves in similar trouble. In the end, taxpayers bore most of the losses, as the banks' creditors and international investors exposed to U.S. mortgage-backed securities were bailed out. At this early stage of the crisis, losses of German banks often came about via special-purpose vehicles operating in Dublin, as the German regulator would not allow such activities to take place in Germany.

BNP Paribas, a large French bank, froze withdrawals from some investment funds on August 9, 2007. Banks that were regarded as fragile began to have problems borrowing in commercial paper and interbank markets.

Seeing the financial system at risk, the ECB introduced Fine-Tuning Operations (FTOs). Under this program, the ECB provided a fixed amount of funds, €95 billion outstanding at its peak, at a variable rate that cleared the market, in exchange for a wide schedule of marketable and non-marketable securities (Runkel, 2022a).

This was the first of many programs to come, under which the ECB made it easier for banks to borrow, at low rates and against looser collateral. Without questioning its usefulness for stemming problems, like all interventions, it had unintended consequences. Borrowing from the Eurosystem started to replace the interbank market, especially for banks that were in trouble or that were considered as fragile by the market. Banks paid rates to the ECB that did not reflect market assessment of their riskiness. That's the point; in a crisis, the ECB disagrees with the market about riskiness. But over the long term, an important incentive to contain risk is suppressed. ECB support also allowed creditors of these banks to take out their deposits without losses. That too is the point. Central banks can stop runs by effectively guaranteeing deposits, so everyone who wants to get out can do so, and others don't feel like they have to join the run. But such expected creditor guarantees, with no corresponding insurance premiums, remove the incentive for creditors to assess risk and burden taxpayers.

How such policy fits in with the ECB's mandate to conduct monetary policy in pursuit of price stability was a tricky question. In a press conference in September 2007, President Trichet evoked for the first time the "separation principle" and introduced a framing for interventions that persists through the present.[8] These loans to banks were not monetary policy stance interventions (i.e., they did not aim at a looser monetary stance). Neither, however, were they directly lender-of-last-resort functions to stop bank runs per se. Emergency Liquidity Assistance (ELA) remained a nonmonetary, national task and thus the responsibility of national central banks, not the ECB. Rather, they were justified as interventions to maintain the transmission of monetary policy, to preserve the functioning of the interbank market, and to ensure that the ECB could use its interest rates to address too high inflation (or "upside risks to price stability").

Following the (in retrospect) relatively peaceful interlude between spring 2007 and spring 2008, the U.S. financial crisis exploded over the summer and fall of 2008. After a summer of large failures, most notably Lehman Brothers, a "run on repo" broke out in October 2008, in which short-term financing via repurchase agreements dried up. A severe recession broke out, and real estate values began to fall around the world, so that mortgage lending losses spread from the small U.S. subprime market to real estate and banks everywhere. Banks in Ireland, and later Spain, suffered more from local real estate collapses than from their international exposure. Initially, the hardest-hit countries in the EU were Latvia and Lithuania (see figure 5.1). At the time, however, they were outside the euro area.

The three major Irish banks (Anglo-Irish, Bank of Ireland, and Allied Irish) had used short-term borrowing, including from international banks and financial institutions, to fund long-term mortgage loans and securities investments. Their combined balance sheet was 500% of Irish GDP (International Monetary Fund, 2010). The Irish banks faced a sudden and massive outflow of their funding. Among others, U.S. money market funds were no longer willing to invest in the banks' asset-backed certificates of deposit. Depositors from around Europe also cashed out.

On September 30, 2008, the Irish government guaranteed all the liabilities of the six largest Irish banks for two years, including bank bonds, a total of €440 billion (Tooze, 2018, p. 189). Some banks, particularly Anglo-Irish, turned out to be insolvent, not just illiquid. Guaranteeing the banks' debts, rather than painlessly stopping a multiple-equilibrium run due to illiquidity, put a major dent in the finances of the Irish state, handing resources from Irish taxpayers to bank creditors.

The troubles of many Irish banks were due in large part to the collapse of the Irish housing market and construction sector and the associated recession. These internal disruptions resulted in large losses of the banks on their loan books, including loans to highly indebted developers and mortgage loans. The sharp fall in property prices also strongly reduced collateral values.

The Irish and Icelandic bank crises reveal a central problem of international banking. If banks in a small country take short-term international deposits to finance long-term illiquid assets, in part international investments, to the tune of multiples of that country's GDP, the banks can exceed the country's ability to backstop the deposits with government-provided deposit insurance or bailout guarantees.

This is not entirely the story of the Irish case, but it is an important lesson for reform of the European financial system. As Europe moves toward banking and financial union, large pan-European institutions cannot rely on national lenders of last resort. The founding structure of national banks and national emergency assistance and regulators fit together. Broadening the former—contributing to break the sovereign-bank nexus, among other reasons—requires broadening the latter or moving to financial institutions that fund themselves with equity, long-term debt, and other securities rather than run-prone, short-term liabilities. The intersection of national bank regulators with the possibility of EU and ECB support poses obvious conflicts of incentives.

The Irish banking crisis also reveals a clear failure of national bank regulation and supervision, which allowed such huge amounts of short-term debt to finance longer-term and less liquid assets.

Although some EU countries, including the Netherlands, Italy, and France, thought that the moment called for an EU rescue fund, the German government turned down the idea, insisting each country deal with its own problems.[9] There would not be any agreement on common European rescue initiatives until early 2010, when euro-area governments offered common financial support to Greece.

After heavy deposit withdrawals at Hypo Real Estate, a German bank that had a major exposure to Ireland via a subsidiary and whose private bailout was failing, German chancellor Angela Merkel in early October 2008 declared that all deposits of German banks were guaranteed.[10] Other countries, such as Denmark, followed.

For the ECB, such political and fiscal support for bank depositors was helpful, as it reduced pressures for large central bank loans or asset purchases to prop up banks. However, the German guarantee was just a political declaration. It did not provide any concrete collateral that the ECB could accept for lending operations to banks. The banks did not receive any money, capital, transfers, securities, or explicit, legally sound guarantees from the government. So it was not fully clear what would happen in the case of a major bank run or solvency crisis, and where exactly the money would come from to stop it.

4.5   Policy Responses

The tensions were increasingly felt in the European interbank market. On October 15, 2008, the Euro Interbank Offered Rate (Euribor) increased above 5%.

The ECB stepped in to provide further support to banks. These actions had the unintended consequence of making the subsequent sovereign debt crisis worse by encouraging banks to buy sovereign debt, as well as financing budget deficits and balance of payments deficits.

The ECB greatly expanded the list of securities that were eligible as collateral in refinancing operations. From 2006 until 2009, the use of collateral doubled from below €1 trillion to about €2 trillion, mainly due to increases of uncovered bank bonds, asset-backed securities, and non-marketable private assets.[11] For the first time, these operations were generally full allotment: Banks could obtain any amount of funds, limited only by the amount of eligible collateral, at the fixed rate. Starting May 2009, the ECB expanded the program to include one-year Long Term Refinancing Operations at attractive rates, which allowed banks to borrow to buy securities and not worry that the interest rate paid on the borrowing might rise.[12] The ECB also continued the expanded collateral policy.[13]

The ECB effectively replaced a large part of the short-term unsecured interbank market, especially for banks perceived as weak or fragile by markets. The resulting increase in bank borrowing from the ECB created large quantities of excess reserves ("excess" relative to regulatory reserve requirements).

Eurozone banks in turn used some of the money to buy sovereign bonds. Euro-area banks (more precisely, monetary and financial institutions, MFIs) held €1460 billion in government debt securities in September 2008. Those holdings increased by €356 billion by December 2009, and by a total of €445 billion by April 2010, the month before the ECB itself started to purchase the sovereign debt of stressed member states for monetary policy purposes.[14]

Banks could borrow money from the ECB and use the money to purchase high-yielding government bonds. Normally, banks must get some of their funding for risky investments by issuing equity, not just by borrowing the funds. But borrowing from the ECB to buy sovereign debt required no additional bank capital, as the sovereign bonds carry no risk weight in capital-adequacy regulation.

Given that the ECB was accepting lower quality collateral, banks could borrow from the ECB at more favorable conditions than from the market. Since the ECB, unlike private lenders, offered the same interest rate to all banks, the weakest banks benefited the most and investment in the weakest sovereigns was the most profitable. And since only government bonds were treated as risk free (not requiring capital), the program skewed incentives toward sovereign debt purchases.

From autumn 2008 onward, banks in so-called periphery countries, Spain, Greece, Ireland, Italy, and Portugal, increased their holdings of domestic sovereign bonds, much more than did those of the "core countries" of Austria, Belgium, Germany, France, and the Netherlands. "The domestic sovereign debt holdings of periphery banks rose from €270 to €781 billion between October 2008 and September 2013, while those of core-country banks rose from €352 to €548 billion, a 131% increase in the former versus a 56% increase in the latter." At the same time, banks reduced their holdings of non-domestic sovereign bonds, particularly in core countries (Battistini, Pagano, and Simonelli, 2014, figures 5 and 6).

The main danger to this "carry trade" profit was a sovereign default. If the assets had longer maturity than the 1-year ECB financing, then there was also some risk that financing rates would rise when the time came to roll it over. In both cases, since some of the point of financing at favorable conditions was to keep banks from losing too much money, it would have been natural to expect further support from the ECB or fiscal authorities.

In the end, neither default nor persistently higher interest rates materialized, so this was a terrific deal ex post for the banks. That is, except for those banks that bought and kept Greek bonds that were maturing after the Greek default in the spring of 2012, whose troubles were to spark the next great intervention.

This trade, using the balance sheets of the banks to buy government debt to lower its financing costs, helped governments in the short term. But the concentration of assets meant that defaults on those bonds would greatly imperil banks, and thereby the respective economies. Because banks were so leveraged compared to other bond purchasers, and unable therefore to take principal losses, upfront orderly debt restructuring was made nearly impossible. The concentration of sovereign debt in domestic banks thus contributed to the depths and costs of the sovereign debt crisis.

5

The Sovereign Debt Crisis

By the fall of 2009, the immediate effects of the global financial crisis had passed for Europe as a whole, leaving only what would turn out to be years of slow-growth recovery.

There was much agonizing about why analysts, central banks, and regulators hadn't seen brewing mortgage risks. But at the same time, official Europe paid little or no attention to brewing sovereign risk. With the wake-up call that systemic banking crises can happen in the contemporary era, Europe's financial regulators still did nothing to address the risky sovereign debt on bank balance sheets. Indeed, the ECB's large-scale loans to banks ended up unintentionally worsening this risk, encouraging larger sovereign debt on bank balance sheets and financing balance of payments.

First Greece, and then Ireland, Portugal, Spain, Italy, and Cyprus suffered a series of crises that linked sovereign debts and financial institutions. In some countries, like Greece and Portugal, a sovereign debt crisis spilled over to a financial crisis. In other countries, such as Ireland and Spain, a banking crisis eventually affected the sovereign as guarantor of the banks.

The sovereign debt crisis is easiest to see in bond markets, as shown in figure 5.1. At the start of 2008, yields of ten-year government bonds of euro-area countries were around 4%, with yields spreads relative to German bonds below one percentage point. Yields on Greek bonds moved above 10% in 2010 and reached almost 30% shortly before the Greek debt restructuring in early 2012. Yields on Irish and Portuguese

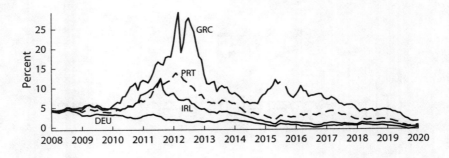

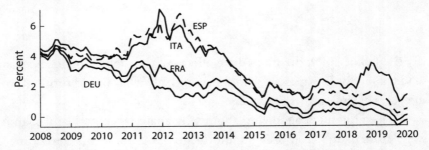

FIGURE 5.1. 10-year bond rates in the euro area. Source: ECB, "Long-Term Interest Rates for Convergence Purposes," https://data.ecb.europa.eu/data /data-categories.

government bonds also increased strongly during 2010 and moved above 10% in 2011.

As people started to worry about sovereign debt, the stability of local banks holding sovereign debt and guaranteed by the same sovereigns, and also foreseeing economic trouble, a run started. Savers and investors increasingly withdrew bank deposits and tried to sell government debt and private investments in order to move their funds to less risky banks and economies. When many people try to sell at once, the value of investments in stocks, bonds, and real estate falls, making the banks' situation even more precarious. Capital flight requires a sharp turn of the country's current account. But making such a switch from net importer to net exporter in a short time is hard. Sovereign debt spills into an economic and financial crisis.

In similar cases outside a monetary union, the IMF often provides temporary financing, which supports a slower adjustment from net imports to net exports, a slower reduction in fiscal deficits, and can keep financial institutions operating. IMF rescue packages usually come with conditions embedded in an adjustment program to reform budgets, clean up banks, and adopt growth-enhancing and export-enhancing reforms.

Absent a euro-area body able to provide that sort of support, without even a mechanism for orderly default, the ECB stepped into the breach, lending to banks that used some of the money to buy government bonds, purchasing bonds of crises countries, and eventually President Mario Draghi's famous "whatever it takes" proclamation. The ECB felt that it was the only institution able to move quickly enough to stem a deeper crisis.

European institutions worked out fiscal rescue packages on the fly. These packages coalesced eventually into EU/IMF economic adjustment programs for Greece, Ireland, Portugal, and Cyprus, and resulted in the creation of the European Stability Mechanism (ESM). Sovereign debt restructuring, in which bondholders and other creditors take losses, was applied to Greece in 2012. This restructring was unfortunately too late since many bondholders were bailed out ahead of it, but it was technically successful. Depositors also took haircuts in Cyprus.

Sadly, this crisis management regime—or, as one would hope, a more refined and strengthened version benefiting from its lessons— does not seem to be ready and politically accepted for use again to tackle the larger sovereign debt issues that may loom in the future. Reviving this reform effort is one of our major recommendations. The alternative is larger and larger ECB intervention, with clear fiscal and monetary implications, along with uncontained moral hazard.

We discuss the crises in part by country, in part chronologically, and in part by focusing on the different methods used to address them. Our focus is monetary-fiscal interactions, so we do not address the details of economic adjustment programs and their implementation. We first describe the various EU and IMF rescue packages, and then focus in more detail on ECB actions.

5.1　Greece

Greece suffered the first and most visible euro-era sovereign debt crisis. Greece was the case for which a resolution method was developed, and the only case in the EU of a sovereign debt restructuring so far. In 2012 and again in 2015, Greece was confronted with major political uncertainty with significant "Grexit" fears. Both events resulted in large deposit outflow and substantial loan support from the ECB for Greek banks.

In October 2009, shortly after George Papandreou and his PASOK party won the elections in Greece, new finance minister Giorgos Papakonstantinou announced in an interview with Reuters that the fiscal deficit in 2009 would not be 6% of GDP, as previously thought, but likely more than 10%. Later, after some cleaning up of the statistics, the official deficit for 2009 was revised upward to above 15%.

Bond markets initially did not react strongly. However, over time, more bad news emerged. Fitch (on October 22 and December 8, 2009) and Standard and Poor's (on December 16, 2009) downgraded Greece's bond ratings.

Statements from the German government reduced hopes for a bailout. For example, Chancellor Angela Merkel said in a December 17, 2009, speech at the German Parliament, "I also say with regard to individual countries with very high deficits: Each individual member state is responsible for healthy public finances."[1] Bond investors started to get nervous. In early 2010, the yield on 10-year Greek government bonds moved above 6.5%, about two percentage points higher than early October 2009 (see figure 5.1). Doubts grew that Greece would be able to roll over its short-term debt—Greece might not find new buyers to provide money to repay maturing bonds.

While the German government was concerned about the domestic politics and moral hazard consequences of a bailout, other member states and the ECB were strongly opposed to any default, haircut, or burden-sharing with private bondholders. In the end, the view that no credit event or default was tolerable, which was also supported by the U.S. administration, postponed the debt restructuring by about two years (Mody, 2018, 236–242).

On February 11, 2010, the heads of state or government of the EU signaled that governments were considering financial assistance to Greece: "We invite the Ecofin Council to adopt . . . recommendations to Greece based on the Commission's proposal and the additional measures Greece has announced. The Commission will closely monitor the implementation of the recommendations in liaison with the ECB and will propose needed additional measures, drawing on the expertise of the IMF. . . . Euro area Member states will take determined and coordinated action, if needed, to safeguard financial stability in the euro area as a whole. The Greek government has not requested any financial support."[2]

While guarded, this wording is similar to the standard language of IMF financial assistance and programs. In spite of the last sentence, a financial assistance–cum–adjustment program with IMF involvement was only a matter of time. The aim to "safeguard financial stability" signaled that financial assistance would come without losses by large private-sector creditors.

In a subsequent statement, ECB president Trichet made clear that he had agreed on an active role of the ECB in potential future program negotiations and monitoring with Greece: "I confirm that the ECB will work with the European Commission in monitoring the implementation of the recommendations by Greece and will work with the European Commission on proposals for necessary additional measures."[3]

It still took a couple of months until all euro-area governments were convinced to use their taxpayers' resources to make whole the holders of Greek government bonds. The bad taste of the 2007–2009 bank bailouts was still fresh. In March 2010, the German finance minister, Wolfgang Schäuble, still floated the possibility of Greece exiting the euro area. In April 2010, however, it became clear that he had changed his mind. He rejected the application of the "no bailout" principle, and stated, "We cannot allow the bankruptcy of a euro member state like Greece to turn into a second Lehman Brothers. Greece is just as systematically important as a major bank."[4]

On April 11, 2010, European governments and the IMF announced that they would set up a financial rescue package and that "the

Commission, in liaison with the ECB, will start working on Monday April 12th, with the International Monetary Fund and the Greek authorities on a joint program."[5]

On May 2, 2010, the Eurogroup (the group of euro-area finance ministers) and the IMF agreed to financial assistance loans to Greece totaling €110 billion for the coming three years, subject to conditionality, in which the Greek government committed to an adjustment program. Euro-area governments committed €80 billion, and the IMF committed €30 billion.

This assistance at last reduced pressure on the ECB. So far, the central bank alone had been supporting Greek balance of payments, mainly via loans to Greek banks. Target2 loans from the ECB to the Greek national bank had already reached €83 billion by April 2010, more than one-third of Greek 2010 GDP. This large Target2 debt also reflects that the ongoing expansion of total Greek bank assets was increasingly financed by central bank loans rather than private-sector deposits. During the twenty months between the Lehman collapse and agreement on the Greek bailout, assets of Greek banks increased by 16%, or €71 billion, about 30% of 2010 GDP, of which €22 billion were additional holdings of government debt.[6]

In sum, the ECB indirectly protected bank depositors and other creditors from losses. These loans also allowed private debt holders to sell their debt to the banks, protecting those investors from default, restructuring, or further price declines.

The fiscal bailout unburdened the ECB, but it was not large enough to allow the ECB to swiftly reduce its funding of Greek banks. To the contrary, as we discuss in the next section, ECB loan support and the related Target2 balances increased further until around mid-2012. From 2008 to mid-2012, central bank funding rose from almost nothing to about 35% of bank liabilities, as deposits fell from 70% to about 50% of liabilities.[7]

The Greek Sovereign Debt Restructuring

During a summit in Deauville, France, in October 2010, a few months after the Greek financial assistance program had been announced, French president Nicolas Sarkozy and German chancellor Angela

Merkel put sovereign default firmly on the table: "France and Germany consider that an amendment of the Treaties is needed. . . . The establishment of a permanent and robust framework to ensure orderly crisis management in the future, providing the necessary arrangements for an adequate participation of private creditors and allowing Member States to take appropriate coordinated measures to safeguard financial stability of the Euro area as a whole."[8]

"Participation of private creditors" means that creditors take losses.

This was not a final EU decision, however. It met strong resistance from some member states, the ECB, and the financial industry. Although the proposed amendment of the Treaties was supported by the European Council (October 28, 2010), it was never implemented.

The Deauville summit was also contentious for other features, which may account for the failure of this reform proposal to take off. President Sarkozy and Chancellor Merkel proposed a security opening to Russia: "Mrs. Merkel said Saturday that a goal of the summit was to improve cooperation between NATO and Russia, . . . 'for the Cold War is over for good.'"[9] France and Germany also proposed strong sanctions for countries that miss debt and deficit targets, including "confiscating EU voting rights."[10] And, politically, they gave the impression that they could decide EU policy on their own.[11]

From October 2010 until mid-2011, several member states and the ECB resisted any explicit default or restructuring.

All in all, after Deauville—itself a year in to the crisis—another almost year-and a half of intense discussion and uncertainty followed. These were detrimental to confidence, political stability, and growth in Greece. The eventual restructuring of Greek sovereign debt was finally politically agreed to in autumn 2011 and implemented in March 2012. (See the excellent discussion of the Greek debt restructuring by Zettelmeyer, Trebesch, and Gulati, 2014.)

The IMF, which uses the euphemism private sector involvement (PSI), provides a good summary of this "largest in history" debt restructuring (International Monetary Fund, 2017, 40):

The private sector involvement (PSI) followed months of negotiations among the Greek authorities, Euro group representatives, and the creditor group led by the Institute for International Finance (IIF).... The IIF's PSI proposal that came in July 2011 provided insufficient debt relief and had to be recalibrated.... Under the PSI, €197 billion of Greek government bonds (GGBs) were exchanged for €62 billion of new debt and €30 billion in short-term EFSF notes, resulting in a debt write-down of €106 billion or 52 percent of 2012 GDP, a haircut of 53.5 percent in nominal terms.

The IMF also calculates that "the decision not to restructure debt at the outset of the Greek crisis" meant all in all, that some €50 billion in maturing bonds were repaid in full. And this does not count bondholders who were able to sell to the ECB or national central banks:

The decision not to restructure debt at the outset of the Greek crisis had already allowed some €40 billion in maturing bonds to be fully repaid in the first year of the SBA. Once the PSI was deemed necessary, the drawn-out negotiations meant that some further €10 billion continued to be repaid in full (Zettelmeyer, Trebesch, and Gulati 2013). By the time of the debt exchange, Greece's debt was largely held by Greek and European banks, and by the ECB (through Securities Markets Program (SMP)–related bond purchases). The ECB, as well as European national central banks, and the EIB, as official creditors, would be excluded from the PSI.

In other words, from December 2009 to the eventual restructuring in March 2012, many creditors received full value for maturing bonds, paid by financial assistance loans from euro-area member states and the IMF. Other creditors had sold their bonds to the ECB. All of this diminished the debt relief that could be achieved by a given haircut. This is one more reason that restructuring should happen quickly in a crisis. But to happen quickly, a plan and an institutional framework must already be in place.

Having Greek banks buy lots of government debt backfired. The capital of Greek banks was essentially wiped out by their bond losses, which led to a recapitalization by the state. That transfer further reduced the net benefits of the sovereign debt restructuring for taxpayers.

The ECB, National Central Banks, and the European Investment Bank (EIB) took no losses in restructuring. It is frequent in a rescue plan or reorganization that new debt must be repaid before old debt. However, these institutions were also protected from losses on their purchases of existing bonds. As we have noted, this provision helps to separate monetary from fiscal policy, as it insulates assets on the ECB balance sheet from default and thus protects the value of ECB liabilities. However, it means that to generate the same reduction in debt owed by Greece, other bondholders had to take larger losses. If the market expects that the ECB and National Central Banks are always made whole, it also means that the purchases do less to remove default risk from private markets, and the effect of such purchases might even be to *lower* the price of bonds held by other people. For this reason, the ECB announced that it would in the future be treated "pari passu" in case of a debt restructuring involving bonds purchases under OMT (2012) and PSPP (2015). As the story makes clear, one difficulty of making up a restructuring plan after the fact is that different creditors can negotiate different treatment.

The restructuring was also too late to stem the steep recession that took hold in the Greek economy, some of which was likely attributable to great uncertainty over how the crisis would resolve.

The 2012 Crisis

The transfers and restructuring still left Greece with a large debt to repay and required a sharp fiscal adjustment from its previous structural deficits. The more than two-year delay in restructuring, from early 2010 until March 2012, meant that the fiscal adjustment had to be larger. What bondholders do not pay, European taxpayers pay via fiscal transfers or ECB monetization, or Greek citizens pay in higher taxes and lower government spending, starting immediately. Taxpayers, recipients of social transfers, and public employees in Greece were thus confronted with a severe fiscal consolidation program.

The Greek public became increasingly dissatisfied with the adjustment program and the government. A problem of fiscal assistance with conditionality is that the public then blames the helper for any subsequent trouble, not realizing just how much worse things would have been without help. The market would have demanded far tougher conditionality to buy debt than the EU and IMF did.

The political situation became more uncertain. Concrete fears about Grexit—an exit of Greece from the euro area—emerged again, especially after Greek prime minister George Papandreou announced in late 2011 a referendum about the bailout program. That came as a shock to other member states and to markets. The *Financial Times*, in a series of long articles about the Greek crisis published in spring 2014, wrote the following about this announcement: "Eurozone bond markets, which had briefly rallied after the Greek debt restructuring was agreed, sold off in a panic. Yields on Greece's benchmark 10-year bond spiked by 16.2 per cent in a single day. More worryingly, borrowing costs for bigger eurozone governments began to approach levels where others had been forced into bailouts: yields on Italy's 10-year bond jumped to more than 6.2 per cent."[12]

Following intense political discussions in Cannes in early November 2011, the referendum did not take place, Papandreou stepped down, and a new government was formed. Lucas Papademos, vice president of the ECB until 2010, became prime minister.

March to July 2012 saw a further increase in Grexit fears. In May 2012, parliamentary elections ended in a deadlock and a political crisis. Grexit risks and political instability undermined confidence, investment, employment, and the implementation of economic and administrative reforms.[13] Peter Spiegel wrote in the *Financial Times* that in early 2012 a secret blueprint was prepared, "a detailed script of how to reconstruct Greece's economic and financial infrastructure if it were to leave the euro."

The plan was drawn up by about two dozen officials in small teams at the European Commission in Brussels, the European Central Bank in Frankfurt and the IMF in Washington. Officials who worked on the previously undisclosed plan insisted it was not a road map to force Greece out of the euro—quite the opposite. Grexit, they feared, would wreak havoc in European financial markets, causing bank runs in other teetering eurozone economies and raising questions of which country would be forced out next. But by early 2012, many of those same officials believed it was irresponsible not to prepare for a Greek exit.[14]

As with the lack of preparation for sovereign default in the euro, there is a justifiable fear that talking about something makes it more likely to happen. But not preparing is catastrophic if it does happen. In our view, preparation is the wiser course. Spiegel continued, "'We always said: it's our aim to keep them inside,' said one participant. 'Is the probability zero that they leave? No. If you are on the board of a company and you only have a 10 per cent probability for such an event, you prepare yourself.'" New parliamentary elections in June 2012 eventually resulted in a center-right government under Prime Minister Antonis Samaras, and Grexit risks began to recede.

Why Did Restructuring Come so Late?

When the Greek crisis hit, upfront creditor losses were excluded. These can include partial defaults, in which investors receive only a partial payment, or debt restructuring, in which creditors get new debt that has longer maturity, pays a lower coupon, or with a lesser principal amount, than the original debt. Creditor losses were excluded mainly due to fears of "contagion" and "financial instability." These words are bandied about as if they have precise technical meaning and well-understood mechanisms. They do not, so to understand and evaluate the fears, we must dig a bit.

German finance minister Wolfgang Schäuble's April 2010 statement, "We cannot allow the bankruptcy of a euro member state like Greece to turn into a second Lehman Brothers. Greece is just as systematically important as a major bank," captures the feeling well.

This central presumption, that sovereign default is the same as default of a large, leveraged, and central financial institution, with the potential to ignite a systemic run and thus threaten financial calamity, gave much of the motivation for the extraordinary interventions of the sovereign debt crisis, as well as the delay in allowing any restructuring. The mentality proved durable and powerful in the years ahead, despite the later successful Greek restructuring, and accounts at least partially for the failure of the restructuring regime to take hold, and the persistence to this day of the expectation that bailouts will almost always come.

If you think for a moment, this fear is puzzling. Sovereigns are not dealer banks. Sovereigns are not hugely leveraged with overnight debt. Their default does not spark a rush by creditors to seize assets or stop their normal functioning. A bank in default cannot buy and sell or make loans. A sovereign in default can continue most operations. Sovereign default is more like the bankruptcy reorganization of a large nonfinancial company. "Financial stability" is not the same as "no large bond investor ever loses any money."

Sovereign default leads to a financial crisis only if it threatens a large number of highly leveraged and central financial institutions, which in turn causes bank failures and their inability to intermediate new credit. In the Lehman analogy, Greece is not the bank; Greek debt is (potentially) the mortgage-backed security.

Some "contagion" is a necessary component of financial calamity. Greece is not that large on its own. To cause a systemic crisis, as in 2008, run-inducing losses on Greek debt at some banks would have to spread to run-inducing losses on other assets, and to creditor runs at a wide swath of banks.

But it's hard to see concretely how sovereign default sparks "contagion." None of the alleged contagion mechanisms of 2008 apply to sovereign debt. Italy's debt is a claim on Italian taxpayers, Greece's debt is a claim on Greek taxpayers. Italy does not hold a lot of Greek debt. Greece defaulting tells you nothing about Italy's economic prospects, nor does it directly cause Italy, as the next domino, to fail. Argentina's repeated defaults spark no contagion to Chile, Brazil, or other Latin American countries. Sovereign debt is an easily measurable asset on bank balance sheets, not an illiquid and hard-to-value derivative. If bank X loses a lot on Greek debt, that event does not induce a run on bank Y, as people know directly what bank Y's exposure to Greek debt is.

What was the concern, then? When one spells it out, one concrete mechanism remains. Despite a huge financial and banking crisis in the rear-view mirror, some large German and French banks were exposed to Greek debt. Those banks, as well as banks from the United Kingdom and the Netherlands, also had substantial exposures to Italy, Spain, and Ireland, and Spanish banks were exposed to Portuguese debt. For example, in the fourth quarter of 2009, French banks had about €625 billion total exposure to Spain, Portual, Italy, Ireland, and Greece, with Spain and Italy by far the largest components. German banks had nearly €500 billion exposure.[15] And of course Greek banks had a lot of Greek debt, so much that their equity was wiped out in the sovereign default.

Even then, bailing a few systemically important banks out of their Greek debt losses would have been a lot less expensive than bailing out all creditors from Greek debt and trying to raise the value of all Greek debt by all holders. Perhaps political leaders were a bit unwilling to bail big banks out quite so soon, but bailing out all bondholders and the Greek government was hardly popular either. To cause a real crisis, we need some mechanism by which a Greek restructuring imperils, say, Italy. What is it?

Since countries are not leveraged banks and lack a direct connection, only one plausible concrete "contagion" mechanism between countries remains. If European authorities allowed a Greek default while banks, markets, and regulators all assumed a fiscal or monetary bailout was likely, bond investors would quickly lower their expectations of a EU and ECB bailout should Italy, Spain, Portugal, and others run into trouble. The Greek default would quickly lower bond values and could even cause a rollover crisis in other countries. The combined losses on all these sovereign assets could spark a widespread financial crisis, challenging the EU's fiscal and the ECB's monetary resources for a colossal bailout. Indeed, the restructuring of Greek bonds, when it came, had a negative impact on the market prices of bonds of other countries, in particular Italian and Spanish bonds.

In this interpretation, then, the vague statements of "financial stability" and "contagion" worries start to make sense. We can also understand officials' reluctance to state mechanisms concretely and their preference to allude to market psychology untethered from rational assessment of risk. Under this mechanism, the threat of financial crisis stemming from a sovereign default, even in a small member state, admits a failure of the euro's architecture: Contagion comes because everyone expects bailouts, despite the founding promises that neither the ECB nor other countries would bail out a country in trouble. It admits a larger and abject failure of banking regulation. With the 2008 banking crisis just in the rearview mirror, bank regulators completely ignored another category of dangerous assets, sovereign debt, indeed still assigning it zero risk weight in capital requirements and ignoring large and increasing debts on important banks' balance sheets. Perhaps in the 1990s one could forgive an attitude that major financial crises are relegated to the distant past or emerging markets, but two years after banks threatened to collapse from real estate investments, did it really take that much imagination to look around and worry about what other large investments might cause trouble?

If this is the interpretation of officials' past and continuing fears—and we know of no other interpretation that makes sense—then the solution is not to stop all sovereign defaults or declines in asset values in perpetuity by ECB or fiscal intervention, with continual allusion to mysterious market dysfunction. Rather, the solution is to reform the financial system so that banks and other run-prone intermediaries are not dangerously exposed to such sovereign risk, and to include a resolution regime so that a resolution in one country does not massively change expectations about how debt in other countries will be treated should those countries run into trouble.

There are other reasons for delayed restructuring as well. Restructuring is politically difficult for the sitting government, even if the policy mistakes were largely made by a previous government supported by other parties. Restructuring can make future borrowing harder. One always hopes that in just a little more time, the government will be able to turn things around or announce some new plans that will calm the markets; maybe paying off some creditors will assuage the others.

Private bankruptcy tends to happen on the day that debt comes due and there is no cash to pay it, and governments face similar incentives. Bank resolution can come more quickly, but only when outside regulators swoop in to force it. Nobody likes to stiff their creditors.

Help, when it came, was insufficient to fully support the Greek economy and bail everyone out. But it is possible to offer too much help. Disincentives lie everywhere. The IMF argues: "Even in the face of a sustained loss of market access, debt restructuring could be delayed because of the ample availability of official financing and the authorities stated willingness to entertain an unprecedented program of fiscal adjustment."[16]

In other words, don't default or send in international help after every little market hiccup. Market turmoil offers useful pressure on governments to straighten things out on their own, and the market test of reforms is better than official conditionality programs. Even missing a few interest payments and suffering some "loss of market access" can buy time if it results in a successful adjustment program. Nobody, least of all international financial organizations, really knows the size of the problem and what a country can do about it, or what it takes for markets to come back. Putting off restructuring reflected optimism about the kinds of fiscal and structural adjustments Greece could accomplish. With hindsight, Greece simply did not have the political and technical capacity to do what it committed to in the adjustment programs, including optimistic assumptions about improvements in tax administration and other reforms.

Delay has costs, however. In its "Ex-Post Evaluation of Exceptional Access under Greece's 2010 Stand-By Arrangement," the IMF staff provides a candid assessment of the problems of delayed debt restructuring:

> Not tackling the public debt problem decisively at the outset or early in the program created uncertainty about the euro area's capacity to resolve the crisis and likely aggravated the contraction in output. An upfront debt restructuring would have been better for Greece although this was not acceptable to the euro partners. A delayed debt restructuring also provided a window for private creditors to

reduce exposures and shift debt into official hands. As seen earlier, this shift occurred on a significant scale and limited the bail-in of creditors when PSI eventually took place, leaving taxpayers and the official sector on the hook.[17]

The balance is delicate. Clearly, however, we cannot expect political leaders to make up a resolution plan on the spot, in the middle of a crisis, especially if decisions must be unanimous. A *mechanism* for resolving sovereign debt needs to be in place ahead of time in order for anyone to expect speedy action when a crisis hits.

The 2015 Crisis

After two crises, the Greek macroeconomic outlook started to improve in late 2013 and the first half of 2014. But Greek banks were still fragile. As Hardouvelis and Vayanos (2023, 4) write, "The first and second recapitalizations were successful in transforming a banking system in which most banks were economically insolvent into one where banks were solvent and partly owned by private investors. At the same time, banks remained fragile and vulnerable to a worsening in the economic situation."

Sadly, the economic situation worsened quickly, and financial fragility returned with a vengeance.

After the election in January 2015, a government was formed by two "anti-program, anti-austerity" parties (Syriza and ANEL). This change created significant uncertainty, which increased until summer 2015: Would the government eventually agree on a new program with its creditors so as to ensure further financial assistance? Would Greece instead drop out of the euro? This event is a good reminder that multi-year programs are always renegotiable and that political parties change.

People started taking money out of Greek banks, and the banks were less able to borrow from other banks. Hardouvelis and Vayanos (2023, p. 25) report that "between the end of 2014 and June 2015, inter-bank borrowing dropped from €38.6 billion to €7.7 billion (a drop of 80.1%) and domestic deposits dropped from €160.3 billion to €122.2 billion (a drop of 23.7%)." These outflows were balanced with an increase in emergency lending from the ECB from zero to €86.8 billion in the same period.

How did this large increase in central bank loans to Greek banks come about? The new Greek government rejected the existing adjustment program. But that program was a precondition for the loans from euro-area member states and the IMF. Without it, member states (via the ESM) and the IMF could not provide further financial assistance, at least without negotiating a whole new program. The Greek economy worsened, default and exit risks increased, and yields on Greek sovereign and bank debt rose.

These events put the ECB into a difficult situation. In line with its rules, the ECB declared that bonds issued or guaranteed by the Greek government were no longer eligible as collateral for loans from the ECB "since it is currently not possible to assume a successful conclusion of the programme review." But the ECB was the last game in town. The ECB instead signaled that banks could still borrow from their national central bank: "Liquidity needs of Eurosystem counterparties, for counterparties that do not have sufficient alternative collateral, can be satisfied by the relevant national central bank, by means of emergency liquidity assistance (ELA) within the existing Eurosystem rules."[18] The Bank of Greece, under Emergency Liquidity Assistance (ELA), a "national task," could accept collateral that the ECB could not accept for "monetary policy loans," and Greek sovereign bonds in particular. The ECB Governing Council set the overall limits of such loans, which it raised in several steps until June 2015. Of course, this deepened the government-bank nexus in Greece, but there were few remaining options.

Thus in the following months the Bank of Greece substantially increased its emergency lending to Greek banks (see figure 5.2). To do so, it created new euros (bank reserves). Greek banks mainly used those borrowed euros to allow investors to withdraw their deposits and other banks to withdraw interbank loans.

As euros were leaving Greece, additional Target2 loans from the ECB were needed to finance the ELA loans provided by the Bank of Greece. The Bank of Greece saw its target debt increase by about €58 billion in half a year toward €108 billion by end of June 2015.

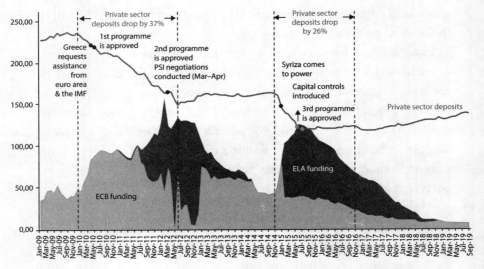

FIGURE 5.2. Private-sector deposits and Eurosystem funding profile of Greek banks, € billion, 2009–2019. Source: Andruszkiewicz et al. (2020), p. 32.

The situation came to a head when a majority of Greek voters rejected an economic adjustment program in a referendum held in June 2015. As a result, the ECB announced it could not even allow additional ELA loans. In a public letter from September 2015, President Draghi explained that "ELA can only be provided against adequate collateral and only to solvent banks. . . . As regards the collateral adequacy, the quality of the assets used by Greek banks as collateral with the Bank of Greece at its ELA operations at the time was closely linked to the ability of the Hellenic Republic to honour its financial obligations. Several events at the end of June 2015 triggered a reassessment of the Greek government's financial prospects."[19] Note Draghi's recognition of a bank-government nexus. A country's banks receive emergency loans from their national central bank, using collateral including the same government's securities. When the banks and the government are in trouble, the national central bank has a big problem.

The Greek government responded by introducing capital controls and a daily deposit withdrawal limit of €60. After some hesitation and internal disputes, the Greek government ultimately agreed to a new bailout package with the ESM in July, which included fiscal consolidation measures and economic reforms. The IMF did not participate with new financing.

For Greek citizens, the cumulative severity of the three crises was enormous. According to Eurostat, GDP dropped by over one quarter and stayed flat through 2016. Unemployment reached 26.5%.

For Greek banks, the 2015 crisis was another big blow. The levels of non performing loans increased further, as many borrowers were unable to repay their debts due to the economic downturn. The Single Supervisory Mechanism (SSM), which had been established in November 2014, required a new asset quality review during the third quarter of 2015. This review led to the banks having to acknowledge a further €10 billion of losses relative to the asset quality review that had taken place just one year before, and agree to large recapitalizations, partly via debt for equity swaps. These moves reduced the value of equity that the government had taken by almost the entirety of the €25 billion it had invested in the previous rescue (Hardouvelis and Vayanos, 2023).

Nonperforming loans continued to grow through March 2016, peaking at an astonishing 48.9% of all loans before starting to drop. As part of the rescue, a thorough review of the governance of Greek banks took place, which improved the independence and capability of their boards of directors.

Hardouvelis and Vayanos (2023, p. 41) extract three lessons from these successive crises. First, "governments should not rely excessively on their banking systems for financing, and banks should limit their exposures to domestic government securities." Second, both EU and financial market monitoring failed to prevent Greece's excessive debt and deficits due to expectations of an implicit bailout. Third, Greece's default was mishandled. Debt restructuring was delayed to mitigate banks' losses, piling them on Greek citizens instead.

What about the ECB's decision to provide substantial loans to Greek banks, via Target2 loans to the national central bank at risk-free rates? Given the significant sovereign and bank default risks, such loans implied substantial subsidies relative to market conditions. They indirectly helped the new Greek government to mitigate the financial and economic impacts of its decision to reject the existing adjustment program. But given the shortcomings of the euro's institutional framework, one can see why the ECB made this decision despite its political and fiscal consequences. Had the ECB, for example, rejected or withdrawn ELA loans at an early stage, a consequent "sudden stop" of private financing might have caused a disorderly default and led Greece to choose to exit from the euro area.

The ESM paid the first tranche to Greece in summer 2015, just a few weeks after a new program had been agreed to. Such a swift disbursement was unusual. It came just in time to allow Greece to pay several billion euros on maturing Greek government bonds.[20] Of course, avoiding default was the point of the program, and avoiding default meant that European resources went straight to bondholders. Those bondholders included the ECB, bonds that the ECB had bought under its Securities Market Program (SMP). A Greek default toward the ECB could have created big problems for the central bank.

Greece entered a third economic adjustment program on August 19, 2015, which ran until August 20, 2018.[21] Greece received €61.9 billion direct additional financial assistance from the European Stability Mechanism (ESM), in return for a broad package of banking, fiscal, and economic reforms to make its debt more sustainable. During the third program, Greece also received significant relief of the debt to the EFSF and ESM, and thus euro-area member states, incurred under previous programs, known as "Official Sector Involvement," reflecting the corresponding losses taken by the "official sector," and eventually taxpayers. This relief was provided through extensions of grace periods, below-market interest rates, interest deferrals, and very long maturities.

The IMF did not participate in financing this third program. The IMF was part of the program negotiations and design, and the IMF Board approved "in principle" a stand-by arrangement (SBA) in July 2017.[22] The SBA never became effective because the IMF insisted on even greater official debt relief from European member states.

All in all, the ECB's decisions and emergency fiscal transfers from other member states likely helped to avoid a larger, more costly crisis in

Greece, and possibly the euro area as well. But all bailouts lead to moral hazards and expectations of future bailouts.

5.2 Ireland

In the course of 2010, Ireland became the next focus of the emerging European sovereign crisis. Rather than years of borrowing to finance government spending and consumption, Ireland's problems stemmed from its housing and banking crisis in 2007–2008 and the way that the Irish government addressed that crisis, including the Irish government's guarantee of bank deposits in the fall of 2008.

Over the years from 2007 to 2010, combined funding from deposits and debt securities of Anglo Irish and Irish Nationwide Building Society (INBS)—both of which would eventually be nationalized and merged to form the Irish Resolution Banking Corporation (IRBC)—fell from €96 billion at the end of 2007 to €23 billion at the end of 2010 (Whelan, 2012). Starting in March 2009, the Central Bank of Ireland agreed to provide Emergency Liquidity Assistance (ELA) loans to both of these institutions against collateral that did not qualify for the usual Eurosystem repurchase agreements. By the end of 2010, these two entities owed about €52 billion to the Central Bank of Ireland and thus the Eurosystem, of which about €28 billion in ELA debts. ELA would eventually reach €40 billion in 2011. Between August 2010 and early December 2010, deposit outflows from the Irish banking system accelerated, in part likely related to rising unemployment and deleveraging. Total customer deposits in its main six banks dropped by 20% (McQuinn and Woods, 2012).

The guarantees to bank creditors provided by the Irish government in autumn 2008 turned into a massive liability for the Irish state. The total cost of the bank bailout for Ireland, including particularly the nationalization of Anglo Irish in 2009 and of Allied Irish in December 2010, was staggering: €64 billion, or 40% of Irish GDP. (See Whelan, 2012, for an excellent discussion of the Irish bailout.) In particular the Anglo Irish rescue was clearly not a case in which deposit insurance bridged a multiple-equilibrium run on illiquid assets or stopped self-confirming expectations, which would not cost the government anything. It was a simple bailout of an insolvent bank, benefiting depositors and bondholders in the end.

Irish government debt rose from 24% of GDP in 2007 to 86% of GDP in 2010, and it would top out at 120% of GDP in 2012. A fateful decision by the government had turned the insolvency of Irish banks into the potential insolvency of the Irish state.

The increase in public debt was not just a result of bank bailouts. During the construction boom, the Irish treasury received enormous tax inflows, particularly from value-added tax revenues on the booming building industry and household consumption, and a stamp duty on the sales of residential properties. When these inflows vanished, government revenues were sharply below expenditures. Even before the EU/IMF program started, the Irish government recognized this fiscal problem and put together its own plan to address the issue. That plan became the core of the adjustment program, insofar as it related to macro-structural issues.

On November 19, 2010, ECB president Jean-Claude Trichet sent a private letter to the Irish finance minister, urging him to ask for a financial assistance program from the euro area and the IMF.[23]

The ECB had understandable reasons to do so. Under ELA, the Eurosystem was providing large amounts of loans to Irish banks, including ELA loans with collateral that the ECB would not accept for normal monetary policy operations. The ECB is allowed to provide loans only to *solvent* banks and against *adequate* collateral.

At the time, the solvency of banks had to be assessed, and was confirmed, by the national supervisor. The quality of collateral was increasingly in doubt due to rising concerns about the solvency of the Irish state, which provided guarantees for collateral that banks provided to receive ELA. But the guarantees of a state that may itself be insolvent leaves an obvious circularity.

In this situation, financial assistance from euro-area governments and the IMF and a credible adjustment program that would ensure the solvency of the state and recapitalize viable banks was the only promising way to allow the Eurosytem to continue providing loans to Irish banks.

On November 21, 2010, the Irish authorities requested financial assistance. In December 2010, the EU and the IMF committed to financial assistance loans of €67.5 billion, conditional on an adjustment program that involved stabilizing the financial system and a sharp adjustment in the government's finances worth eight percentage points of GDP. No sovereign debt restructuring was contemplated.

5.3   Portugal

Portugal was different from many other crisis countries. Portugal saw virtually no growth, including productivity and employment growth, during the first decade of the euro (Blanchard, 2007). Its construction sector actually contracted. Reis (2013, p. 144) writes, "Portugal in the 2000s experienced neither a housing boom like Spain and Ireland, nor as rampant an increase in public debt as Greece, nor does it suffer from Italy's chronic political instability."

As in Greece, Portugal had big trade deficits and inward capital flows during the early years of the euro. The stock of net foreign assets was −101% of GDP by 2007, with a change in 8 years of −78.5 percentage points of GDP. Wages grew, making exports harder and imports easier. Portuguese banks took foreign deposits and loaned them out in Portugal, channeling around 50% of this debt (Reis, 2013). Much of the debt went to finance consumption goods.

Public debt also grew substantially from 2000 to 2007, from about 54% to 73% of GDP. Retirement pension increases accounted for the entirety of the increase in government expenditure.

When these private capital flows started to decrease, public financing via Target2 balances partly took over. Rather than pay for imports with money borrowed from banks or investors abroad, the Portuguese central bank simply owed the corresponding euros to the foreign central banks via the ECB.

As international creditors continued to abandon the country, Portugal's public finances collapsed. Starting with a high structural deficit, that deficit increased due to the severe recession and to efforts to prop up its banks. Some of the largest banks, Millennium, Banif, and Banco

Espirito Santo, were rescued in 2012, 2013, and 2014 for a total of almost €10 billion. Portugal's 2009 and 2010 deficits were 9.9% and 11.4% of GDP. Public debt grew strongly from 73% of GDP in 2007 to 114% of GDP in 2011 (and peaked at 133% in 2014).

The perilous situation of the government, in turn, worsened the solvency of the banks, for whom Portugal's bonds were 23% of their assets.[24] Portugal entered a classic bank-government feedback loop.

As the situation became untenable, on May 16, 2011, Portugal agreed to a €78 billion bailout in exchange for a commitment to cut its deficit, recapitalize its banks, and undertake 223 structural reforms. The conditions of the bailout were to be monitored by the troika of the European Commission (EC), the European Central Bank (ECB), and the International Monetary Fund (IMF). Again, the EU chose a bailout, with some conditionality but no debt restructuring.

In spite of the bailout, Portugal's interest rates kept rising until January 2012, peaking at 13.85%.[25] At the time, no one was really sure that Portugal would not default chaotically, or even withdraw from the euro. The bailout did not immediately restore private investors' confidence on the ability of Portugal to eventually repay its debt.

5.4 Spain

In 2011, bond markets increasingly realized the dire situation of Spanish semi-public savings banks, or *Cajas*. These banks had borrowed heavily and invested in their local housing booms. The housing market collapsed, wiping out the value of their assets. The *Cajas* were also poorly governed, involving a complex web of influence between developers, politicians, and lenders (Cuñat and Garicano, 2010). Their collapse led to a "vicious cycle of failing banks, unsustainable fiscal deficits, rising borrowing costs, contracting output, rapid job loss, and severe financial market turmoil" (International Monetary Fund, 2014b, p. 3). Most *Cajas* were small, badly governed, and their equity was not traded in stock markets. As a result, private recapitalization by selling new equity, finding new equity investors, or selling the whole bank to new investors was essentially impossible.

On July 22, 2012, the Eurogroup accepted Spain's request for a program to finance the rescue of its savings banks with up to €100 billion. The Memorandum of Understanding included "the conduct of an asset quality review and stress test for the large majority of banks in Spain; the recapitalisation, restructuring and/or resolution of weak banks; and the transfer of problem assets to an asset management company," as well as the performance of "a burden-sharing exercise that imposed losses on junior bank creditors—mostly retail investors—and a downsizing of the banks requiring public support. Sector-wide conditionality involved several measures to strengthen the regulatory and supervisory framework" (Baudino, Herrera, and Restoy, 2023, p. 3). To ensure that the burden-sharing took place, bank restructuring plans could be approved only by the European Commission (according to the State Aid Banking Communication) after burden-sharing had been implemented, although only by holders of bank-subordinated debt and not senior bond holders or depositors. This step has been estimated to have reduced the cost of the subsequent restructuring plans by approximately one fourth (Lienemeyer, Kerle, and Malikova, 2014). The IMF participated, but only by providing expertise and technical support, not by providing loans. The program was narrower than the other programs, as Spain did not request, and the Eurogroup did not demand, a macroeconomic adjustment program.

The Memorandum of Understanding did require Spain to "comply fully with its commitments and obligations under the EDP and the recommendations to address macroeconomic imbalances within the framework of the European Semester," and stated that "Progress in meeting these obligations under the relevant EU procedures will be closely monitored in parallel with the regular review of program implementation." However, these were parallel and not new conditions.[26]

Consequently, there was no detailed conditionality for financial help on fiscal and structural polices. There was only financial-sector conditionality concerning the banking system, and notably the governance of the Spanish savings banks: The old *Cajas* could not have controlling interests in credit institutions, and their boards would have to be subject to "fit and proper" tests. The Memorandum stated: "The Spanish authorities will prepare by end-November 2012 legislation clarifying the role of savings banks in their capacity as shareholders of credit institutions with a view to eventually reducing their stakes to non-controlling levels. Furthermore, authorities will propose measures to strengthen fit and proper rules for the governing bodies of savings banks and to introduce incompatibility requirements regarding the governing bodies of the former savings banks and the commercial banks controlled by them."

5.5   Italy

Italy was the largest of the euro member countries to run into financial market trouble due to concerns about its debts. The Italian treasury bill rate peaked in November 2011 at 6.4%.[27] Its 10-year bond rate spiked to 7.05%, while Germany's was 1.87%.

But Italy was unwilling to ask for an adjustment program. On November 4, 2011, at a G20 summit in Cannes, Italy was confronted with pressure to request financial assistance and enter an euro area/IMF adjustment program.[28]

A week later, Prime Minister Silvio Berlusconi stepped down and Mario Monti became prime minister of a so-called technocratic government. The Monti government implemented far-reaching fiscal reforms, including major changes to the pension system. These even burdened workers who were close to their retirement age by changing the basis of pensions from the end-of-career salary to total earnings and by raising the pension age.[29] The reform also increased real estate taxes and introduced several structural reforms, including in the labor market.

Monti's reforms eventually passed into law in December 2011. Italian interest rates fell (see figure 5.1), with the Treasury Bill rate bottoming out at 1.13% in March 2012. Italy ran small primary surpluses until the Covid recession. Its main problem remained persistently weak growth and a large stock of debt, rendering it vulnerable to interest rate increases.

Italian bond prices then dropped (and yields rose) significantly again in the run-up and the aftermath of Greece's restructuring, in which remaining Greek bondholders took haircuts. In June 2012, the Italian treasury bill rate rose back to to 3.39%. The 10-year rate rose from a low of 5.04%, while Germany's was 1.83%, to 6.0% (1.2%) in July 2012.

The Greek debt restructuring had an intended side effect—to make it clear that debt-holders would not always be made whole by EU, IMF, or ECB funds. Higher Italian interest-rate spreads were a natural consequence of the larger probability of default or restructuring and the lower probability of a bailout. However, from the perspective of the Monti government it was bad luck, and seemingly unfair, as the yield rise had nothing to do with any change in Italian policy. It was an external event. It counteracted the positive effects of reforms and fiscal consolidation initiated by the Monti government. Yes, higher default premia in reaction to the Greek debt restructuring were also due to the high public debt and structural economic problems that prime minister Monti had inherited. But this did not help Monti, who lost the next election, in February 2013.

5.6 Cyprus

The crisis in Cyprus started in mid-2011, resulting from banking troubles as in Ireland. From October 2011 onward, two large Cypriot banks received Emergency Liquidity Assistance from the Central Bank of Cyprus, effectively financed by the ECB.

The Greek crisis was a key trigger. Cypriot banks' Greek branches experienced large non performing loans. And the eventual write-downs ("private sector involvement," PSI) of Greek government debt in the March 2012 restructuring resulted in further losses of Cypriot banks, rendering one of the banks insolvent.

The Cypriot government requested financial assistance from the euro area and the IMF on June 25, 2012. However, it took nine months of negotiations, bank balance sheet assessments, and political uncertainty until agreement was reached between the Cypriot authorities, the Eurogroup, and the IMF.

On March 19, 2013, the Cypriot parliament rejected the agreed adjustment program. This program would have imposed a levy on all bank deposits to recapitalize banks. This step was perceived to violate deposit insurance.

Cyprus experienced a spiraling banking crisis, and finally a run. The government closed the banks for two weeks and imposed capital controls.

The parliament's rejection posed a challenge for the ECB. Under the Outright Monetary Transactions (OMT) program, the ECB may purchase sovereign debt only when such a program is in place. And the Eurosystem had large exposures to the Cypriot banking system, mainly via Emergency Liquidity Assistance. Some Cypriot banks were economically insolvent; the value of their assets was less than the value of their liabilities. Without a program that included a significant losses by creditors, including depositors, only a large bail-out would save the banks. However, the Cypriot banking system was eight times the size of the Cypriot GDP, and bank capital needs amounted to 60 percent of GDP, larger than Argentina in 1980 or Ireland in 2008.[30] Cyprus did not have the fiscal capacity to bail out all of the creditors of its banks or to fully recapitalize them. Thus, any effective bank bailout would raise much further the risk of a sovereign default. Without a program, the ECB could not buy sovereign debt under OMT. And with undercapitalized and economically insolvent banks, and no program, the ECB could no longer even offer Emergency Liquidity Assistance.

Against this background, on March 21, 2013, two days after the Cypriot parliament had rejected the EU/IMF program, the Governing Council announced the following decision on Emergency Liquidity Assistance requested by the Central Bank of Cyprus: "The Governing Council of the European Central Bank decided to maintain the current level of Emergency Liquidity Assistance (ELA) until Monday, 25 March 2013. Thereafter, Emergency Liquidity Assistance (ELA) could only be considered if an EU/IMF program is in place that would ensure the solvency of the concerned banks."[31]

On March 25, the Eurogroup accepted a somewhat revised adjustment program, provided that unsecured deposits in two large banks were "bailed in" to finance the resolution of the Laiki Bank and the recapitalization of the Bank of Cyprus.[32] Together, those banks had assets of four times GDP.

Cyprus received a €10 billion bailout in exchange for a IMF/EU program. That program involved a significant bail-in (i.e., losses) for many depositors. The program also involved the closure of Cyprus's largest bank. Politically, a factor possibly explaining this one bail-in of depositors in the whole crisis was the fact that a large share of them belonged to wealthy Russians. As the *New York Times* put it, "The exercise was meant to banish what Germany and other Northern European nations viewed as dirty Russian money from Cyprus's bloated banks."[33]

Creditor losses in Spain and both creditor and depositor losses in Cyprus were important watersheds. There was no subsequent widespread run or crisis. Sadly, these elements in particular seem to have fallen by the wayside in the subsequent backtracking from reforms.

The Cypriot case also tested the new tool allowing the direct recapitalization of the banks by the ESM, rather than by the already-stressed Cypriot government. Although taxpayer-funded recapitalizations of private banks remain a contentious tool, nonetheless in that instance such recapitalization by the ESM could have helped to reduce the sovereign-bank doom loop and the ECB's consequent exposure. However, the Eurogroup did not agree to use this tool for Cyprus or any other case.

There was no haircut on government bonds, but the Cypriot program also included a small domestic debt restructuring. This involved an exchange of domestic sovereign bonds maturing within three years for new bonds with the same coupon but extended maturities. The restructuring triggered a temporary selective default rating by Fitch and Standard & Poor's, which was reversed once the transaction was concluded. There was not much market reaction.

5.7 Lessons

Two nostrums pervade opinion about the euro: Sovereign default or restructuring is an unthinkable calamity, and any bank depositor ever losing any money is an unthinkable calamity. Greece proves the first wrong, and Cyprus proves the second wrong. Those lessons seem not to sink in, though.

These crises emphasize the interrelated problems of banks and sovereigns. First, banks are loaded up with undiversified sovereign debt, so a sovereign default means a banking crisis. Banks are encouraged to do so by zero regulatory risk weights. If banks just had internationally diversified sovereign debt portfolios, with conventional equity buffers, much of the fear of financial turmoil surrounding sovereign default would be addressed. It would be better still if sovereign debt were held directly by investors rather than via bank deposits, in diversified mutual funds, or by pension funds and other unleveraged institutional investors. Second, international and pan-European banks are implicitly guaranteed by domestic sovereigns. However, states like Ireland and Cyprus may not have the resources to effectively guarantee deposits. Large international banks need either a large deposit backstop or a less fragile financial structure.

The problems remain. As one sign of continuing banking malaise, market price-book valuations for European banks broadly fluctuated during the following decade around 50%, even in good times. That is, investors assessed the true capital of those banks around 50% below the accounting capital, which bank regulations use as a basis for capital adequacy rules.

Clearly, delinking banks and sovereigns is a critical part of reforming the euro. We return to this issue in chapters 10 and 11.

We see in these histories the emergence of a new and reasonably successful crisis management regime. When a sovereign gets in trouble, the EU and IMF can step in to provide temporary fiscal support, aimed at specific uses. They condition help on an adjustment program by which the country cleans up its banking system and macroeconomic situation. And they impose a significant sovereign debt restructuring and losses by bank creditors, including depositors.

One might argue that the fiscal support of ESM packages left behind the philosophy of the no fiscal bail-out commitment. An ESM program may require an upfront debt restructuring, and the assistance often takes the form of loans, though admittedly at low interest rates, and the loans may subsequently be partially foregiven. Still, an element of fiscal transfer remains, from member state taxpayers to troubled governments and to bondholders. A pure no-bail-out means default, however, and staring at the messy facts of crises, the EU decided to stretch the no-bail-out principle. Conditionality and program rules attempt to address moral hazard, and in the end do so better than an incredible threat to refuse any support.

One can complain that the system needs improving, about the form of adjustment programs, and so forth. Yes, the system emerged over time, and all of the programs were not perfect. But the outlines of an institutional framework for dealing with bank and sovereign crises were forming. The main lesson of our later history is that this effort stalled, and this important progress now seems largely forgotten.

5.8   The ECB's Securities Market Program

We shift focus now to the role of ECB bond purchases during the sovereign debt crises.

On May 10, 2010, the ECB introduced the Securities Market Program (SMP), under which it began to buy sovereign debts. The SMP mainly consisted of discretionary purchases of sovereign debt of specific stressed countries—initially Greece, Ireland, and Portugal, and starting in summer 2011, also Spain and Italy. By mid-2012 the ECB had bought about €210 billion in public bonds from the five countries.

The SMP represented a remarkable U-turn by the ECB. Only three days before President Trichet had publicly stated that the ECB would not purchase any sovereign debt. The ECB press release offered the following explanation of the program:

> The objective of this programme is to address the malfunctioning of securities markets and restore an appropriate monetary policy transmission mechanism.
>
> In order to sterilise the impact of the above interventions, specific operations will be conducted to re-absorb the liquidity injected through the Securities Markets Programme.[34]

Here, the ECB justified purchases as remedying market malfunction and, most of all, to ensure monetary policy transmission. "Sterilization" and "liquidity injection" mean that the ECB will either sell other bonds or reduce its lending to banks so that the overall quantity of reserves (base money) does not rise.

President Trichet explained further, citing the "separation principle," in his Summer 2010 Jackson Hole speech:

> This puts in perspective the separation that central banks are making between their policy interest rates and monetary policy stance— namely the standard measures—and, in particular, the full allotment mode in the supply of liquidity, the longer term refinancing of commercial banks by the Central Bank or the purchases of securities— namely the set of non-standard measures. The monetary policy stance is always designed to deliver price stability in a medium and longer term perspective. The non-standard measures have a clear purpose: ensuring that the standard measures themselves are transmitted as effectively as possible despite the otherwise abnormal functioning of some markets. All the non-standard measures taken during the period of acute financial market tensions . . . are . . . by construction, temporary in nature.[35]

The ECB's mandate is monetary policy with a goal of price stability, not fighting sovereign default or sovereign yield spreads that reflect default probabilities. Both statements defend ECB intervention as part of the ECB's mandate. The justification is the idea that elevated sovereign spreads reflect markets that are somehow malfunctioning, and that this malfunction affects the ECB's ability to control inflation in the EU via the ECB's interest rate and general bond-buying policies.

In the spring and summer of 2011, the ECB increased policy rates from 1% to 1.25% in April and to 1.5% in July to reduce inflation, while around the same time, starting SMP purchases of Italian and Spanish government bonds to lower their sovereign spreads. Since the latter are also expansionary Quantitative Easing operations, one may also understand the former as a form of sterilization, or an instance of the separation principle.

The SMP proved extremely controversial. Jürgen Stark, the German member of the ECB executive board, resigned in 2011 in protest over his belief that the program constituted monetary financing, and hence a breach of the EU treaties.

Buying sovereign debt, as well as lending to banks against sovereign collateral, also necessarily positioned the ECB at the heart of discussions about stabilizing and recapitalizing banking systems, and even on macroeconomic and structural reforms (Brunnermeier, James, and Landau, 2016). The ECB tried to use the Securities Markets Program bond purchases to informally impose conditionality on countries (i.e., to force fiscal and structural reforms). The ECB included a general reference to fiscal commitments in the May 10, 2010, press release on SMP: "In making this decision we have taken note of the statement of the euro area governments that they will take all measures needed to meet [their] fiscal targets . . . in line with excessive deficit procedures and of the precise additional commitments taken by some euro area governments to accelerate fiscal consolidation and ensure the sustainability of their public finances."[36]

The ECB stepped up the pressure for fiscal and structural reforms. This was done through confidential letters sent on August 5, 2011, from Presidents Trichet and Draghi (at the time president of Banca d'Italia) to Prime Minister Silvio Berlusconi, and from President Trichet and Bank of Spain governor Miguel Angel Fernández Ordoñez to Spanish prime minister Rodriguez Zapatero. The letters outlined the reforms that were to take place in exchange for the ECB buying bonds of these two countries.[37]

One can understand why the ECB acted in this way. It felt the pressure of crisis. From public statements in the Greek debt crisis, it appears that ECB wanted to avoid sovereign debt restructuring, consequent losses for banks, and the associated financial stability risks at almost any cost. A euro exit by any country could have been a life-threatening event for the common currency. The ECB felt that it was the only institution capable of moving quickly enough to stem the crisis. No action from member states was in sight, either to provide resources or to impose the kind of conditionality needed for countries to get out of trouble. So it lent to banks and bought sovereign debts. The ECB was then exposed, indirectly by its holding of low-quality sovereign and nonmarketable private collateral and then directly from its SMP purchases. The ECB saw that lending and buying without any conditionality would be a recipe for bad incentives. The same institutions that were not providing any help were certainly not about to impose the kind of reforms that would be needed as conditions for ECB support. So the ECB had to try on its own.

Still, with such letters, the ECB was doubly stretching its mandate. It was not only buying sovereign debt with newly created money, but it was giving advice to, and even trying to impose policies on, fiscal and political authorities in stressed member states.

Like many improvisations taken in the heat of a crisis, the effort runs into the classic problems of discretionary policy. If countries fail to reform and threaten again to default, and if they figure out how much the ECB wants to avoid default for its own reasons, then the ECB's threat to withhold more funds is not credible. Effective conditionality needs precommitment that the ECB will do things that it will not want to do ex post, a rearrangement of the situation so that sovereign default is not so damaging to the ECB's interests, or the effective arrival of a cavalry that will impose conditionality by other means.

5.9 Whatever It Takes

In the end, the EU and IMF did rally to offer help with conditionality through the European Stability Mechanism (ESM). But by summer 2011, Italy and Spain had not agreed to an adjustment program, as Greece, Ireland, and Portugal had done. Spain officially asked for financial assistance from the euro area via the ESM only on June 25, 2012, and refused to accept wide-ranging conditionality beyond the reform of financial market institutions. Italy never asked for it.

On November 1, 2011, Mario Draghi replaced Jean Claude Trichet at the helm of the ECB. He quickly shifted the ECB's position, reversing course on interest rates, bringing the deposit facility rate down from 0.75% to zero by July 2012.[38] He also announced an ambitious Long-Term Refinancing Operations program starting in December 2011.

Under this program, banks could borrow for three years at a fixed 1% interest rate, with a wide set of collateral including stressed country sovereign debt.[39] Banks had the option to end the loan after one year. The low fixed rate for a long period allowed banks to invest the funds in illiquid or risky debt without fear that their funding costs would rise.

Thus encouraged, European banks, particularly Spanish and Italian ones, engaged actively in the "Sarkozy trade:" take out cheap loans from the ECB to buy high-yield sovereign bonds, with no risk weight, and thus no need to raise capital.[40] Italian banks bought €45.6 billion in the first two months of 2012, and Spanish banks €38.7.

The move helps the sovereign, which can issue more debt at lower prices, but only by endangering the banks that hold that debt. In the Greek crisis, Greek debt put French and German banks at risk. Now Italian and Spanish risks became more concentrated in Italian and Spanish banks. Rather than spreading risk around the EU, a default would now crater the defaulting country's own financial system. The prospect is if anything even more frightening to the ECB. Banks became hostages against sovereign default.

Thus, in spite of President Draghi's loosening, the euro crisis entered a new and potentially more severe phase in the first half of 2012, with Italy hovering on the verge of default. Many people feared that such a default would lead to a chaotic breakup of the euro. Default and redenomination risks pushed up Italian yields. The restructuring of Greek debt in March 2012 likely also drove up yields on Italian debt by making haircuts more thinkable and full bailouts less likely. In contrast to Spain, however, Italy still rejected a euro-area (ESM) financial assistance program.

In response to the deteriorating crisis, at a conference in London on July 26th, 2012, President Draghi made what became his most famous pronouncement: "Within our mandate, the ECB is ready to do whatever it takes to preserve the euro. And believe me, it will be enough."[41] This speech is widely seen as the turning point of the eurozone crisis, with many crediting Draghi for saving the euro.

A "whatever it takes" commitment has the potential to cut off an acute crisis, whether a self-fulfilling debt crisis equilibrium or even a simple insolvency, if people believe the commitment. In turn, that belief requires that agency offering the commitment (here, the ECB) has the will and the means to actually do whatever it might take. Many banking and foreign exchange crises have not been stopped by pronouncements, as people did not believe the firepower or the will was there. In the case of the ECB, the firepower of the printing press was evidently enough to buy all outstanding Italian debt if needed. And Draghi convinced markets that the will was there too.

Is it the ECB's job, though, to compress risk and default premiums of sovereign debt? In his speech, Draghi explained that risk premia "charged on sovereign states borrowings . . . have to do . . . with default, with liquidity, but they also have to do more and more . . . with the risk of convertibility."

But the limited mandate concerned him: "To the extent that the size of these sovereign premia hampers the functioning of the monetary policy transmission channel, they come within our mandate. So we have to cope with this financial fragmentation addressing these issues." The ECB does not have a clear mandate to stop sovereign bond defaults, no matter how chaotic. So he phrases the action in terms of monetary policy "transmission" toward the single price stability mandate, and "fragmentation," although acknowledging that default premia can be real rather than "dysfunction." Going forward, markets interpret ECB references to "transmission" and "financial fragmentation" to mean that the ECB will likely act to limit or reduce default, liquidity, or exit premia in sovereign bond yields.

5.10   Outright Monetary Transactions

President Draghi's new policy was implemented via the "Outright Monetary Transactions" (OMT) program, announced by the Governing Council of the ECB in August 2012 and approved in September 2012. The ECB would buy public short-term debt bonds in the secondary market, provided that the issuing country committed to an adjustment program with the European Stability Mechanism (ESM)—the fund that EU countries had set up only months before to provide fiscal support—and ideally also with the IMF as well, in order to provide, in IMF parlance "strict and effective" conditionality. Deciding on that conditionality would not be the ECB's job, and the ESM's fiscal backstop added to the ECB's resources.

Markets and most observers had understood from the famous "whatever it takes" speech by Mario Draghi, stating that the aim of the program was to reduce the chance of default, redenomination, or euro exit, and with that the yield premia being charged against those risks.

Conditionality aimed to limit the risk that, should the ECB actually have to buy large quantities of bonds, a country such as Italy or Spain would not be able to repay those debts. It also aimed to limit the moral hazard of issuers and bond investors to ignore the market signals and issue or buy even more debt under a perpetual "whatever it takes" guarantee. A good conditionality imposes the same conditions that the country would have to work out by itself to reassure bondholders.

Farming out conditionality to the ESM and the IMF is a way to try to precommit that the ECB could not extend the guarantee if countries didn't do their part and a new crisis erupted. Having a third party impose a condition is a clever precommitment device. In the words of Mario Draghi:

> The conditionality associated with the program to which governments and the European authorities agree is a crucial element in being able to preserve monetary policy independence. It is important in providing the ECB with adequate assurance that interventions supporting sovereign debt bond prices do not mutate into financial subsidies for unsustainable national policies in the medium term.
>
> By way of drawing a parallel between OMTs and our standard liquidity operations: as the credit provided to banking counterparties cannot be, and must not be, interpreted as an injection of capital into failing banks; in the same vein, under OMTs, in compressing the premium for the risk of redenomination, the ECB cannot and does not intend to provide financial support to governments which reinstate solvency conditions which have not already been approved ex ante.[42]

The Governing Council of the ECB decided in September 2012 that an ESM program with "strict and effective" conditionality was a necessary precondition for activation of country-specific bond purchases by the ECB. The country would commit to a package of reforms and fiscal targets. The financial assistance program would have to be agreed by the Board of Governors of the ESM (comprising the euro-area finance ministers) and be assessed and then monitored by the European Commission with the ECB acting in liaison with the Commission. The IMF was also invited to join the program and its financing. In 2016, the ECB announced that it would limit the scope of its own involvement in program discussions and monitoring to "macro-critical developments, headline fiscal targets and sustainability issues."

Moreover, an explicit fiscal backing by euro-area governments would be included in the conditionality deal. This could take the form of "a full ESM macroeconomic adjustment program or a precautionary program (Enhanced Conditions Credit Line), provided that they include the possibility of ESM primary market purchases."[43] The participation of the ESM, an intergovernmental organization, was intended to help the member countries to demand reforms from the member state in trouble, in line with agreed commitments. It also allowed the ECB to more credibly threaten to stop supporting a country via OMT purchases, since it would not be alone in making the decision and there was another source of financing.

The ECB's freezing of Emergency Liquidity Assistance when Cyprus turned down the assistance program shows that the rules could be effective constraints. Most of all, the *fiscal* backstop helped to separate the monetary policy aspects of the intervention—temporary lender of last resort, backstop liquidity provider, and other factors—from the messy question of how much crisis interventions were really loans, or to what extent they morphed into transfers. These steps also helped the ECB to stay closer to its mandate and maintain price stability without monetary financing of sovereign debts.

However, the fiscal commitments were intentionally a bit vague. They specified that a program and mechanism would be there, but not how much fiscal support could be provided. This tension continues.

Explicitly unlimited fiscal guarantees can bite, as they did in Ireland. But a limit tempts markets to speculative attacks larger than a limit. Limits are sometimes important to keep together the political coalition supporting the program, as not all members want to sign an unlimited guarantee. Specifying a mechanism but not a limit makes it easier to invoke the mechanism in a crisis, leaving its size to be negotiated later.

If not perfect, these features of the OMT are a substantial improvement relative to the previous SMP and show the institutions of the EU learning from experience.

As fiscal transfers became more likely, monetization became less likely. The ECB could more credibly maintain that it would not monetize or inflate away debts, but provide only temporary "liqudity" to "stabilize" interbank and bond markets. The Greek bond haircut in 2012 and bail-in of large bank deposits in Cyprus in 2013 also contributed to make debt monetization less likely.

But whether monetary or fiscal, the combined vision of no sovereign purchases, no bail outs, and no fiscal transfers was over. Only the balance between fiscal versus monetary bailouts and how best to contain the moral hazard remains an evolving project. Program conditionality and rules attempt to do that. And the previous regime, with strict promises not to help that nobody believed, was evidently not effective.

"Whatever it takes" is often interpreted as a Mosaic commandment, words alone that made a flood recede. In fact, President Draghi's pronouncement rested on an overall framework with concrete procedures and conditions under OMT. These, together with creditor losses in Greece and Cyprus, kept the waters from swiftly rushing back even higher. By requiring that euro-area member states agree to provide financial assistance loans in exchange of reforms before OMT purchases, the ECB reduced the risk that the central bank bond purchases would "mutate into financial subsidies for unsustainable national policies" (in the words of President Draghi on May 2013), which would have violated the prohibition of monetary financing. It also gave a strong incentive for the member states to agree on ESM packages swiftly rather than wait around and hope the ECB would take care of any emerging problems.

6

Institutional Reforms

The sovereign debt crisis was not just a story of temporary expedients. The mechanisms to offer fiscal support with conditionality evolved toward a permanent institutional structure, with elements to combat moral hazards. People recognized the deficiencies of the banking system and the fiscal rules, and reform projects began.

The period between the sovereign debt crisis and inflation proved to be a calm between two storms, in which much progress on this agenda could have been made. It would also have been a good chance for troubled countries to enact fiscal and microeconomic structural reforms. President Mario Draghi's "whatever it takes" was linked to important reforms, such as a concrete proposal to create a single European banking supervisor, as well as his expectation that "much more of what is national sovereignty is going to be exercised at supranational level."[1] Indeed, just one month before "whatever it takes," on June 29, 2012, at a Euro Area Summit in Brussels, heads of state and governments from all euro-area member states had made a promise in the the first sentence of their statement: "We affirm that it is imperative to break the vicious circle between banks and sovereigns."[2]

By and large, however, reform projects eventually stalled, and a more ambitious program to address the shortcomings in the design of Economic and Monetary Union has not started. The European Stability Mechanism (ESM) structure has not been refined and strengthened; ECB sovereign purchases have abandoned the requirement for ESM program participation; debt and deficit rules are ineffectual; and banking reform has stalled.

This failure left monetary policy more and more exposed in fighting subsequent crises. As former German finance minister Wolfgang Schäuble explained: "Mario Draghi always said the ECB can never replace what the member states should do. But as long as the member states don't do it, the ECB must do what it can."[3]

6.1 Fiscal Rules

The original debt and deficit rules did not work when, among others, France and Germany blew through them. The effort to loosen the rules in 2005 to make them more flexible but thus more likely to be followed also did not work. So between 2011 and 2013, the EU tightened debt and deficit rules and surveillance mechanisms three times, with the "six pack," the "Fiscal Compact" (an intergovernmental treaty), and the "two pack." Among other provisions, states were to enact new balanced budget rules, sanctions for excessive deficits would become more automatic, a qualified majority of countries would be needed to block European Commission proposals for sanctions, and a new debt reduction rule would be introduced in which debt would gradually converge to 60% of GDP within 20 years (European Central Bank, 2012).

This burst of reforms aimed to restore market confidence in sovereign debt. They also contained a "macroeconomic imbalance procedure" to correct "imbalances" such as large current account deficits and "competitiveness" problems such as high wages and low productivity.

Compliance by the member states remained low, and sanctions did not work. For instance, while member states must progress to their medium-term budgetary objective and maintain it once reached, by 2019, seven member states had never reached it in the previous 20 years (Belgium, France, Italy, Poland, Portugal, Slovenia, and Slovakia). On a given year, a given country was as likely as not to be following the rules, according to the data of the European Fiscal Board (EFB), an independent institution within the EU.

The EFB found that successive reforms have made the rules more complex and opaque: "The sources of unnecessary complexity include: (i) an excessive reliance on unobservable indicators; (ii) badly timed use of flexibility encouraging pro-cyclical fiscal policy; (iii) a tendency towards postponing fiscal adjustments to the outer years of the stability and convergence programs."

The EFB also found that "During the first five years of the macroeconomic imbalance procedure, the number of EU countries experiencing macroeconomic imbalances gradually rose from 12 to 19."[4]

However, the Commission did not launch any excessive imbalance procedures.

6.2 The European Stability Mechanism, Conditionality, and the Troika

We have alluded previously to the emergence of EU and IMF fiscal support with conditionality. Here, we tell the story in more detail, with an emphasis on how the institutions evolved.

To deliver financial assistance loans in the sovereign debt crisis, member states initially set up the Greek Loan Facility in May 2010. This facility consisted of bilateral loans from euro-area countries to Greece, amounting to €52.9 billion. The European Financial Stability Fund (EFSF) was created in June 2010, via a separate international treaty outside the EU. This fund was originally intended as a temporary backstop. It had a lending capacity of €440 billion. It was organized through a company based in Luxembourg as a "Special Purpose Vehicle." The EFSF would borrow money in financial markets and use the money to provide assistance to member states. Its debt issues were backed by joint and several guarantees of the euro-area member states. It was limited to back-to-back lending with a liquidity buffer. In July 2011, its lending capacity was increased to €724 billon.[5]

In October 2012, this crisis mechanism was made permanent and became the European Stability Mechanism, or ESM.[6] The ESM received instruments broadly similar to those of the IMF: to make loans, with conditionality on macroeconomic performance, budget, and structural reform. Unlike the IMF, the ESM can issue securities, which are joint and several liabilities of EU members according to their capital key. The ESM had an authorized capital of €704.8 billion, with €80.5 billion paid in. The rest, €624.3 billion, was committed callable capital. Aiming for a triple A rating, its maximum lending capacity was restricted to €500 billion.[7] Despite the abundance of resources relative to lending, however, it failed to obtain the highest credit rating. Between 2010 and 2018, the ESM and EFSF together provided €295 billion in loans to Ireland, Portugal, Greece, Spain, and Cyprus.

From the beginning, some observers doubted whether the ESM had received sufficient capital and guarantees from governments of member states to address a crisis in one or two of the larger member states without upfront debt restructuring. The funding needed for a program for Italy or Spain could run at over €1 trillion. Gros and Mayer (2012, p. 1), for example, argued that "even the ESM might not be able to raise at very short notice the huge sums that might be required to prevent a breakdown in the financial system." Kapp (2012) calibrated the necessary size of the fund at somewhere between one and two times the proposed size. Though the "committed callable capital" of €624.3 billion is impressive, it is mostly not yet disbursed. The member states would have to borrow it, during what would likely be a chaotic time.

In addition to limits on the ESM's ability to stop a default, there is always the question whether it would choose to do so. A country might also reject conditionality or fail on its conditionality promises.

There is a point to limiting the size and terms of a bailout fund such as the ESM. The EU, with highly indebted member states, faces a similar dilemma as regulators of highly leveraged banks. If the EU commits that no government bondholder shall ever lose money, it faces moral hazard: bondholders have no incentive to monitor governments, and governments have less incentive to borrow and spend responsibly. The EU can try to patch up those incentives with debt and deficit limits and conditionality, as regulators try to patch up deposit insurance with asset risk regulation and capital requirements. But that is an imperfect remedy for moral hazard. Limiting the size of a bailout fund, rather than "whatever it takes," can be seen as part of an additional effort to remedy moral hazard by limiting the EU's commitment.

The limits can also be seen as buying some credibility. Perhaps people believe the EU will ride to the rescue with €700 billion, but they will not believe larger promises. Limits are also useful to assemble a coalition of member states that may not be entirely happy to sign an unlimited fiscal guarantee. However, limits are limits, and they can be exceeded. If there is a limit, that means there are some events in which the country will default. Limits on the ESM's firepower will thus increase pressure for monetization via the ECB.

The *nature* of conditionality has been contentious, as the IMF's conditions for supporting countries in fiscal trouble have been contentious. The right combination of spending cuts, tax reform, microeconomic liberalization, social program reform, and other interventions to get an economy moving again and a government solvent will always be contentious. By supporting conditionality in principle, we do not necessarily cheer each element of particular programs, and we especially do not require the reader to endorse the details of each program.

Conditionality is politically contentious as well. The country must enact and support the program for a number of years, and typically through a tough economic time. It is understandable that some governments and their citizens regard ESM adjustment programs as creating too much stigma, too much trouble, too much pain, and too much interference with their sovereignty. They are likely to think that different measures would be more effective, and more support and more time should be given. Conditionality makes the foreign supervisors a convenient target for criticism. Such was the case with the troika in the European debt crisis.

The obvious counterargument is, "If you don't want our money, go ahead and default." Or better, "Go ahead and find out what kind of structural adjustment and reforms program it takes to convince private markets to lend to you again." But the ESM never said that, mechanisms for orderly default remained missing, and everyone understood that the euro-area member states were also protecting their own bondholders, banks, and economies. The perception of a north-south political tussle, southern austerity to repay debt to nosy northerners, remained. It undercut political support, and thus the durability of structural adjustment and conditionality promises.

The political decisions on financial assistance and adjustment program conditionality were taken by the finance ministers of the euro area and the IMF. These took place in meetings of the Eurogroup and, after its establishment, in the Board of Governors of the ESM. The troika, formed by the EU Commission, the ECB, and the IMF, often get blamed. But their role was really only to be a "technocratic" instrument in charge of analysis, discussion with authorities, and monitoring of implementation. However, it was easy to shoot the messenger, and treat the troika as a scapegoat.

There needs to be a clear institution and mechanism that can impose conditionality, address the moral hazard of fiscal transfers, arrange the fiscal transfers, and monitor the conditions. It is not easy work. A predictable procedure and outcome will also help to address these objections. Governments will know what's coming and perhaps take action to avoid it in the first place. It's harder to lay blame for following common rules and procedures than for apparently discretionary decisions.

The ESM and the troika reflect worthy attempts to balance the various incentives, moral hazards, and unintended consequences of other possibilities. We think the mechanism can be improved, and we discuss improvements next. Sadly, during the subsequent decade, even this progress seems to have been forgotten.

6.3 Banking Reforms

At the same time that it endorsed the rescue of Spain's financial system, the European Council agreed on June 29, 2012, to set up a Single Supervisory Mechanism (SSM) under the umbrella of the ECB.[8] One year later, on June 27, 2013, it further agreed to "complete the Banking Union" to ensure financial stability. The Banking Union was meant to consist of three pillars: a single Europe-wide banking supervisor; a single resolution mechanism avoiding state-run bailouts of insolvent banks; and a single deposit insurance.[9]

The SSM was established on November 3, 2013, and was fully operational by November 4, 2014. Prior to assuming its supervisory role, the ECB undertook a comprehensive assessment of the 130 main banks in the Eurozone, as required under Article 33(4) of the Council Regulation on the SSM. This assessment was published on October 26, 2014.[10] The change in supervision, together with the asset quality review, reduced pressure on monetary policy by providing incentives for banks to improve the resilience of their balance sheets, and hence strengthen the banking system.

But banking union, and more generally financial union, were never fully completed. The SSM's "single" supervisory framework remains fragmented: while the ECB has central authority, national supervisors retain local reporting lines, causing coordination issues. Its scope excludes market conduct, insurance, anti-money laundering (AML), and third-country branch supervision, leaving these tasks to national authorities. Less significant institutions are also under national oversight. International banks face a patchwork of national regulators beyond prudential supervision, as EU directives are unevenly implemented, creating overlapping supervisory bodies. This often leads to conflicts between "home" and "host" supervisors, even within the banking union. Banking resolution was put in place on paper, but never fully exercised its powers. European Deposit Insurance (EDIS) has never passed the stage of a legislative proposal. Moreover, no progress has been made on reducing the incentives for banks to concentrate their lending on their own sovereigns. The EU Council's promise from 2012 to break the "vicious circle between banks and sovereigns" has not been fulfilled.[11]

7

The Zero Bound

At the end of 2014, the worst of the sovereign debt crisis had passed. However, euro-area economies were still growing very slowly, and inflation declined below the ECB's target range. The ECB, like many other central banks, embarked on further "unconventional monetary policy," steps beyond simply lowering interest rates. These policies included interest rates below zero, forward guidance about future interest rates, expanded lending to banks at low rates and with easy collateral, and massive asset purchases, primarily of government debt. While these steps were clearly aimed at traditional monetary policy concerns, many have fiscal implications. That is particularly true for the ECB, as these steps can imply fiscal transfers between member states. Asset purchases especially, and looser bank lending to a lesser extent, also further stretched the traditional boundaries on ECB action, setting an important precedent for later interventions.

7.1 Asset Purchases (Quantitative Easing)

The ECB lowered the main refinancing rate to 0.05% and the deposit facility rate to −0.20% on September 14, 2014.[1] Lowering interest rates below zero is difficult and controversial for many reasons. Facing this "zero lower bound," or the looser "effective lower bound" that interest rates cannot be too negative, the ECB turned to asset purchases, buying bonds in return for newly created reserves.

The ECB started to purchase securities under Asset Purchase Programs (APP) in October 2014. In the first months the ECB only bought covered bonds (Third Covered Bond Purchase program CBPP3) and small amounts of asset-backed securities (in the Asset-Backed Securities Purchase program).[2] These securities include collateral, which protects the ECB against credit risk. On January 22, 2015, the ECB announced the Public-Sector Purchase Program (PSPP), a new part of the APP, to purchase sovereign debt. In March 2015, the ECB substantially increased net monthly purchases from about €10 billion to €60 billion. In 2016, the ECB increased net monthly purchases further, to €80 billion. The ECB also started buying corporate debt in the Corporate Sector Purchase Program (CSPP), also part of the APP. The bulk of the overall APP purchases (85%) were public securities under the PSPP, amounting eventually to around €2,500 billion. These programs are the counterparts to "Quantitative Easing" undertaken in the United States and the United Kingdom.

Net purchases in all of these APP programs ended in January 2019. They were reactivated in President Draghi's last governing council meeting on September 2019, as announced in a speech in June 2019.

Most government bonds purchased under this program and later ones, including the Pandemic Emergency Purchase Program PEPP, were acquired by national central banks, which normally bought the public bonds of their government. Interest income was not shared. As a result, national central banks of countries with high sovereign yields made significant profits, which they distributed to their treasuries. The treasuries in effect got to borrow at the risk-free overnight rate, not the much higher market rate on long-term debt.

The question of whether the asset purchase programs are legal was raised again. In its Weiss judgment (*Weiss and Others*, C-493/17, EU:C:2018:1000) on the legality of the Public Sector Purchase program (PSPP), the European Court of Justice ruled that the program was legal, and in so doing established important precedents.[3]

Unlike Outright Monetary Transactions (OMT), which were meant only for those countries that were a part of an adjustment program with the European Stability Mechanism (ESM), the PSPP allowed the ECB to purchase debt securities throughout the euro area. Whereas OMT was designed to lower yields and the probability of default on the debt of specific countries, the PSPP was intended to stimulate the economy and raise inflation, in the context of the zero lower bound, for all members of the single currency. Its intent thus fell more clearly into the ECB's general monetary policy effort directed at the price stability mandate, regardless of whether it may have had fiscal side effects.

But monetary policy *intent* alone did not automatically make the program legal, nor did that intent limit the fiscal side effects of the program. The ECB has a mandate to focus on price stability, but also restrictions on what tools constitute monetary policy to that end. Dropping money from helicopters or confiscating money from Europeans' pockets would also influence the price level, but these tools clearly exceed the ECB's mandate.

The European Court of Justice concluded that the PSPP was legal, even though the program involved buying sovereign bonds, because the ECB imposed on itself important limits in the program's implementation. There were many limits, but two are most relevant.

First, the ECB's PSPP purchases of sovereign debt followed each country's capital key based on GDP and population. Thus, the split of ECB purchases across countries was mechanical and did not focus on countries with fiscal problems.

Buying in proportion to a capital key follows a principle of "market neutrality," whereby the ECB aims to raise or lower all bond yields, not to raise or compress spreads between bond yields. It may not have that exact effect, as some country's bonds can be more affected than others by such purposes, and purchases by capital key are greater or lesser fractions of debt outstanding in each country. Yet the mechanism still follows a market-neutral spirit, in that purchases are not conditioned on spreads.

The ECB also implemented issuer limits. In its original announcement, the PSPP could not buy more than 25% of any specific issue or more than 25% of the total outstanding debt of any country. One rationale behind these limits is that the ECB did not wish to have a too decisive, or even large role as a bondholder in the event of the sovereign's default.

In the ECB's November 2015 expansion of the PSPP, this limit was extended to 33%. The new limit was set at 33% because, as a part of the ESM treaty, countries had to set up common rules for the restructuring of sovereign debt, and these included a 33% limit on collective auction clauses. Such clauses state that a 66% majority of bondholders must accept a restructuring before all other bondholders are obliged to accept it. If the ECB were to hold more than 33% of any country's debt, it would necessarily be the deciding vote on any restructuring. The ECB tries to stay out of fiscal policy.

The Court decision emphasized the importance of these issuer limits. The Court did not validate that the ECB had chosen the right figure of 25% or 33%. The Court specified only that any issuer limit should prevent the ECB from owning the totality of any given issuance or issuer. Under this looser interpretation, many have argued that the ECB should again increase its issuer limit. For example, the Bank of Japan has a 50% limit.

The ECB soon found that increasing purchases would at some point violate the capital key or country and issue limits. The ECB decided to give priority to the capital key, even if this meant buying more than 33% of the sovereign debt of countries with low levels of debt, like the Netherlands and Luxembourg. This conflict shaped the ECB's response to the pandemic.

7.2   Subsidized Loans to Banks

In general, we speak of a subsidized loan or a loan at favorable conditions if the interest rate on an ECB loan to a bank is below the marginal market funding costs for the same bank using the same collateral. Initially, it was understood that the ECB should not subsidize or recapitalize weak banks. Any such action was a responsibility of national fiscal authorities and could violate the separation of fiscal and monetary policies and the prohibition on monetary financing. President Draghi made this principle clear when explaining the aim and design of the ECB's Outright Monetary Transactions (OMTs) in 2013: "By way of drawing a parallel between OMTs and our standard liquidity operations: as the credit provided to banking counterparties cannot be, and must not be, interpreted as an injection of capital into failing banks; in the same vein, under OMTs, in compressing the premium for the risk of "redenomination," the ECB cannot and does not intend to provide financial support to governments which reinstate solvency conditions which have not already been approved ex ante."[4]

However, during the subsequent period of persistent low inflation, large-scale lending to banks started to involve incentives (including bonuses) that effectively allowed banks to obtain large amounts of funds at below-market rates, and later partly even at financing costs below the interest rate at which banks could deposit such money at the ECB. In this way, the ECB indirectly provided risk-free arbitrage profit opportunities to banks. The balance sheet costs of such loans are eventually shifted to taxpayers via lower future central bank profits, and thus lower future dividends paid to governments.

To secure such subsidized loans in Targeted Long-Term Refining Operations (TLTRO), first implemented in the second half of 2014, banks had to meet certain thresholds. Primarily, they needed sufficiently strong lending to the non bank private sector, excluding mortgages. However, such thresholds were relatively easy to fulfill for most banks.

On March 7, 2019, the ECB decided to launch a new series of quarterly targeted longer-term refinancing operations (TLTRO-III), starting in September 2019 and ending in March 2021. Banks could borrow from the ECB at low rates, initially with a maturity of two years. The ECB explained that "These new operations will help to preserve favourable bank lending conditions and the smooth transmission of monetary policy."[5] These loans to banks (TLTROs) were part of a package that was designed to provide "significant monetary policy stimulus" and that "will support the further build-up of domestic price pressures and headline inflation developments over the medium term."

At an ECB press conference following this announcement, a journalist asked: "The TLTROs are also kind of subsidies for banks, especially for weak banks. A lot of these banks are paying dividends to their shareholders and bonuses to their senior managers. Do you think this fits together with the subsidies?" President Draghi replied, "If there were no subsidies, then nobody would take up the TLTROs." He further explained, "The issue is not whether there is a subsidy or not; there is a subsidy. The issue is whether the TLTRO fulfils monetary policy objectives and helps the transmission of monetary policy. We believe it has always done that, it's been very effective, as a matter of fact, in reactivating the banking sector in the eurozone and in transmitting . . . the better lending conditions to firms and households, to the private sector in the economy. I think that's the yardstick of successful TLTRO."

Given that the duration of TLTRO loans to banks are up to three years, with interest costs to banks calculated from past deposit rates and "as low as 50 basis points below the average interest rate on the deposit facility over the period from June 24, 2020, to June 23, 2022," banks also had an incentive to delay the repayment of TLTRO loans to the ECB when interest rates on the deposit facility started to increase. This happened over the course of 2022.

Again, we present this discussion as fact, not as criticism. These programs were intended as monetary policy, to spur bank lending and to lower interest rates. Monetary policy has fiscal effects. Some critics view low interest rates themselves as a subsidy to the financial industry. The policies stretched the traditional tool limits and served as precedents. We point out those effects, which may not have been obvious.

7.3 2016–2019: Low Inflation Continues

In spite of a massive expansion of the Eurosystem balance sheet, inflation remained stable and mostly a bit lower than the ECB's target at the time of close to but below 2%. (That target was replaced by a symmetric 2% target in mid-2021.) Some economists conclude from the episode that Quantitative Easing really has no significant effect on inflation after all; a liquidity trap is a liquidity trap once we are satiated in reserves, adding more reserves does nothing; and whatever small declines in long-term bond yields central banks were able to achieve reflect the exact "segementation" that keeps those rates from affecting the rest of the economy. Others think that QE offset even larger deflationary pressures and believe that even more QE should have been attempted.

During and after the sovereign debt crisis, the ECB had been calling upon fiscal authorities to restore sound public finances, especially in countries with high public debt. But with inflation lower than the target and the ECB's interest rate and asset purchase tools seemingly ineffective to nudge inflation back up to the objective and keep it there, thoughts in the wider policy community naturally turned to fiscal expansion. The ECB understandably did not call on high-debt countries to reverse course and get in trouble again. And the ECB did not publicly call on countries with fiscal space to help with fiscal expansion, even to compensate for countries that the ECB was asking to cut down on debt. While President Draghi in August 2014 did call for fiscal authorities to support demand in general, this was the exception.

In autumn 2020, ECB president Christine Lagarde, looking back, acknowledged the potential importance of fiscal policy:

> When central banks have to use balance sheet policies extensively, there is an inevitable strengthening of the interplay between monetary and fiscal policies. . . . Indeed, one explanation for the superior inflation performance of the United States relative to the euro area in recent times is that monetary and fiscal policies were more aligned. From 2013 to 2018, fiscal policy in the euro area tightened by around 2.5 percentage points of GDP, compared with a loosening of around 0.8 percentage points in the United States. ECB analysis for the euro area finds that, while monetary policy was supporting inflation during this period [2013–2018], it was being offset by demand headwinds.[6]

Overall, however, the ECB largely respected another tradition of monetary-fiscal separation: central bankers don't opine too much on fiscal policy. They neither speak too loudly in demand of stimulus nor complain too loudly when fiscal authorities overdo it. At best, they notice fiscal policy as sources of demand that they must offset and adapt to, along with other shocks. The ECB largely held to this separation, despite the widespread calls in parts of the policy community for fiscal expansion to boost demand, under the banners of "secular stagnation," "hysterisis," "r is less than g," and "modern monetary theory," as well as good old-fashioned Keynesian multipliers. When those calls were finally answered in 2020–2021, they quickly produced a large inflation. The ECB also largely held to this separation despite its struggles to raise demand and inflation by conventional and unconventional policies. The ECB's mandate for price stability rather than a joint mandate to support employment as well helps, and it was respected in this regard, as the point of most calls for fiscal expansion was to raise output and employment without inflation, rather than to boost inflation up a half percentage point to return it to target.

8

The Pandemic

The Covid-19 pandemic, which began in early 2020, led to huge monetary and fiscal policy responses. The pandemic was an economic crisis,
not just a public health crisis. Authorities feared financial and economic
meltdown, motivating immense policy responses.

Monetary policy included a large expansion of ECB bond purchases,
in the Pandemic Emergency Purchase Program (PEPP). This program gave substantially more flexibility for the ECB to purchase debt
issued by member states with high interest-rate spreads. As with all
purchase programs, these purchases were made with newly created
euros in the form of reserves (deposits) that banks hold at the central
bank, convertible to cash. The ECB also aimed to make borrowing easier ("ensure . . . supportive financing conditions"), explicitly including
governments among the sectors that can benefit.[1]

Fiscal policy saw large deficit-financed spending, mostly transfers to
people and businesses in the member states, as well as guarantees for
loans to firms. It also saw a major fiscal innovation at the EU level: the
issuance of joint European debt to finance cross-border fiscal transfers
in a program called Next Generation EU, agreed upon in 2020.

8.1 Monetary Response

In March 2020, a week after the first Covid-related lockdowns in Italy,
the U.S. Federal Reserve cut interest rates from 1.5% to 0. In its March
12 meeting, the Federal Reserve also announced a $1.5 trillion balance

sheet expansion that included $600 billion in asset purchases on the same day. On March 10, the Bank of England announced a 0.25% rate cut and a new funding scheme for small and medium-sized enterprises.

The ECB did not change policy rates in its March 12 meeting. Unlike the Federal Reserve, the ECB had not raised rates, and its deposit facility rate was unchanged at −0.5% since September 2019. There wasn't room for much further lowering. However, the ECB announced a comprehensive package of monetary policy-easing measures. The ECB encouraged banks to borrow more from the ECB. The ECB launched new Long Term Targeted Refinancing Operations (TLTROs), ECB loans to banks that ended up amounting to almost €400 billion, considerably more favorable interest rates on outstanding TLTROs, and committee work on further "collateral easing measures to ensure that counterparties continue to be able to make full use of the funding support."

The ECB increased the envelope for the existing Asset Purchase Program (APP) by €120 billion to be spent throughout 2020. While there was flexibility on the monthly purchases and the distribution of the purchases across the different asset classes, including the Public Securities Purchase Program (PSPP), the cross-country distribution of such bond purchases remained bound by each country's capital key.

The ECB encouraged fiscal authorities to implement an "ambitious and coordinated fiscal policy response . . . to support businesses and workers at risk." It saw its own role in supporting "liquidity and funding conditions for households, businesses and banks and . . . [helping] to preserve the smooth provision of credit to the real economy." It anticipated that the pandemic would "slow down production as a result of disrupted supply chains and reduce domestic and foreign demand, especially through the adverse impact of the necessary containment measures."[2]

In the press conference following the Governing Council meeting, President Christine Lagarde reacted to a question on how the ECB would respond to higher government bond spreads: "More debt issuance coming down the road depending on the fiscal expansion . . . will be determined by policymakers. Well, we will be there . . . using full flexibility, but we are not here to close spreads. This is not the function or the mission of the ECB. There are other tools for that, and there are other actors to actually deal with those issues."[3]

"We are not here to close spreads" is likely the second most memorable and impactful statement by an ECB president (after "whatever it takes"). This statement led to the single largest daily yield increase in Italian sovereign debt in history. The jump in yields revealed suddenly just how much continuing expectation of ECB intervention, an implicit "ECB put," was keeping Italian and other spreads low in the first place.

The importance of such expectations likely came as a surprise to many experts in EU institutions, including President Lagarde herself. She likely meant the statement as a simple reminder of the current regime, and certainly not a market-moving revelation.

As a result of the jump in yields, some commentators criticized President Lagarde for her statement. This criticism, however, overlooks the fact that in March 2020 President Lagarde found herself in an extremely difficult situation.

A few months after she took office at the ECB, President Lagarde was confronted with the highly uncertain economic implications of the pandemic. She also inherited a strong and long-standing ECB communication that eschewed any direct role of the ECB in lowering default risk premia or yield spreads. ECB bulletin articles and speeches of board members in prior years did not analyze how ECB bond purchases and commitments would compress credit risk spreads, not even as a side effect. The talk was about "taking out duration risks" to lower-term premia for government bonds of all member states.

Her predecessor, President Mario Draghi, had stressed in 2013 that ECB purchases of troubled member states' sovereign bonds under the OMT program had to have as a precondition European Stability Mechanism (ESM) program conditionality. In his statements, this element was crucial to "preserve monetary policy independence." He promised that the ECB would not attempt to reduce spreads related to solvency risks: "The ECB cannot and does not intend to provide financial support to governments which reinstate solvency conditions which have not already been approved ex ante."[4] President Draghi had acted and communicated in line with this commitment when fiscal plans and statements of politicians of a new government in Italy had resulted in a substantial widening of spreads in autumn 2018. He then pointed to the responsibility of fiscal policy and the role of the fiscal rules and the European Commission, but he did not promise any ECB support to lower Italian spreads.

Thus, President Lagarde was consistent with standing ECB doctrine when she stated that the closing yield spreads was not the mandate of the ECB, but of "other actors," meaning the national fiscal authorities, the ESM, and the European Council and Commission.

So why did yields spike? Given that no preparations for an ESM bail out or a smooth debt restructuring of a large euro-area country had been made, and previous statements notwithstanding, market participants expected the ECB to do "whatever it takes" to compress spreads, including bond purchases of countries that are not part of an ESM conditionality program. President Lagarde's seemingly innocuous statement surprised those participants.

President Lagarde quickly issued a correction in a CNBC interview the same day. It was footnoted in the aforementioned ECB press release so that we could not miss it: "I am fully committed to avoid any fragmentation in a difficult moment for the euro area. High spreads due to the coronavirus impair the transmission of monetary policy. . . . The package approved today can be used flexibly to avoid dislocations in bond markets, and we are ready to use the necessary determination and strength."[5] Market participants understood the first two sentences to make it clear that the ECB is committed "to avoid . . . high spreads."

Why reverse course so suddenly? Once yields spiked, not least of Italian sovereign debt, could the ECB just have announced that it expects Italy, the country that was hit hardest by the pandemic, to join an ESM adjustment program before the ECB can help with country-specific bond purchases? Understandably, "strict and effective" conditionality in the middle of the health crisis was not on the table. And a fiscal transfer mechanism among member states that could have been swiftly activated did not exist. So the ECB must again have felt that it had to step into the vacuum. By doing so, it effectively announced a policy that, if spreads turned out to be related to default risk and not just market malfunction, would shift sovereign default risks to the Eurosystem's balance sheet.

On March 18, after a late-night meeting of the Governing Council, the ECB announced the Pandemic Emergency Purchase Program (PEPP), with an initial quantity of €750 billion, to be implemented immediately. President Largarde added a "no limits" pledge: "Extraordinary times require extraordinary action.[6] There are no limits to our commitment to the euro." The ECB explained that the PEPP was "established in response to a specific, extraordinary and acute economic crisis, which could jeopardise the objective of price stability and the proper functioning of the monetary policy transmission mechanism."[7] But "*no* limits" can easily be interpreted to mean *no* limits.

The ECB also stressed that it "will ensure that all sectors of the economy can benefit from supportive financing conditions that enable them to absorb this shock. This applies equally to families, firms, banks and governments." The explicit mention of "governments" in its promise to ensure supportive financing conditions, which was not included in the statement after its previous regular meeting a few days before, is another innovation to monetary-fiscal interaction in reaction to the pandemic.[8]

Did the ECB lower yields symmetrically, or did it end up lowering spreads? In one recent study, Costain, Nuño, and Thomas (2022) observed that "The highly asymmetric reaction of euro area yield curves to the announcement of the ECB's pandemic emergency purchase programme (PEPP) is hard to reconcile with the standard 'duration risk extraction' view of the transmission of central banks" asset purchase policies. They develop a "no-arbitrage model of the term structure of sovereign interest rates in a two-country monetary union." Calibrating their model to Germany and Italy, they find that the channel they call "default risk extraction . . . accounts for most of the impact on Italian yields. The programme's flexible design substantially enhanced this impact."

Why did the ECB create a new program rather than use existing ones? A good guess is that the ECB wished to remove the self-imposed limits of those programs, and Outright Monetary Transactions (OMT) in particular.

The Pandemic Emergency Purchase Program differs from previous purchase programs in several key properties:

First, the pandemic program was not limited to a particular type of security.

Second, the existing purchase programs were bound by the capital key and included issuer and issue limits. The ECB desired flexibility to purchase bonds from particular states, and potentially in larger quantities. In the official decision (March 24, 2020), the ECB stated: "A flexible approach to the composition of purchases under the PEPP is nonetheless essential to prevent current dislocations in the aggregate euro area sovereign yield curve from being translated into further distortions in the euro area risk-free yield curve, while also ensuring that the overall orientation of the program covers all jurisdictions of the euro area."[9]

While the ECB announced that the benchmark for purchases of sovereign debt would still be the capital key, it allowed itself deviations from this benchmark: "Purchases under the new PEPP will be conducted in a flexible manner. This allows for fluctuations in the distribution of purchase flows over time, across asset classes and among jurisdictions." This flexibility clearly allows the ECB more room for monetizing debts and squashing spreads of countries in trouble.

Third, under the PEPP, the ECB would also start purchasing Greek sovereign debt. This reversed a previous ECB decision not to purchase debt below investment grade (Credit Quality Step 3) unless the sovereign issuer is in an ESM adjustment program.

Fourth, the ECB also removed the limitation that it could buy no more than 33% of the debt of any particular issuer.

Fifth, with the encouragement of member states to borrow and spend, the PEPP had an intent to hold down yields on new debt issues, making sovereign borrowing easier. This intent differs from previous programs, including OMT, aimed at rollover difficulties, the functioning of secondary markets, or market prices of outstanding long-term debt.

Unlike the OMT design, the ECB may have seen no possibility for fiscal authorities to swiftly provide transfers or financial assistance linked to an ESM program. This is natural, as issuing new debt cheaply is different from heading off a rollover crisis. There would be no point to conditionality. The ECB's decisions also seem consistent with the prevailing view of fiscal and monetary authorities around the world, that now was no time to worry about how debts will be repaid, especially with the experience of a decade of intractably negative real interest costs that most officials thought would never end.

With the PEPP's flexibility, however, the ECB allowed itself to buy sovereign bonds from countries with high interest rate spreads, with no capital key limitations. The goal of issuing new debt to finance pandemic spending was supported by spread compression and implicit guarantees on existing debt.

The PEPP announcement did the trick. The pandemic did not cause a debt crisis. Spreads went down again. Governments could borrow huge amounts at low rates.

As a result of the looser limits, the PEPP seems to have displaced earlier programs. Euro-area member countries have little incentive to borrow via the European Stability Mechanism (ESM). As later Italian prime minister Giorgia Meloni said in a press conference in 2022: "I fear the fund will never be used" as the conditions are "too stringent."[10]

In sum, in these six days in March 2020, almost all the previous restraints on bond buying came off, and we saw a significant further blurring of boundaries between fiscal and monetary policy. The ECB's U-turn on communication, from "we are not here to close spreads" to "no limits," and the strong financial market reactions to those announcements, revealed how important expectations about future ECB purchases of sovereign bonds are for bond yields, and thus the funding costs of euro-area member states, especially those with with high debt, default spreads, and significant debt sustainability risks.

To be absolutely clear, we do not criticize cross-country solidarity or transfers for member states that are particularly hard hit by a pandemic or a natural disaster. But we think that such support should be decided and designed by governments or a European fiscal institution, not by an independent central bank, and not via interventions that, as an unavoidable side effect, protect the wealth of investors holding outstanding bonds.

The constant innovation of new programs with steadily looser limits leads one to wonder just what the point of self-imposed limits was. In part, the motivation was surely to stem moral hazards and to try to dissuade markets and governments from expecting support beyond the limits. But now, with self-imposed limits and constraints breached or circumvented over and over again, many observers surely have concluded that if the ECB finds a self-imposed limit to be inconvenient ex post, it will just invent a new program with looser limits. In part, the limits may have been internal, for the ECB to persuade itself that bond buying was going to be a limited emergency response to particular situations, not a regular practice. Perhaps buying debt with ever-loosening limits was a natural "boil-the-frog" process of finding out how much bond buying the ECB can pursue internally, politically, and in public opinion. Or perhaps each crisis seemed larger than the last and required a less-limited response, although then it is time to ponder just why crises are getting larger and larger. Most likely, a bit of all four.

A clear lesson is that while institutions such as the ECB can invent crisis-fighting tools on the fly, institutions are never very good at inventing on the fly durable precommitments to constrain their own future actions. It is also interesting that an innovative central bank, supporting expansionary fiscal policy, which was the clear policy of all the member states, still felt the need to describe its actions in terms of market "dysfunction," "fragmentation," and monetary policy "transmission." The ECB does not seem to be facing any legal challenges.

Clearly, the ECB will continue to intervene in debt markets. Indeed, helping the sovereign to issue debt at low rates by promoting a liquid market and trading sovereign debt for money, and establishing mechanisms that help the sovereign commit to repayment, have been central purposes of central banks going back to the founding of the Bank of England in 1694.

We can read this short history as the ECB discovering such a purpose, despite a quite different founding philosophy, but not yet in a clearly defined and systematic way that controls the moral hazards scattered around conjoined monetary and fiscal policies. Clearly, there must also be some mechanism in the reformed EMU to deal with sovereign defaults and the repeated problem that yield spreads rise, and debt gets harder to roll over, in anticipation of sovereign defaults. The balance between liquidity and fiscal support will always be difficult. The habit of repeating a fanciful story ("fragmentation" and "transmission"), when we all know that the point is to lower spreads, impedes a lot of serious thinking and debate about what the true problems are and how one might fix them.

8.2 Fiscal Response

Three months after the ECB's pandemic bond-buying program was decided, the European Union agreed on a fiscal response of a similar size to the initial PEPP, the Next Generation EU, "to address the challenges posed by the COVID-19 pandemic, the Commission will be authorised to borrow funds on behalf of the Union on the capital markets. . . . The funds borrowed may be used for loans up to an amount of EUR 360 billion in 2018 prices and for expenditure up to an amount of EUR 390 billion in 2018 prices."[11]

This was the first major issuance of explicit European Union debt (to be repaid by December 31, 2058, at the latest). No existing European legislation provided for a fund like this.

A portion of these funds would finance existing EU programs. But the main component of these funds was the Recovery and Resilience Facility (RRF), which directly financed "reforms and investments" in the member countries, with EU approval. The "reforms and investments" are geared to "Make their economies and societies more sustainable, resilient and prepared for the green and digital transitions, in line with the EU's priorities; [and] address the challenges identified in country-specific recommendations under the European

Semester framework of economic and social policy coordination. The RRF is also crucial for implementing the REPowerEU plan—the Commission's response to the socio-economic hardships and global energy market disruption caused by Russia's invasion of Ukraine."[12]

Part of the funds—up to €385.8 billion—would provide *loans* to member countries, which were supposed to be eventually repaid by the receiving country. In addition, *grants* of up to €338 billion were predominately allocated to countries with high debt and/or relatively low GDP per capita.

Repayment of this new EU debt is to be covered by future contributions from member states, and potentially by new EU resources. The EU increased the ceiling for the total EU budget (the "own resource" ceiling) from 1.2% to 1.4% of gross national income (GNI), as well as an additional temporary increase of 0.6% of gross national income to cover the liabilities in connection with the EU borrowing until 2058 or when the liabilities are repaid, whichever comes first. Hence, adding up both increases, the EU total ceiling (or "headroom," in EU parlance) increased from 1.2% to 2% of the European Union GNI.

To repay all these liabilities, the EU decided on one new own-resource, a small plastics levy, with estimated revenue of €7 billion per year. Beyond that, the EU declared its desire to come up with new own-resources, including a Carbon Border Adjustment Mechanism, a digital tax, a tax on the Emissions Trading System, and a Financial Transactions Tax. So far, however, these taxes remain just an intention. The EU has not specified how concretely revenues to pay back bondholders will be raised or how they will be distributed across EU member states.

Since the EU did not put in place its own taxation to finance repayment, this bond issue is not yet the harbinger of a European fiscal authority. EU member states did not agree, beyond plastics, to shift sovereignty over concrete taxes or tariffs to the EU. They also did not agree to a concrete legal obligation for each member state to pay back a defined share of the debt issued and spent by the EU Commission. The bonds are to be repaid by contributions of member states, which are not defined ex ante. The Commission states: "The EU budget headroom hence serves as a guarantee that the EU will be able to make repayments under any circumstances," but expenditure "headroom" does not state where the money comes from.[13]

Many observers long for Europe to come to institutional arrangements reminiscent of those that emerged in the 1790s in the United States, for the EU to become at least somewhat a "United States of Europe." Alexander Hamilton, the first U.S. Treasury secretary, famously arranged that the federal government would take on state debts from the revolutionary war, and have the taxation power to repay those debts. The Articles of Confederation, in which member states supported the federal government via contributions, had proved dysfunctional. The U.S. Constitution gave the federal government the power to tax and spend on its own authority, and thus to repay debts. The NGEU/RRF bond issue is a first step, but clearly not a "Hamiltonian moment." It is still long way from that set of fiscal institutions.

The vagueness about how debt will be repaid also creates a statistical gap. The new "EU debt" issued to finance the grants does not appear in the official debt figures of the EU member states, although they have a collective specified duty to repay EU bonds if the "own resource" taxes are not enough. The aggregated debt of all EU member states thus omits €360 billion of their promised contributions to pay off the EU debt.

9

Inflation, War, and Tightening

In spite of several crises, low growth, and adverse shocks during the first two decades of the euro, inflation was low and measures of medium-term inflation expectations did not rise (see figure 9.1).

From 1999 to 2007, Harmonized Index of Consumer Prices (HICP) inflation was mostly close to the ECB's 2% upper bound. This was a remarkable achievement, given that the euro was a new monetary union among (initially) eleven fiscally sovereign member states, which had very different inflation histories and economies.

During the financial and sovereign debt crises inflation was more volatile, broadly in a range between zero and 4%, but still on average around 2% and following a normal boom-bust-recovery pattern.

From early 2013 onward, inflation declined to around zero in 2015–2016, but it gradually came back to around or slightly below 2% in 2017–2018. Whether because of or despite negative interest rates, forward guidance, and quantitative easing, it is natural to view the outcome as a success for the ECB.

In 2020, the first year of the pandemic, HICP inflation fell to around zero again. As in 2008, this is a remarkably small decline given the magnitude of the economic collapse.

Core inflation, which excludes energy and food prices, barely budged from the 1–2% range the whole time. Given that inflation is measured to at best a one-percentage-point accuracy, these small movements are not particularly meaningful.

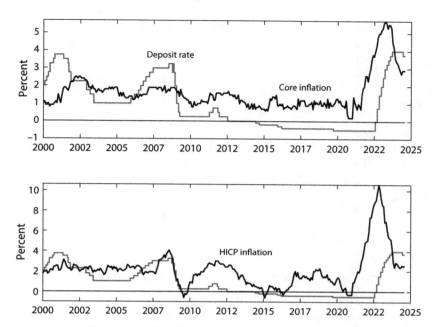

FIGURE 9.1. Inflation and ECB deposit rate. *Top*: Harmonized Index of Consumer Prices (HICP), excluding food and energy. *Bottom*: HICP including food and energy. Annual percentage changes. Source: European Central Bank, Data Categories, https://data.ecb.europa.eu/data/data-categories.

9.1   Inflation Returns

Inflation returned with a vengeance starting in mid-2021. The timing was particularly unfortunate for the ECB. After a decade of worrying about low inflation and the effective lower bound on interest rates, and during the reduction of inflation of the Covid economic contraction, the ECB embarked on a systematic policy review. The review was launched in January 2020 and the outcome was announced on July 8, 2021. The central objective of the new policy framework was to *increase* inflation. The ECB raised the target to symmetric around 2%, from the original 0 to 2% band or the 2003 close-to-but-below 2% target. The ECB also announced that it would tolerate moderately higher inflation on occasion. Since expected future inflation is a primary determinant of today's inflation, much of the point of the ECB's announcement was to raise inflation expectations, and thereby stimulate aggregate demand and increase inflation immediately. In the ECB's words, "The Governing Council considers that price stability is best maintained by aiming for a 2% inflation target over the medium term. This target is symmetric, meaning negative and positive deviations of inflation from the target are equally undesirable. When the economy is operating close to the lower bound on nominal interest rates, it requires especially forceful or persistent monetary policy action to avoid negative deviations from the inflation target becoming entrenched. This may also imply a transitory period in which inflation is moderately above target."[1] The announcement also featured an "ambitious climate change action plan," a new focus of ECB policy.

The ECB's policy review to some extent mirrored the U.S. Fed's policy review that was finalized in August 2020 and resulted in "flexible average inflation targeting."[2] Also with an eye to increasing inflation and with zero bound worries in mind, the Fed committed to reacting slowly to any inflation that might emerge, and to allow greater than target inflation in the future to make up for any previous inflation below target. If people believed the promises of this framework the framework could lower their expectations of future interest rates, lower current long-term rates, raise expected inflation, and thereby stimulate the economy and raise current inflation. Central banks were also worried about their credibility. Even if 1.7% inflation is not objectively a disaster, they worried that not being able to raise inflation to 2% would lower public confidence that they control inflation at all. If one is critical of the ECB, at least one should recognize that the same ideas pervaded central banking circles globally.

In hindsight, this move came at exactly the wrong time. We can see now that inflation had already started to increase significantly. The new strategies were elaborately constructed defenses against hypothetical zero bound deflationary spirals. But the threat was already advancing on the opposite front.

Figure 9.1 includes inflation and the ECB deposit rate through this episode. Inflation is the one-year growth rate of the price level, as is customary to reduce noise, but thereby lags actual (change from a day ago) inflation by about six months.

One can see the normal cyclical pattern of inflation that declines in the recession and returns to normal early in the recovery. But then inflation started to rise in the first quarter of 2021. Year-on-year inflation breached the 2% target in mid-2021, with higher monthly rates. By December 2021, inflation had increased to 5%, then 6.1% in the first quarter of 2022, and kept rising. The same pattern holds in the United States, starting about a half year earlier, in February 2021.

9.2   The Monetary Policy Response

Although inflation broke out in early 2021, the ECB, like the U.S. Fed and many other central banks, responded hesitantly. The ECB did not budge the deposit rate even up to zero until July 2022, when inflation was over 8%, a full year after inflation broke out. This delay is unusual. Even in the inflationary 1970s, most central banks did not wait so long to respond to higher inflation with higher interest rates.

ECB bond buying did decline. In December 2021 the ECB announced an end to net purchases under its Pandemic Emergency Purchase Program (PEPP) program by March 2022, as the pandemic was over and the economy was recovering in the V-shape fashion expected of a supply shock.

But overall the ECB maintained its accommodative monetary stance for 2021 and the first half of 2022 while inflation kept rising. This stance included negative interest rates, moderated but continued net purchases under the Asset Purchase Program (APP), an extension of the reinvestment horizon for the PEPP until the end of 2024, announced in December 2021, and generous lending or "liquidity provision" to banks in Targeted Long Term Refinancing Operations (TLTRO). In March 2022, the Governing Council communicated that it would "assess the appropriate calibration of its two-tier system for reserve remuneration," in which it offers lower interest on some reserves than others, such that "the negative interest rate policy does not limit banks' intermediation capacity in an environment of ample excess liquidity."[3] Translation: while some reserves (deposits at the ECB) pay a higher rate than others, the ECB worries that banks are sitting on reserves rather than lending to the private sector. The announcement hints that lower rates might soon apply to a larger share of reserve deposits to encourage banks to lend the money instead.

In February 2022, with inflation already surging, Europe received a second shock: the Russian invasion of Ukraine, which promised additional economic uncertainty, especially regarding energy. That event may have led to additional delay in monetary tightening.

In March 2022, the ECB's Governing Council's language was still broadly consistent with easing and its long-stated forward guidance: "The Governing Council expects the key ECB interest rates to remain at their present levels until it sees inflation reaching 2% well ahead of the end of its projection horizon and durably for the rest of the projection horizon, and it judges that realised progress in underlying inflation is sufficiently advanced to be consistent with inflation stabilising at 2% over the medium term."[4] Translation: Inflation may be surging now, but our forecasts show it going away on its own, and we're not going to move until our forecasts show inflation reaching 2% a few years out.

The ECB mentioned here that "fiscal measures, including at the European Union level, would also help to shield the economy." In assessing fiscal policy, the ECB was still worried about *lack* of demand, not excess stimulus, though the pandemic borrowing and its monetization were just in the rearview mirror, the V-shaped recovery was proving the Covid recession to be a supply rather than a demand shock, and inflation was surging.

Some observers speculate that the ECB felt that loose policy was necessary, given its past forward guidance promises to keep interest rates low, even after inflation rose to and somewhat above target, promises designed to combat (then) low inflation and deflation risks. Having promised to keep rates low in the face of inflation somewhat above target, in this view, the ECB felt that its credibility would be undermined by reacting quickly. Indeed, President Lagarde stated in

2023 that she had "felt bound by our forward guidance" and regretted not raising rates sooner.[5] But ECB officials did not stress this in 2021–2022, and if they were buying a reputation for credibility in their promises by deliberately damaging their credibility for stopping inflation surges, they surely would have said something about it to drive the message home.

Another possible explanation for the ECB's unusually slow reaction to inflation is that like other central banks, the ECB misperceived what was happening. The ECB likely assumed that the recession was mostly due to lack of demand, as in 2008, and might last as long, rather than the temporary disruption of a pandemic. The ECB saw the subsequent inflation surge as being largely due to transitory factors, such as base effects, supply bottlenecks, relative demand shocks (more goods, less services), and energy price shocks, or price increases confined to specific sectors. In broad terms, these are all temporary relative price changes. The ECB seems to have thought that consequent measured inflation would fade away quickly, or even reverse, without it having to respond at all.

The new policy framework and the long-standing medium-term forward-looking philosophy contributed to delay. Even without past forward guidance promises, the ECB only reacts to forecasted future inflation, not past misses, and only to medium-term inflation, not the short-term effects of transitory shocks. In the new framework the ECB may additionally tolerate some above-target medium-term forecasted inflation, and acts decisively only if long-term expectations might become "unanchored."

However, the same transitory supply-shock stories were told in the 1970s, especially regarding oil price shocks as the source of inflation, in an era that understood inflation much less well. Nonetheless, central banks of that era raised interest rates more swiftly, if not enough.

ECB forecasts, like those of the U.S. Fed, confidently forecast that inflation would return promptly to the 2% target, without policy response, at each point of inflation's rise. For example, the ECB's March 2022 projections for annual headline inflation were still reassuring: 2.1% inflation in 2023 and 1.9% in 2024, and the ECB reported that

"The Governing Council sees it as increasingly likely that inflation will stabilise at its two per cent target over the medium term."[6]

The ECB began to change its language in April 2022, citing "flexibility": "The Governing Council stands ready to adjust all of its instruments within its mandate, incorporating flexibility if warranted, to ensure that inflation stabilises at its 2% target over the medium term."[7] Note that the "medium term" orientation continues, which allows substantial further inflation in the short term.

Inflation rose further to 8.6% in June 2022 and showed no signs of abating. Hilscher, Raviv, and Reis (2024, p. 5) calculate measures of inflation expectations based on option prices. They report that: "While the mean of the distribution of expected inflation moved little, leading policymakers at the time to conclude that expectations were anchored . . . , the tails showed a sharp deanchoring."

It finally became clear to the ECB that monetary policy had to tighten: Quantitative easing had to stop, and interest rates needed to rise. In its June 9, 2022, meeting, the ECB announced that it would end its Asset Purchase Program (APP) by September 2022, though reinvestments of maturning bonds under the Pandemic Emergency Purchase program (PEPP) would continue. Most of all, the ECB announced that it would start raising key interest rates from July 2022 onward. The ECB also abandoned forward guidance promises to keep rates low and replaced them with a more flexible and state-contingent communication strategy. The ECB stated that "The Governing Council undertook a careful review of the conditions which, according to its forward guidance, should be satisfied before it starts raising the key ECB interest rates. As a result of this assessment, the Governing Council concluded that those conditions have been satisfied."[8]

9.3 Inflation's Surge and Easing: Sources and Lessons

How central banks failed to see inflation before it broke out, and even while it was surging, is finally attracting some soul-searching. See, for example, the examination of the United States by Chahad et al. (2022) and Levy (2024). Maybe the models are wrong. Maybe there are shocks that central banks have overlooked. Maybe inflation is inherently unforecastable. We need to know. If we do not understand what went wrong, there is no way to fix policy mistakes, process, data collection, modeling, or fiscal and monetary policy institutions to avoid a repetition of the event.

The source of this unexpected inflation is contentious. Many politicians rounded up the usual suspects: greed, monopoly, and profiteering. More serious analysis varied on the effects of supply shocks, energy price shocks, war, monetary policy, and fiscal policy. A recent ECB staff analysis (Arce et al., 2024) concludes that "inflation since 2021 has been driven by both supply and demand factors, with the former playing a primary role." This paper does not attempt to explicitly model the role of monetary and fiscal policies, which the authors recommend for future study.

The debate over the source of inflation hides a larger question: Does inflation control by the central bank require diagnosis of the shock and different responses for different shocks? One's inclination is to say "of course it does." For example, the central bank should diagnose and respond differently to "supply" versus "demand" shocks, "real" versus "financial" shocks, and so forth. But given that the nature of the shocks is still hotly debated three years later, requiring central banks to diagnose and respond differently to shocks in real time is obviously a challenging task.

Simple rules like the Taylor rule (without shocks or time-varying natural rates) prescribe the same response to inflation, no matter the shock. Though such rules are less than perfect-information optimal, such an approach may be more realistic in real time.

Modelers would still want to know, however, that such rules do reasonably well when confronted with multiple shocks, and analyzing the shocks ex post is a crucial component of that more theoretical knowledge.

More importantly, if it is hard for the *decisions* of monetary policy to condition, in real time, on the source of shocks, the *institutions* of monetary policy should be well adapted to multiple shocks. If

2021–2023 inflation was driven by a big fiscal shock or a big supply shock, we need monetary policy rules, habits, and institutions that will contain inflation next time.

The surge of inflation was clearly not due to an expansionary movement of central bank interest rates. The ECB's policy rate was unchanged. A decade of zero to slightly negative rates before the pandemic did not create even 2% inflation, let alone 10% inflation. The drop to zero interest rates in 2012 did not cause any inflation. If one wishes to blame the interest-rate setting component of monetary policy, it must be for failing to react to a shock that comes from elsewhere. Pandemic asset purchases to support the fiscal expansion are a more likely partial culprit, which we return to later in this discussion.

Supply Shocks and Monetary Response

The pandemic itself was a supply shock: An economy under lockdown can't produce much. There wasn't inflation immediately, in part because the pandemic also compressed demand. Even when lockdowns did not forbid economic activity, people didn't want to spend much money in restaurants, hotels, or airplanes with a contagious pandemic raging. But that demand suppression, unlike the case of regular recessions or financial crises, is more like the demand suppression of a snowstorm. It goes away when the pandemic ends. The V-shaped recession is consistent with that diagnosis.

Post-pandemic global supply chain bottlenecks and energy supply disruptions were also real, and they are not superficially implausible causes of the 2021 inflation. But supply shocks alone do not tell the complete story of inflation. Supply shocks per se only cause changes in *relative* prices. If the economy can produce fewer cars or TVs, then the price of cars or TVs must rise relative to restaurant meals and wages. But the latter could fall rather than the former rise. How does a relative price shock raise all prices and wages?

Moreover, a supply shock alone gives a transitory rise in a price *level*, not a transitory rise in the inflation *rate*. If car factories close, the price of cars rises. But when the factories open again, the price of cars falls back to where it was. A period of car deflation follows the car inflation. We have seen a rise in *inflation* that seems finally to be easing, but no commensurate deflation that brings the price level back to where it was.

In the end, for prices to rise, demand must be there as well. People must still have the money and desire to buy the goods under supply shock. A supply shock translates to general inflation, and a permanent rise in all prices, only when and because the shock is *accommodated* by monetary and fiscal policies.

We focus on monetary policy first. Facing a relative price shock, such as an energy supply disruption, the central bank can choose whether to have higher energy prices or lower prices of everything else, and no inflation. Since central banks believe price and wage cuts to be more damaging than rises, they choose a higher overall price level. The central bank lets other prices rise too, so higher energy costs feed through to higher costs of goods that use energy. This accommodation is the standard analysis of the 1970s energy price shocks, for example.

By leaving interest rates at or close to zero in the face of inflation approaching 10%, then, the ECB and other central banks accommodated the supply shocks, let them spread throughout the economy, and provided the necessary demand. This accommodation need not have even been a conscious, discretionary decision. It is a natural result of the habits, traditions, rules, or framework followed by the ECB and other central banks. The ECB follows an inflation target, with a "medium-term orientation;" it reacts strongly only if long-term expectations are in danger of no longer being "anchored;" and it lets "bygones be bygones," meaning that it does not try to remedy past undesired inflation or deflation. It does not bring the price level back, but rather simply aims to get future inflation, the rate of change of prices, back to its 2% target, no matter how much the price level has increased in recent years.

So, if inflation initially and unexpectedly rises, the ECB will normally not try to push inflation back to 2% within a quarter or year, especially if it sees a transitory shock behind the inflation. The ECB will only try to bring inflation back in the "medium term," by which time the price level will have risen more than 2%. And the ECB will be in no hurry to bring inflation back either, so long as its measures of medium- and longer-term inflation expectations remain unchanged, or "anchored" in central banker jargon, at the inflation target. It certainly will not allow the natural period of *deflation* to emerge as the supply shock reverses.

Supporting this view, ECB Board Member and Chief Economist Philip Lane presented interesting results of a counterfactual analysis using some of the ECB's New Keynesian models.[9] In these model simulations, an earlier or stronger increase in the policy rate would have resulted in significantly lower real growth and inflation during the years from 2022 to 2024.

In standard New Keynesian models, a "supply shock" shows up as a shock to the Phillips curve, in which inflation is driven by expected inflation, the output gap, and a shock:

$$\pi_t = \beta E_t \pi_{t+1} + \kappa x_t + u_t.$$

Such a shock apparently raises inflation, without subsequent deflation. Via the persistence of the shock, and via the model's dynamics, including the policy rule, such a shock can produce protracted inflation. Balke and Zarazaga (2024) and Smets and Wouters (2024) are two excellent recent papers that evaluate the importance of such shocks in accounting for the inflation episode, finding an important role for such supply shocks.

However, the same accomodation issue arises in these models. New Keynesian models appear to be models of inflation only, without a price-level anchor. But if you look closely, they do.[10] These models assume that either the money supply or unbacked fiscal expansion rises to allow the change in the price level that emerges. As in our intuitive discussion of a microeconomic supply shock, the supply shock causes inflation only because of the endogenous monetary or fiscal accommodation.

The supply shock is the carrot, which causes the monetary or fiscal horse to pull the cart of inflation. Is this really a carrot effect, or a horse effect? If we label shocks by the external event that induces monetary or fiscal policy response, why call it a supply shock rather than a pandemic shock or a lab-leak shock? Those were the ultimate first movers. But that label does nothing to illuminate the mechanism that actually caused inflation to move, or the policy alternatives that might have led to less inflation (and potentially worse real outcomes), given the same pandemic and supply disruptions.

Confusion between relative prices and the price level pervades discussion of inflation. Inflation is not about individual prices going up. Inflation is an increase of the level of all prices, a fall in the value of currency.

If supply and relative-demand shocks, accommodated by monetary policy, are to blame, that fact will require a reevaluation of the policy framework. Again, these are by themselves relative price shocks, not inflationary shocks. Monetary and fiscal policy choose to let some prices and wages rise even more rather than let any prices or wages fall. But a dynamic economy in a union of heterogeneous states will always have some important prices and wages that want to rise relative to others. If all prices and wages must rise so that none must fall, there will be a permanent bias toward inflation, and this sort of episode will recur. The strong popular reaction against inflation makes it pretty clear that regular bouts of inflation are bad for the economic and political health of the monetary union.

Thus, if this is the story, monetary policy in the union must get over the fear of local declines in some prices and wages. In part, this simply requires a return to the original philosophy, namely that the EMU worries about the union-wide price level, not making sure that no individual country, industry, or sector sees price or wage declines. In part, though, it needs a deeper reflection. Deflation is thought to be bad because prices and wages are sticky downward. This is the single friction in modern macroeconomic thinking, the single reason that undesirable recessions and unemployment happen. Well, then, rather than focus only on monetary policy to inflate all prices and wages so that none must fall, why not try to remove some of the stickiness that makes falling prices and wages painful? The EU and its member states are full of microeconomic policies that impede downward price and especially wage adjustments. Simple microeconomic reforms would have useful macroeconomic consequences. Countries that bind themselves to a single monetary standard lose the option to inflate and devalue their way out of uncompetitive prices and wages. Doing so requires that "internal devaluation" be easier. This too was part of the founding philosophy of the EMU, which has been on hold.

Finally, if an unprecedented inflation was really due to supply shocks, then central banks including the ECB should be spending a lot more time monitoring and analyzing supply shocks. Central banks often use "demand" almost as a synonym for "output," and regard "supply" as at best a very slow-moving object, along with "potential" output and the natural interest rate "r star." Well, if this inflation came from a fast-moving supply shock that central bank forecasts, models, and analysis completely missed, then there should be a team of economists looking for the next fast-moving supply shock and integrating that into central bank forecasts and analysis. One might say that inflation is the natural and optimal response to supply shocks (not our view). But the fact that analyses and forecasts by ECB (and all other central banks) completely missed inflation suggests that this inflation was not a conscious choice.

Fiscal Shocks

The second main story for the burst of inflation comes from fiscal policy. The underlying shock, of course, was the pandemic, so fiscal policy like monetary policy is a response or accommodation rather than a bolt of lightning from the blue. But in this narrative, the large burst of spending financed by public borrowing, potentially together with the ECB's monetization of much of that borrowing, is the central policy choice leading to inflation.

Between the end of 2019 and the end of 2023, the combined nominal government debt of the nineteen EU member states of the euro area increased by about €2.4 trillion. This is about a 20% rise in debt, and 20% of the aggregate 2019 GDP of about €12 trillion.

We do not intend this discussion to be critical of pandemic spending. People hit by a pandemic and a locked-down economy need government support. Whether it was done efficiently or not is a debate for another day. Our only question is whether this spending and the form of the borrowing that financed it caused inflation.

Even the fact of fiscally caused inflation is not always bad policy. Some commenters welcomed a Lucas-Stokey state-contingent default via inflation to fund what they regard as the huge necessary expenditures of a pandemic. Hall and Sargent (2022) show that a sharp bout of inflation accompanied the massive fiscal expansions of the previous two world wars. In wars, governments spend an enormous amount of money. They raise those resources by printing money, devaluing outstanding debt via inflation, and holding down interest rates. Hall and Sargent argue that the Covid and post-Covid expansion is like a third such war. (However, Lucas and Stokey, 1983 describe inflation at the beginning of a war, not after its conclusion, as happened in all three cases. Why people buy debt knowing that it will be inflated away is a bit of a puzzle in this interpretation.)

Suggestively, the price level started rising soon after the debt expansion started and it also rose about 20% from end-2020 to end-2024. This increase implies that the price level overshot by almost 12% the price level that would have resulted if the ECB had met its 2% target in these years. Approximately 12% of the outstanding longer-term public debt has been inflated away, equivalent to default with a 12% haircut.

Traditional Keynesian analysis and the more recent fiscal theory of the price level give two different accounts of how this fiscal expansion led to inflation, as discussed next.

KEYNESIAN ANALYSIS

In traditional Keynesian analysis, deficit spending has a uniform multiplier effect on aggregate demand. When aggregate demand exceeds aggregate supply or "potential," the price level rises. The substantial fiscal stimulus times a multiplier (often 1.5) is larger than whatever remaining insufficient-demand output gap was left as of 2021. Larry Summers famously made this simple case for the United States in a series of op-ed pieces starting in May 2021.[11]

In this standard Keynesian analysis, the central bank can and should offset excess fiscal stimulus by promptly raising interest rates, and by doing so, it can fully control any resulting inflation. Thus, in this view the ECB, like other central banks, made a serious mistake by encouraging fiscal stimulus, by buying and monetizing so much debt, and then by not raising the rate promptly with the stimulus itself, and certainly a few months later when inflation rose. It only takes a back-of-the-envelope analysis to compare deficit spending with any reasonable guess of the GDP gap to realize there was too much spending.

As many central banks initially misdiagnosed inflation as "supply" shocks that would go away on their own without policy further action, they and governments also misdiagnosed the huge fall of output and employment during the pandemic as lack of "demand," requiring only every possible demand stimulus to reverse. One may be charitable, as it was not an easy time to be a central banker. There was a big debate on this question, as well as whether the pandemic would produce an L-shaped or V-shaped recession.

If this is the story for inflation, and we do not wish a repetition in the next crisis, central banks need to pay more attention to *fiscal* shocks and supply shocks and more carefully coordinate monetary and fiscal policy. If all it takes is deficit × 1.5 relative to the GDP gap, there is very little excuse for bank forecasters and policymakers to have been so surprised by inflation. Yet to date, the ECB, like most central banks, has largely been silent on the possibility that a massive fiscal expansion was the central driving force of inflation. Much of the public silence is of course motivated by a desire to retain central bank independence and the separation of monetary and fiscal policies. You don't criticize us, and we don't criticize you. But that discretion does not mean that central banks cannot internally be as attuned to inflationary fiscal shocks as they are to financial shocks, and now (hopefully) supply shocks.

FISCAL THEORY ANALYSIS

The fiscal theory of the price level offers a different analysis of how a large fiscal expansion causes inflation. In this theory, inflation occurs when the government issues debt, including money, without a convincing plan to repay that debt. Debt is like stock in the government. When people hold more debt than they think the government will repay, they try to get rid of the debt by spending it, driving the price level. The process stops when debt is inflated away to the real value that people believe the government can and will repay. Cochrane (2023b) explains, and applies this theory to explain the surge and easing of inflation after the pandemic fiscal expansion.

Keynesian analysis looks at the *flow* of deficits as the driver of aggregate demand, and expected repayment is not central to that analysis. Fiscal theory looks at the *stock* of debt relative to its expected repayment.

It is crucial in this story of fiscal inflation that people do not trust new debt to be repaid. It is difficult to measure that expectation independently, just as it is difficult to measure a decline in dividend expectations that underlies a stock price decline. But several features of the Covid expansion are salient, especially compared to earlier borrowing that did not result in inflation such as that following the financial crisis in 2008.

In and following 2008 there were long discussions of how debt would be repaid, including using "austerity" measures to pay down debt in Europe. In 2020–2022, politicians showed little concern for that question. To the contrary, such policies were largely ruled out. The Next Generation EU program is a good example: This debt was issued with no concrete plan for repayment.

Some politicians, if they addressed the issue at all, pinned their hopes on structural reforms and public investment, the latter requiring still more borrowing. For example, at the end of 2021, the French president, Emmanuel Macron, and the Italian prime minister, Mario Draghi, wrote together:

> We must deepen the reform agenda and accompany these transformations with large-scale investment in research, infrastructure, digitisation and defence . . . There is no doubt that we must bring down our levels of indebtedness. But we cannot expect to do this

through higher taxes or unsustainable cuts in social spending, nor can we choke off growth through unviable fiscal adjustment. Instead, our strategy is to curb recurrent public spending through sensible structural reforms. And, just as the rules could not be allowed to stand in the way of our response to the pandemic, so they should not prevent us from making all necessary investments.[12]

About a year later, on November 28, 2022, with inflation in the euro area moving to around 10%, Reuters reported: "Germany's Finance Minister Christian Lindner said . . . he expects the country's debt to GDP ratio to climb to around 70% after the energy crisis but said the government would not raise taxes. 'Germany is already a maximum tax country,' he said at a tax forum."[13]

Comparing the onset of the pandemic to 2007, debt-to-GDP ratios were higher, fiscal space was smaller, Europe had been through sovereign debt crises showing the limits of many countries' borrowing ability, and fiscal rules against future deficits and promising debt repayment were much less credible and largely suspended from 2020 to 2023. The "general escape clause" of fiscal rules had been triggered due to the pandemic crisis. "Modern Monetary Theory," "secular stagnation," perpetually negative interest costs on debt, and "debt doesn't matter" captured the international economic zeitgeist. During the early 2020s, the EU, ECB, and member states all announced, or predicted, ambitious climate expenditures, also to be financed by more borrowed money. But since substituting green for brown energy produces less carbon dioxide but no more tax revenue, that spending also risks adding to unfunded debt expansion.

The expansion of public debt during the financial and sovereign debt crises was also followed by ten years of sharply negative real interest costs on debt, which lower debt as effectively as primary surpluses. There is little prospect today of real interest rates going down unexpectedly by an *additional* two to three percentage points.

Barro and Bianchi (2023) look across OECD countries, and find a strong correlation between countries' cumulative inflation and their cumulative fiscal expansion. They find that about 80% of effective government financing came from the inverse effect of unexpected inflation on the real value of public debt, whereas only around 20% reflected conventional public finance. Bianchi, Faccini, and Melosi (2023) find that the increase in U.S. inflation was largely due to an unfunded fiscal shock.

A second puzzle is that inflation eased, despite interest rates far below the inflation rate, and without a recession. Standard monetary doctrine, requires interest rates above recent inflation, along with a fall in output, to lower inflation, repeating the painful experience of the early 1980s. Cochrane (2023b, 2024) also shows that easing of inflation without high interest rates or recession is natural in the fiscal theory, in response to a one-time fiscal shock, and for the same reason. Once a one-time fiscal expansion has been inflated away, inflation stops, even if the central bank does nothing. Thus, the fact that inflation eased with interest rates still far below inflation is a second argument in favor of the fiscal theory mechanism.

Central banks still matter in fiscal theory. For a given sequence of primary surpluses, higher interest rates can lower inflation immediately, though at the cost of somewhat higher future inflation. Raising interest rates promptly when inflation breaks out is still good policy under fiscal theory.

In this way, the fiscal theory view is kinder to the ECB. Inflation would have come and would have eased no matter what the ECB did. Raising interest rates sooner might have lowered inflation initially, but at the cost of more persistent inflation. ECB monetary policy could not have completely stopped inflation.

How can we avoid a repetition of this event? If we are not to repeat bouts of inflation with every fiscal expansion, the EU needs stronger institutions to guarantee that debts will be repaid by taxes, not inflation. The original EU had promised such institutions, and we emphasize that they must be rebuilt.

Some of those institutions involve the ECB, such as the prohibition on buying sovereign debt directly from the government. Even in fiscal theory, repaying debt with money or with debt that pays less than market interest causes inflation, and expectation of that event causes inflation sooner.

In the face of intractable bad news about future surpluses, default can substitute for inflation to bring the real value of government debt back to the present value of surpluses. The separation of monetary and fiscal policies in the EU is essentially designed to preserve this possibility.

The fiscal theoretic perspective thus warns us that inflation can erupt from unbacked fiscal expansion, even with the most hawkish central bank. The fiscal as well as monetary institutions of the EU matter centrally to avoiding inflation.

Debt and deficit rules, both at the union level and better yet strongly supported voluntarily by member states, are supposed to give debt holders confidence that debt will be repaid without inflation or default, allowing governments to borrow in times of stress. But these rules are evidently not working. Temporary deficits are not the issue. Governments can and should borrow in times of stress. What counts to stopping inflation is that bond and money holders believe that governments will repay debts. Repaying debts requires decades of small primary surpluses. It requires permanent structural changes to tax, spending and growth-oriented microeconomic policies when debts have risen after big deficits. Inflation is a sign that both existing EU debt rules and voluntary rules, norms, and traditions are not enough.

The very simple versions of fiscal theory of the price level that have been explored so far make little distinction between central bank money and interest-paying debt. Money is just very short-term debt that may pay lower interest due to a liquidity premium. Otherwise, they are equivalent government liabilities. Current models also make no distinction between transfers and purchases. So, given expectations of repayment, government purchases financed by interest-paying debt have almost the same inflationary impact as writing checks to people financed by new money creation. Intuitively, the latter seems more inflationary, and in this case the large monetization by ECB (and the U.S. Fed) is partly to blame for the surge of inflation. That intuition reflects natural frictions. Monetization may signal less repayment than selling interest-bearing debt in securities markets. The latter is set up to signal repayment; the former not. Sending people checks gives money quickly to those most likely to spend it, although we still must account for why those who get the new money in the second round do not save it. Who gets the money and the form that it takes clearly may matter to the overall decision to spend or save it. Formalizing these channels with heterogeneous agents and different expectations for different securities is an interesting avenue that has not yet been formally pursued within fiscal theory.

9.4 Easing Inflation, and Synthesis

Inflation eased pretty much coincident with the first interest rate increases. The easing of inflation without a period of high real interest rates and recession, unlike the disinflation of the early 1980s, poses a puzzle. Generally, 1% or 3% interest rates do not represent significant tightening when inflation is 7% or even 10%! Conventional macroeconomic doctrine says that inflation, once started, will spiral away until interest rates rise substantially above inflation, and only by causing a recession, reducing inflation via the Phillips curve. The early 1980s stand as the classic case, but 2022–2023 refutes that doctrine.

Some cheer how wonderfully effective monetary policy is, that the mere beginning of rate rises to positive numbers, while inflation raged at 8%, was enough to turn the tide and produce a "soft landing." But did the ECB and other central banks truly stop the tide with relatively small actual rate rises, or did they jump in front of the parade as it neared the finish line? Fiscal theory, strongly, and Keynesian fiscal stimulus and supply-shock stories, to a lesser extent, say that inflation would have eased on its own, although rate rises help on the margins.

A painless disinflation requires some action that reduces inflation expectations, such that even interest rates many percentage points below actual inflation represent positive real rates. (In the Phillips curve $\pi_t = \beta E_t \pi_{t+1} + \kappa x_t + u_t$, inflation can fall via the first term on the right-hand side rather than the second one.) Fiscal and supply-shock stories act through this mechanism. Analysis that attributes the end of inflation entirely to the beginning of central bank interest rate rises without lower output requires a signaling effect: By raising rates, the ECB signaled its commitment to do whatever it takes, even repeat

1980–1984 if need be. That commitment lowered expected inflation, and lower expected inflation eased inflation immediately through the forward-looking Phillips curve. But many central banks have had to fight much harder in the past, as in the early 1980s, and many small signaling actions and loud promises have had little effect in stemming past inflations. Faith that small actions can stem future inflation should not be unquestioned. Cheap signals, heard once, can be misread or overused next time.

It is likely that all these mechanisms played a role in the rise and easing of inflation. There were supply shocks, energy shocks, and a pandemic with associated lockdowns. None of these is inflationary per se, but they do induce monetary and fiscal accommodation and expansion, which are inflationary. There was monetary accommodation, in the form of an unprecedentedly slow interest rate reaction to inflation and in the form of massive purchases of sovereign debt. There was an immense fiscal expansion. The expansion featured large Keynesian flow deficits, which were particularly powerful since so much money was directly transferred to people. It also featured an increase in sovereign debt with little to no concrete plans for eventual repayment of that debt. Inflation went away rather painlessly as its driving impetus went away, including the pandemic itself, consequent supply shocks, and the immense fiscal stimulus that the pandemic wrought, as well as a sign from central banks that they were not asleep at the wheel about inflation.

Fortunately, all three of these inflation stories offer roughly similar lessons for institutional reform if we wish to avoid repetition of the episode, though with different emphasis on interest rate policy, bond buying policy and limits, and EU fiscal policy institutions.

9.5 The Transmission Protection Instrument and Flexible Purchases

As the ECB started to raise interest rates, it announced a new bond-buying program, the Transmission Protection Instrument (TPI), on

July 21, 2022. This is a highly significant new program, greatly liberalizing the ECB's rules, traditions and expectations surrounding sovereign debt purchases. It is a fitting capstone to our story of eroding barriers between monetary and fiscal policy. The announcement proclaimed, "Subject to fulfilling established criteria, the Eurosystem will be able to make secondary market purchases of securities issued in jurisdictions experiencing a deterioration in financing conditions not warranted by country-specific fundamentals, to counter risks to the transmission mechanism to the extent necessary."[14]

Under the TPI, the ECB allows itself to buy bonds from troubled sovereigns experiencing high yields, unconstrained by the capital key or other country-specific limits. Unlike the previous Outright Monetary Transactions (OMT) program, which remains one of the ECB's tools, TPI does not require the country being helped to participate in a conditionality program overseen by the European Stability Mechanism (ESM), the European Commission, and possibly the IMF, and to have the *fiscal* backstop that such institutions provide.

Precisely because of its greater "flexibility," the TPI seems destined to largely replace the OMT for dealing with country-specific sovereign debt problems. Market participants and governments thus likely expect the TPI to be the dominant bond-buying program in the future.

During the first half of 2022, when markets started to anticipate an increase in interest rates, long-term rates started to rise. Sovereign debt spreads started to rise as well, particularly for Italy and Greece. After the ECB's June 9, 2022, announcement of a likely increase in interest rates at its next regular meeting in July, spreads between Italian and German debt widened further. The yield on 10-year Italian bonds rose to 4.17% on June 14.

This event has a natural interpretation, as a long-feared monetary-fiscal interaction emerged: Higher interest rates mean higher sovereign debt-service costs. Higher debt-service costs push a high-debt country closer to default, and its risk premium and thus spread rises further still. Higher sovereign spreads also once again imperil banks and leveraged financial institutions that hold concentrated positions on the domestic sovereign. Fear of sovereign risk premiums might have been part of the

ECB's reluctance to raise interest rates more strongly and swiftly in the first place, effects known colorfully as "sovereign debt dominance" and "financial dominance." (To be clear, this and the following statements are not the ECB's interpretation of events.)

Markets might have counted on perpetual ECB support to tamp down spreads. But then they saw that sovereign purchase programs would end as the pandemic passed and economies recovered; they saw an inflationary rather than a deflationary environment; and they saw that the ECB wanted interest rates to go up. Default premiums then naturally feed into market prices.

For whatever reason, as the ECB wished to raise rates amid high inflation, sovereign spreads were rising faster than the ECB may have wished. One might think that the point of raising short rates was to raise long rates, so additional rate rises are swift "transmission," but the ECB apparently wished only to raise the level of all rates, not more in some countries than others, and it wanted to dampen demand without financial turmoil. ECB Board member Isabel Schnabel explained later: "In the conditions prevailing at the time, the necessary interest rate steps could therefore have led to disproportionately higher interest rate adjustments in parts of the euro area . . . the announcement of the TPI is likely to have been an essential precondition for the ECB to be able to increase rates to such a large extent."[15]

Indeed, the ECB found itself in a difficult position. The pandemic, the energy price shock, and the related fiscal expansions had further increased vulnerabilities in high-debt countries. How could the ECB raise interest rates significantly and end Quantitative Easing to contain inflation, without triggering a sovereign debt crisis, causing financial instability, or simply crimping new government borrowing in the weakest parts of the eurozone? The answer was to raise rates, to gradually phase out bond purchases from all countries while announcing a new tool for buying bonds from fragile countries.

This move came in two steps. On June 15, the Governing Council of the ECB surprised markets by holding an unscheduled, ad-hoc meeting. After the meeting, the ECB reiterated its pledge to "act against resurgent fragmentation risks," and announced that it had decided to "apply flexibility in reinvesting redemptions coming due in the PEPP portfolio, with a view to preserving the functioning of the monetary policy transmission mechanism, a precondition for the ECB to be able to deliver on its price stability mandate . . . accelerate [staff work on] the completion of the design of a new anti-fragmentation instrument."[16]

Markets got the message. They translated the ECB's announcement to "act against resurgent fragmentation risks" as follows: The ECB was back, and indeed, it is here to lower spreads in this environment too. Spreads on Greek and Italian bonds immediately fell after the announcement.

But PEPP flexibility and a staff study were not enough. Spreads rose again in early July 2022 due to heightened political uncertainty in Italy. Following the news of Mario Draghi's resignation as Italian prime minister on July 15, 2022, the spread between Italian and German bonds rose again, to 2.19%. Some market participants noted that this level had been enough in the past for the ECB to intervene.[17] However, prospects for a fiscal mechanism to support Italy did not materialize. Member states were unable to agree on a new joint fiscal instrument. That staff study had to bear fruit quickly. The TPI was born.

What is to wean sovereigns, bond investors, market participants, banks, bank regulators, bank creditors, financial institutions, and governments from their evident reliance on ECB intervention, which makes the whole system so fragile that the ECB feels forced to intervene and to loosen any self-limiting rules, time and again, possibly fully eviscerating the boundaries between monetary policy and cross-state fiscal transfers? We take up these questions when analyzing the present situation in chapter 10.

10

The Unsustainable Present

A brief summary: In a currency union without fiscal union, over-indebted countries must be allowed to default just like companies. If the central bank will always step in to avoid default or yields rising in fear of default, key incentives for countries to behave in a fiscally responsible manner are lost, and the central bank will have to intervene frequently. The union will experience inflation, and eventually may risk dissolution after one too many bailouts. If the union wishes not to see defaults or repeated bailouts and inflation, countries must run such conservative fiscal policies that they never risk default and their sovereign spreads never rise on that risk. But the union must find some mechanism to restore countries' incentives to follow such policies.

The euro was set up with a clear understanding of this incentive problem. The ECB was prohibited from buying sovereign debt directly from governments. Though secondary market purchases were legal, in its first decade the ECB did not buy any sovereign debt. A no-bail-out principle would stop other member states from bailing out sovereign debt. Debt and deficit limits, along with good will and responsible behavior, would ensure that no country got in trouble in the first place.

But the initial setup of the euro did not include any mechanism for resolving sovereign debts, analogous to corporate bankruptcy code and procedure; it did not have a mechanism for imposing haircuts quickly while the original investors are still around; it did not include any European mechanism for helping troubled sovereigns, such as standard IMF programs, even to avoid potential multiple-equilibrium runs; and it did not address the problem that banks could load up on sovereign debt and become hostages.

We have speculated on the natural reasons for these lacuane. The more default is painful ex post, the more countries will work to run sober fiscal policies ex ante. A restructuring mechanism that is too painless will be used too often, just as painless central bank interventions will arrive too often. Even talking too much about default mechanisms can make it more likely that countries will use them. In the late 1990s, financial and sovereign debt problems in advanced economies seemed remote. Too much attention to unlikely events would have been awkward in bringing countries together, like discussing a severe pre-nuptial agreement during an engagement. Better for default to be unthinkable and unmentionable.

Already in the early 2000s, Germany and France undermined the credibility of the fiscal rules. Then came a series of unexpected events and crises: the financial crisis, the sovereign debt crisis, stagnation and slow growth at the zero bound, and the pandemic, war, and inflation. In each case, the ECB, other EU institutions, and many national governments (who could have complained about the ECB's actions, but mostly cheered instead) thought that the previous precommitments not to act would have led to disaster, and so took actions outside the traditions and philosophy of the founding design. Although each expedient was considered temporary, many ended up not being temporary, and most people did not believe them to be one-off exemptions, after which the union would return to the previous design. As a result, each change substantially altered expectations about policy going forward. Some member states deviated more and more from fiscal rules and reference values for public debt. Key reforms, implemented and announced during the sovereign debt crisis, withered on the vine. Larger and larger bond purchases and greater market expectations of a spread-compressing ECB put followed.

Again, we do not criticize these ECB decisions. They were taken in the heat of unprecedented events, without adequate tools and institutions to combat the crises. We do, however, bemoan the lack of institutional reforms to strengthen the monetary union framework and to put the genie back in the bottle during the calms between storms. Perhaps this too is understandable. In each case, the ECB did stem the crisis. A great crisis, that the ECB cannot contain, has not yet happened. Europe has had a big surge of inflation. But that event has been widely attributed to supply shocks or fiscal expansion, not mainly to ECB monetization. Thus, it is not a salient impetus for reform. It is natural to think that ECB intervention works and will always work, so why worry? Why change anything?

That view ignores the question, just why we are having so many crises, and why does each one seem to require larger and larger ECB intervention? Today's historical counterfactual is not yet avoidance of a final euro-wide crisis. Had incentive-restoring institutional and structural reform happened in the calm years, the counterfactual is instead a euro area with smaller sovereign debts, greater growth via microeconomic reform, and less need for more and more ECB intervention. In this counterfactual world, when President Christine Lagarde said that "we are not here to close spreads," markets would have said "of course not," and would not have reacted strongly to her speech. The ECB then would not have felt forced to announce new and more generous contingent country-specific purchases. But that counterfactual is not widely appreciated, so it has not motivated difficult institution-restoring reform.

However, the limits of the current regime must become evident sooner or later. In this chapter, we do not assess the short-term impact of policy decisions to stem crises. Instead, we look at the incentives created and the medium-term consequences. We lay out the case that the present status quo is not sustainable going forward, and that reform must happen before the next, larger crisis. That crisis may be the one, finally, that is beyond the ECB's ability to contain.

Many of these points are not novel, and many are echoed by other commentators, including ECB policymakers. For example, in prescient speeches, then ECB Board member Benoît Cœuré stressed in 2012 how to improve the EMU architecture: "We cannot design insurance and forget about its impact on incentives." In 2019 he said: "in an environment in which policy space is significantly smaller today than it was before the crisis," our response "should not be about blurring the lines between monetary and fiscal policies."[1] More recently, in 2024 ECB Board member Isabel Schnabel provided an overview "of the costs of QE."[2]

But when one puts all these points together and focuses on their importance for the euro and its institutions, a starker and clearer picture emerges.

10.1   Unsustainable Fiscal Policy

A Surge in Public Debt

Joining the EMU has not, as originally envisioned, led countries to low debt and deficits. Of the twelve countries that joined the euro area by 2001, in 2023 only three—Ireland (44%), Luxembourg (26%), and the Netherlands (45%)—were below the 60% of GDP reference value enshrined in the Maastricht Treaty.[3] Of the rest, Greece (164%), Italy (135%), France (110%), Spain (105%), Belgium (103%), and Portugal (98%) have the largest debt-to-GDP ratios. In contrast, eleven of the fifteen EU countries that joined the euro area at a later stage or not at all have debt below that limit. Although obviously everything else is not equal, this evidence suggests that the blurring of the fiscal-monetary separation in the euro area may have undermined incentives for sound fiscal policies.

Incentives to run prudent fiscal policies are different across countries. Size seems to matter: Some countries appear to be too big to discipline. The two biggest countries, Germany and France, already refused to follow fiscal rules in 2002 and 2003, and the European Commission was unable to do anything about it. A famous quote of Jean-Claude Juncker, president of the Commission between 2014 and 2019, and as such the person in charge of enforcing fiscal rules, illustrates this point: "Asked why the Commission, on several occasions, had turned a blind eye to French infractions, Juncker admitted candidly in an interview with the French Senate television Public Senate that it did so 'because it is France.'"[4]

Italy has had perpetual fiscal problems. Its debt surged to 155% of GDP in 2020, and has fallen to below 140% mainly because inflation devalued debt in real terms. It would be hard to argue that actual and expected ECB interventions to combat Italy's interest-rate spread have not contributed to Italy's insufficient implementation of the serious fiscal and microeconomic reforms necessary to bring its debt down or its GDP up.

Because of its past problems, we have perhaps unfairly used Italy as an example for thinking about debt problems. However, looking forward, France could be the source of the next unexpected fiscal problem. Its debt is smaller as a percent of GDP than Italy's, but its long-term finances face particular challenges. And many other euro-area countries, as well as most of the advanced world including the United States, the United Kingdom, and Japan face similar fiscal challenges. When thinking of debt problems, think not just of a single large country in the eurozone, but contemplate also the possibility of a global turn against sovereign debt and the consequences of such an event for the eurozone.

Conditionality, where it applied, does seem to have helped to bring down debts over the medium term. During the euro crisis, Greece, Ireland, Portugal, and Cyprus, middle-sized countries with very high fiscal deficits, entered full EU/IMF adjustment programs. In 2023, three of these countries achieved a fiscal surplus, and the deficit in Greece was 1.3% of GDP, well below the euro-area average of 3.5% of GDP. Given the size of its sovereign debt problem resulting from its bank bailout, Ireland is noteworthy for having brought its debt down. At the same time, the largest euro-area countries had sizable deficits, in particular Spain (3.5%), France (5.5%), and Italy (7.2%). Neither Italy nor Spain were part of a full IMF/EU adjustment program. (Spain, as we have seen, had a program, but limited to the financial sector.)

There are, of course, other reasons for this large debt accumulation, which is also seen in many other countries outside the euro. EU governments grappled with four "once-in-a-century" crises. The buildup of sovereign debt in the last three decades largely occurred in these episodes.

However, one cannot chalk up the entire rise in debt to global bad luck. Several EU member states, and others just outside like Switzerland, still have low debt levels. Yes, higher deficits in crises are often good policies. But how *much* a country borrows and spends to fight a crisis and *how* it spends are both decisions, and those decisions are influenced by fiscal incentives. Spending to fight the four crises has often been poorly targeted. Governments supported a wider array of private firms, banks, and asset prices than what was necessary. "Financial stability" does not mean that nobody ever loses money.

More importantly perhaps, temporary deficits in a crisis should be countered by structural surpluses outside crisis times to bring down debt and prepare for future shocks. Spending overall is hardly efficiently crafted, taxes are not well designed to raise revenue with minimum distortion, and pro-growth policy remains a distant aspiration, especially in high-debt states.

Euro-area governments enjoyed a fiscal bounty from low and then negative real interest rates on their debt. Countries could have used this gift to decisively lower their debt-to-GDP ratios. Instead, many reacted to low interest rates and strong debt demand by borrowing more and putting off fiscal and structural reforms.

Debt Sustainability

The debt-to-GDP ratio grows at the real (after-inflation) interest rate, minus the real GDP growth rate and minus the difference between tax revenues and government spending (the real primary surplus) as a fraction of GDP:

$$d\left(\frac{b_t}{y_t}\right)/dt = (i_t - \pi_t - g_t)\frac{b_t}{y_t} - \frac{s_t}{y_t},$$

where b is the value of debt, y is GDP, i is the nominal interest rate, π is inflation, g is the real GDP growth rate, and s is the primary surplus, tax revenue minus spending, not including interest payments. (We abstract from long-term debt here. That changes the dynamics but not the basic long-run message.)

All of the components of the dynamic public debt equation pose concerns for the future. Euro-area debt rose from about 70% of GDP to about 90% from the formation of the euro to today. This aggregate hides substantial heterogeneity. In France and Spain, for example, debt rose from around 60% of GDP in 1999 to around 110% of GDP and 105% of GDP, respectively, in 2023. The real interest rates that governments must pay on their debt $(i - \pi)$ are more likely to rise than to fall further into negative territory. Just how long the ECB can and will suppress risk premiums in interest rates increasingly seems a key question for how long debt remains sustainable.

The sharp unexpected inflation starting in 2021 wiped several percentage points off the debt-to-GDP ratio. But inflation can only unexpectedly wipe out debt. Repeated and thus expected inflation forces an equal rise in the nominal interest rate.

Growth g has been sluggish in many euro member states, especially in countries like Italy that also have high debts b/y and pay higher interest rates $i - \pi$. Over the past decade, taxable real income growth in the euro area has limped along at an average of roughly 1.3% per year.[5] There is little reason to think that taxable income growth will accelerate in Europe over the next decades, especially in the fiscally challenged countries, at least without a revolutionary change in structural microeconomic policies.

Although we tend to focus on debt, the underlying problem is spending sustainability. A 100% debt-to-GDP ratio, on the heels of four major crises, would be entirely sustainable in economies that are growing smartly, whose governments are spending wisely, taxing efficiently, attracting investors at low real interest rates, and generating steady primary fiscal surpluses. Contrariwise, even defaulting or inflating away current debt entirely would not fund the perpetual deficits of current economic policies, and less so the larger deficits that will come in the next, inevitable, "once-in-a-century" crisis. Indeed, such a default would make planned future borrowing impossible and worsen rather than aid Europe's fiscal trap.

Substantial increases in tax rates that can generate additional long-run multi-decade revenue are also unlikely, especially in the slow-growing high-debt countries. Government spending is half of GDP on average in the euro area.[6] In a country whose government spends half of GDP, the long-run average tax rate must be half of income. For everyone who faces a lower rate, someone else must face a higher rate. Growth disincentives surely start to kick in at such tax rates. And several countries spend more than half of their GDP. France spends about 57%.

Tax disincentives come from all taxes put together, the total wedge between producing something worth a euro and how many euros of good or service one can buy with the after-tax result. Combining payroll or social insurance taxes, corporate taxes (which are all passed on to people, as consumers, workers, or savers), income taxes, value-added taxes (i.e., sales taxes), and phaseouts of government benefits with income, marginal tax rates are well in the range that reduces incentives to work and invest, and more importantly reduces incentives to invest in human capital, choose difficult but rewarding careers, or start and grow companies—all the things that are crucial to multidecade growth.

The central fiscal problem is governments that spend half or more of GDP. And there will be increased demands for spending. The regular demands of a welfare state are already troublesome for fiscal sustainability. Rapid aging and ultra-low birthrates means these demands will continue to grow. The European Commission estimates that by 2050, one in three Europeans will be over the age of 65. A Eurostat study estimates the implicit unfunded pension liabilities of France at four times annual GDP, of Italy at 4.3 times, and of Spain at five times annual GDP, all as of 2021. If we count these promised payments as debt, these countries actually have debt-to-GDP ratios of more than 500%.[7] And these calculations omit much other promised spending, in particular on health care. Over decades, something has to give.

In the past, pensions were lower, people didn't live as long after retirement, and there were more children and young workers to support each retiree. Generous pay-as-you-go pensions are simply not sustainable with fertility rates that are around half the replacement rate.[8]

Pension promises are hard to reverse, especially in an aging society. France's turmoil over raising the pension age to sixty-four rather than sixty-two, with a remaining life expectancy well in the mid-eighties, is a sign of this difficulty. But countries that face fiscal crises often do end up cutting pensions when paying them becomes impossible. Brazil and Russia are recent examples. When pensions are cut suddenly in a crisis, the pain is so much larger as people have not had time to adjust their work and savings. Italy's 2012 pension cuts are an example of the former, while pension reforms in Germany in the early 2000s, which gradually shifted the retirement age up to sixty-seven, is an example of the latter. But neither of these reforms is close to the scale of what will be required in the future.

Immigrants can substitute for children in financing a welfare state. But Europe's immigrants are not weighted as much as they could be to skilled young working families who contribute positively on net to government finances.

Pensions at least promise a quantifiable and forecastable amount of money. Health care keeps getting more expensive. In part, that is because health care keeps getting better. Expensive new drugs can save lives. In part, health care is underpriced, leading people to use more routine and ineffective care than they would choose if they were paying the bill, even the bill for private insurance.

The current path of European climate policy involves enormous new public spending. The European Green Deal Investment Plan "will increase funding for the transition, and mobilise at least €1 trillion to support sustainable investments over the next decade through the EU budget and associated instruments."[9] The new era of competition with the United States and China on green industrial policy subsidies could open the public spigots further. Europe could choose a much more cost-effective climate policy, however.

The energy disruption following the Russian invasion of Ukraine emphasized the need for more resilient supply of conventional energy as well. "In 2021, the EU imported more than 40% of its total gas consumption, 27% of oil imports and 46% of coal imports from Russia," according to the EU Commission.[10] It is also a security imperative for Europe to diversify its energy supplies. Germany's swift construction of a natural gas terminal is a good example. Now, energy investment need not require public funds, merely public and regulatory acquiescence. But in Europe it typically does involve substantial public investment.

Energy is expensive in Europe, making many energy-intensive businesses uncompetitive. Energy prices surged further in the first year of the Russian war against Ukraine. Many countries responded to high prices with energy subsidies. Subsidized demand in the face of inelastic supply does not increase the quantity, but just increases the price for those not receiving subsidies. And subsidies add to the public bill. Even the European cap and trade system known as the Emission Trading System, even though it is cheaper and more efficient than most green industrial policies, and indeed can raise revenue, nonetheless makes energy more expensive. Energy-intensive businesses will clamor for subsidies or protection, move abroad, or shut down.

Security will cost money. Just reaching the NATO commitment of 2% of GDP needs a substantial increase in many countries. Spending effectively on renewed equipment and active and effective forces may require a good deal more.

It is widely perceived that current defense spending is insufficient. Spending needs include military equipment, cybersecurity, and development of new systems given the rapid change in military technology. Insufficient defense spending weakens Europe against Russia, China and other threats and increases future social and economic costs related to geopolitical threats. Most current fiscal analyses omit such costs. Given the new threats, fiscal rules need adjustment to temporarily exempt increased defense spending, while reinforcing commitments to repay debts and make long-lasting adjustments. A specific exemption is better than simply suspending all rules as happened during the pandemic.

Economic security is now on the front burner. Friend-shoring or re-shoring of sensitive goods is expensive. And once subsidies and protections get wrapped in a security blanket, costs can explode.

Hopefully, Europe will avoid the siren songs of protectionism, economic nationalism, and industrial policy that are now being sung across the Atlantic. If not, they will add to spending and detract from GDP.

Most worries about debt sustainability envision a slow erosion of borrowing capacity, interest rates that rise slowly, and force a painful adjustment over a few years. Reality is likely to be harsher. Given that governments need to roll over significant amounts of debt every year, the end comes in a run-like crisis. Higher spreads make debt less sustainable and lead to even higher spreads. Crises are by definition unpredictable—otherwise, they would have happened already. Small changes to country fundamentals can lead to such events.

But the largest, less frequently stated, worry about high debt and future spending should be the lack of fiscal space that they imply for individual countries, and even Europe as a whole, to respond to the next shock. We have seen four "once-in-a-century" crises in fifteen years. A fifth or sixth, perhaps even larger, crisis will surely arrive. Imagine, for instance, that China blockades or invades Taiwan, Pacific trade stops, and the world teeters on the edge of war. Imagine that a new pandemic erupts—one that kills, say, 5% of the population, not a fraction of 1%. Imagine that the Middle East breaks out to a widespread war, or Russia attacks the Baltics, or other EU member states. Or suppose that Russia attacks Austria, which is in the EU but not a member of NATO. These or similar events are unfortunately not unthinkably unlikely. They could spark an economic and financial conflagration even larger than the crises of the last fifteen years.

European governments will want to borrow trillions of euros once again, for stimulus, for financial bailouts, to insure suffering populations, and perhaps for sudden surges in vital military or public health expenditures. The ECB will likely buy lots of debt and lend to banks to support these efforts, with newly printed euros.

The economic consequences of higher debt in such a crisis might not be so bad if European countries had substantial fiscal buffers and good long-run growth prospects, and thus could easily borrow more at low rates. But we already have seen signs of limited borrowing ability and limited fiscal space. In some countries, spreads rise when there is bad fiscal news. The pandemic borrowing led to inflation, suggesting that another such round of borrowing would lead to more inflation. Who will buy all this new debt, or hold quietly the newly issued ECB money?

Assume that the institutional weaknesses and shortcomings have not been addressed by EU member states and institutions. The most fiscally fragile member states will get in to trouble first, with spreads widening and markets for their debt shrinking. Their banking systems will once again teeter. Once again, EU officials and governments will regard bondholder losses as unacceptable and threatening larger "financial stability." But will other member states that are already struggling to borrow for themselves step in again, and promptly this time, for a big transfer to highly indebted states? With no well-worked-out institution that credibly ensures the efficient use of such transfers, it is surely unlikely.

Once again, the ECB will likely step into the breach. Now the ECB will have a much easier institutional track to intervention. It has won the acceptance of an essentially unlimited tool to purchase sovereign debts via the Transmission Protection Instrument (TPI). And the ease and apparent past success of ECB lending and bond-buying will likely lead the rest of Europe to avoid painful fiscal transfers or restructurings and just let the ECB handle it, which the ECB will then have to do because there is no alternative.

But there is a fiscal limit to the whole EU, even if governments with some fiscal space will bail out the fiscally weaker member states via a new Next Generation EU program, and there is a limit to what the ECB can do. We may have just seen that limit: The Covid fiscal expansions led or at least contributed to inflation in Europe as in the United States and the United Kingdom, as people were unwilling to hold that much extra debt and money. If people see a quick repetition of 2020–2022 on hand, the ECB may already be fighting inflation when it feels the need to buy bonds of weaker member states once again.

In this case, Europe will be faced with a crisis that fragile states and financial institutions expect a bailout, but the bailout fails; states are unable to borrow to handle the crisis, and the ECB cannot buy massive amounts of debt without pouring gasoline on the fire of an inflation that threatens the euro's existence. If a crisis comes in which everyone expects a river of borrowed money, but governments cannot realistically borrow, the crisis will be enormous.

Europe is not alone. The United States, the United Kingdom, Japan, and other countries have high debts and unsustainable spending plans. A Europe-wide sovereign debt crisis might come in the context of a global sovereign debt crisis. And, at the risk of being too pessimistic, it is worth remembering that many political upheavals have followed debt crises, including the French Revolution.

So here we are. Debt is 90% of GDP in the euro area, with many countries well above that level. Growth is anemic, demographics discouraging, spending desires accelerating, the era of low real interest rates quite possibly over, and the incentives for member states to reform poor.

New Fiscal Rules

The European Commission, recognizing the inadequacy of existing debt and deficit limits, proposed a new fiscal framework on April 26, 2023. After amendment, it was approved by the European Parliament and became effective in April 2024.[11]

The new rules maintain the Maastricht Treaty's 60% debt and 3% deficit ceilings, but significantly alter the Stability and Growth Pact (SGP). The key difference is in the underlying operational mechanisms. The new rules introduce country-specific adjustment paths, to be determined through a debt-sustainability analysis (DSA) by the Commission and negotiated bilaterally with each member state. The paths involve one operational target, a net expenditure path, excluding interest payments until 2027, over a four- to seven-year horizon. The longer horizon applies if the government commits to reforms and investments to improve growth and align with EU's objectives.

After the end of this four- to seven-year adjustment period, the projected debt-to-GDP ratio must follow a "plausibly downward path" or stay "below 60% of GDP over the medium term."[12] The procedure also includes some numerical rules. A "debt sustainability safeguard" prescribes that countries with more than 90% debt-to-GDP ratio must reduce that by 1 percentage point per year,[13] and a "deficit resilience safeguard" mandates that countries with structural budget deficits over 1.5% of GDP must show annual structural primary balance improvements of 0.4% of GDP, or 0.25% with an extended adjustment period.[14]

We are doubtful that this framework will work in a credible and time-consistent way, as it does not consider the main incentives of the actors involved. The previous rules did not fail because they were too simple, and needed a country-specific bilaterally-negotiated stochastic debt simulation. The previous rules failed "because it is France," as Commission President Jean-Claude Juncker put it. The same could have been said of Germany or Italy. The EU was unable or unwilling to force countries to abide by the simple and transparent rules they had agreed to and then found inconvenient, even in the mild early 2000s. New, more complex, and less transparent rules do nothing to address this central problem, no matter how pretty they are on the planning table. Indeed, they arguably make the problem worse, for several reasons.

The new rules rely explicitly on bilateral negotiations with the Commission. That raises the risk of political pressure, especially from larger member states capable of threatening vetoes or otherwise causing trouble for the Commission on crucial decisions.

The rules ignore the central problems of time-consistency and precomitment. Reform commitments are supposed to be implemented over multiple-year horizons, significantly beyond the horizon of most elected officials. What are the incentives of a government to stick to promises for reforms and consolidation plans made several years ago, if they ex post appear politically too costly? How can a government's promise to implement an important but politically difficult labor market, tax, or pension reform be enforced if a new government with different priorities is elected? Will the Commission then go against the outcome of a democratic election and insist that a policy be implemented, even when the majority of voters just rejected it?

Fines or similar sanctions that would need to be imposed by the EU Council did not work in the past and likely will not work in the future. When the Commission is trying to save a country in financial distress, it is not likely to levy substantial fines and penalties that only add to the country's deficit. The rules do not come with a plan for an orderly debt restructuring. Default remains unthinkable. The Council thus has little threat to offer if a country simply refuses.

The rules largely ignore the large government liabilities that are implicit in public pay-as-you-go pension systems. A country that promises greater future pensions may escape the Excessive Deficit Procedure, which focuses on current deficits. For example, a "reform" of the pension system in Spain, supposedly to pursue commitments with the EU under the Next Generation EU plan, will increase future pension expenditures, according to the most recent Ageing Report of the European Commission, by 3.3 percentage points of GDP by 2050 and by 5% of GDP by 2070, one percentage point per decade.[15]

Debt and deficit plans normally assume that nothing bad will happen. Surely at some point over a seven-year adjustment period and the following ten years, some new shock may hit, justifying a new exemption and starting the cycle all over again.

The rules do not have any precommitment devices. Precommitment could be increased, for example, by the involvement of strong national independent fiscal institutions.[16] Despite initial plans from the EU Commission to include this provision, member states have made this role voluntary.

Complexity is the enemy of transparency and enforceability. A complex stochastic simulation can be argued with, especially ex post. A binding rule that triggers unpleasant actions demands clarity. Speed limits are fixed numbers. You do not enter bilateral negotiations with the police over a stochastic simulation of your driving abilities, tailored to your car, the weather, traffic on the particular road, and produce a seven-year plan for slowing down. As Schuberth (2024) puts it, the new rules are "Baroque almost to a point of bizarreness. . . . The DSA [Debt Sustainability Analysis] is highly judgemental, replete with self-fulfilling features, and hence is ill-suited for the operationalization of hard fiscal rules."

The fiscal targets derived from the debt sustainability analysis are sensitive to small changes in technical assumptions and model parameters, including real interest rates, economic growth rates, and behavioral changes by consumers and taxpayers. None of these are known with any precision. This fact means that there is a large degree of discretion and room for negotiation. For example, one parameter is the plausibly downward trajectory of the debt-to-GDP ratio, where plausible means a 70 percent probability of decline according to the Debt Sustainability Analysis. Probabilities are driven by the variance of assumed shocks, a number that is easy to argue with. Optimistic assessments of long-term potential growth and the growth impact of future reforms are also easy ways to change numbers.

The safeguards on excessive deficit and expenditure growth lack precise metrics, challenging effective enforcement. Given how poor forecasts of potential growth, real interest rates, and fiscal consolidation have been in the past, and given how simple debt and deficit limits have utterly failed to constrain member states in the past, the whole exercise seems a pipe dream of detailed technocratic mastery loose in an uncertain and contentious political game.

However, there is a contrasting view in which all these deficiencies might be to some extent advantages. Clearly, the simple and transparent debt and deficit rules did not work. Countries ignored them, and the EU was not powerful enough to impose sanctions for their violation. A complex procedure with bilateral negotiations allows enough wiggle room that every country will in the end be found in compliance, and public sanctions will not be triggered. But in the negotiating process, more or less pressure can be brought to bear so that countries do quietly reform. That process might be politically more effective for the EU to actually produce member state reforms. However, if this is the case, then certification of compliance is essentially useless as a bright line on which the ECB can condition bond purchases.

Fiscal Challenges to Monetary Policy

After rising above 4% in October 2021 and hitting 10.6% a year later, HICP inflation continuously fell to 2.4% in November 2023. It hovered around 2.5% through the first half of 2024, fell to 1.7% in September

2024, and stood at 2.4% in December 2024. Forecasts point to inflation returning to 2% during 2025. But then again, forecasts always point to steady reversion to the ECB's 2% target, even when inflation is ramping up to 10%.

Most analysts seem to regard the recent inflation as a one-time event due to something special about the one-time Covid shock. There is almost no worrying about another inflation shock, or how the ECB and other central banks should react differently next time either to diagnose or offset the shock.

Monetary policy is likely to have a harder time containing any future inflation. Expectations are likely to move more quickly. In the conventional analysis of monetary policy, "anchoring" of expectations is crucial. Inflation equals expected inflation plus output gap plus shock, so goes the Phillips curve ($\pi_t = \beta E_t \pi_{t+1} + \kappa x_t + u_t$). So long as expected inflation $E_t \pi_{t+1}$ remains "anchored," current inflation won't go too far away and will come back on its own following a shock. Indeed, most measures of medium-term expectations did not move much in the recent surge, although bondholders and depositors were sorely disappointed in that expectation and lost a great deal of money in real terms.

If inflation breaks out again in the next decade or two, won't bond investors, as well as people and businesses setting prices and wages, remember the 2021–2023 episode and react much more quickly? Once burned, twice shy. One can expect a much faster inflation breakout, and the need for the ECB to act more decisively, no matter the costs to banks, indebted sovereigns, and the chance of inducing a recession. There are three terms in the Phillips curve, after all, and if inflation expectations move the ECB must either induce a recession—lower x_t—or pray for a better shock u_t.

Similarly, putting on a fiscal theory hat, bond investors also may have learned a sharp lesson about huge fiscal expansion in a crisis, with no resolution of long-run fiscal problems. A new fiscal blowout in response to a shock is likely to produce a quicker response in long-term interest rates and inflation than last time. In current fiscal theory models, central banks can and should slow a fiscal inflation with a moderately persistent rise in interest rates (see Cochrane, 2023b, figure 5.2; Cochrane, 2024, figure 4). And the more quickly the bank acts, the more successful that policy is. If bondholders, price-setters, and wage-demanders expect inflation more promptly as a result of the current experience, the ECB will again have to act more decisively, despite the costs of doing so.

The ECB's huge bond portfolio and strong expectations that it will step in to support a still fragile and overleveraged financial system, as well as fragile sovereigns, may stand in the way of tighter monetary policy. Higher real interest rates, both from monetary policy and default spreads, make default more likely in the familiar default-risk feedback mechanism. Higher interest rates and falling bond prices imperil banks via falling asset values, as happened in 2021–2023, once again. And falling bond prices lower the value of the ECB's own assets. "Fiscal dominance," "financial dominance," and "sovereign default dominance" may hobble any attempt to significantly tighten by selling assets or raising interest rates.

Why Not Inflation?

Some readers may ask: What's wrong with inflation? In particular, some economists have argued that the bout of inflation following the pandemic, war, and energy disruption was at least in part a good thing, given the major challenges amid a limited fiscal space. In response to "once-in-a-century" shocks, let current bondholders finance public expenditures by inflating away some of the value of their debt, rather than place the burden entirely on future taxpayers and people who will suffer from lower growth given the economic distortions of taxation. Inflation is an effective partial default, but without the financial and legal disruption that actual default occasions.

Why not keep at it, some might think? Another bout of inflation would reduce troublesome debts. Keeping interest rates low and a large balance sheet would directly ease government finances.

This advice ignores the many distributional consequences of inflation. With high unexpected inflation, workers suffer lower real wages for some time. Net savers with bank deposits or other nominal claims lose real wealth, while people who have financed real investments such as real estate and machinery with long-term nominal debt see a windfall gain as the real value of their debt falls.

Most of all, the inflation tax does not work if people come to expect it. Another bout of inflation would convince bond investors that inflation is a regular policy, and therefore to demand an inflation and risk premium ahead of time. The ability of European countries to borrow real resources in the next crisis, and of the ECB to buy large amounts of debts without causing high inflation almost instantly, will sharply diminish. More deeply, recurring bouts of inflation will damage public trust in institutions and European integration. Inflation rewards precisely those who have little trust in the central bank and fiscal discipline and thus invested in real assets rather than nominal assets, or used asset purchase programs to sell their bonds to the central bank before inflation took off. Price stability was the first and most important foundational promise of the common currency. Bouts of inflation and devaluation did not turn Greece or Portugal into flourishing economies with large fiscal space in the era before the euro.

Thus, consistent with the Maastricht Treaty, monetary policy must maintain its core mandate: price stability. The ECB needs to ensure stable inflation at its target. The institutional framework of the euro must be reformed so that the ECB *can* achieve that target, even if shocks like Covid reappear.

The Transmission Protection Instrument

The Transmission Protection Instrument (TPI), announced in July 2022, is the ECB's newest program for buying sovereign debts of individual countries. It removes the restriction of Outright Monetary Transactions (OMT), announced in 2012, that requires participation in an external financial assistance and conditionality program agreed to by euro-area finance ministers via the ESM before ECB interventions. Chapter 9, section 9.5 describes how the TPI came into being, as a means for the ECB to raise interest rates and sell assets in general but to buy debt of stressed sovereigns to lower or cap spreads at the same time.

So the ECB crafted a new program, loosening previous rules, that met the exigencies of the moment. The TPI announcement helped the ECB to swiftly raise policy rates to fight high inflation. However, the program was not centrally designed to manage consequent disincentives and moral hazards.

The ECB is not blind to moral hazard. It does not like being constantly called on to intervene in markets and provide quasi-fiscal support, as President Largarde's "We are not here to compress spreads" revealed. Each time it was forced into action by the apparent fragility around it, vulnerabilities accumulated during previous crises, and lack of better institutions. Each of the successive bond buying programs have included conditions and limits to try to precommit the ECB against arbitrary future intervention, and thereby to try to convince countries, banks, regulators, and market participants not to count on eternal ECB intervention. The TPI is no exception. The question is whether the TPI's limits will succeed where previous ones have failed.

One common limitation on bond purchases is that a central bank should support debt of countries whose bonds are suffering "illiquidity," a "multiple-equilibrium" run, or some certifiable market dysfunction, but not of countries whose debt and policies to repay that debt together risk debt sustainability, driving high default risk premiums. This parallels the advice to lend only to solvent but illiquid banks going back to Bagehot. If debt is not sustainable, the central bank should not intervene until policy changes or upfront restructuring to make the debt sustainable are in place. It is usually desirable for fiscal and political authorities to prompt those changes, not the central bank. In practice, of course, sustainability is not easy to determine. This is not the only moral-hazard-limiting criterion, but it is a common one.

To emphasize, the point of such bond-buying limits is mainly to contain moral hazard. A crisis brought about by insolvency is just as bad as a crisis brought about by illiquidity or market dysfunction, and possibly worse. It is also curable with bailout. And they are hard to tell apart in a crisis. But a precommitment not to intervene in case of insolvency attempts to force other actors to avoid insolvency, or forces fiscal and political actors to take over any transfers to address it.

It's clearly better if fiscal authorities, or a European fiscal institution, are responsible for solvency determination and designing conditionality. It is better yet if they provide financial support from fiscal resources, possibly after a debt restructuring. (Indeed, this was the essence of the ECB's OMT program.) Otherwise, the ECB itself has to assess whether fiscal and structural policy plans are credible and sufficient; and it may have have to do so thoroughly, given what is at stake.

So the ECB may have to discuss the plans of the troubled government with political leaders and assess the plans' credibility and effectiveness; the ECB has to assess and announce if government policies no longer suffice, and then stop its TPI interventions, likely leaving the country to default and suffer a deep recession, if such default is delayed or disorderly. But avoiding default and recession was, of course, the whole reason for the TPI bond purchases in the first place. The ECB might even be drawn into negotiating and implementing a kind of conditionality: The country concerned will surely ask what could allow the ECB to continue with interventions, including divisive issues such as taxes, social program spending, public employment, subsidies, labor protections and more, and push back on the difficult items. The ECB may then have to judge how much burden can realistically (or should?) be borne by taxpayers or citizens, rather than bondholders. Beyond credibility, all of these actions thrust the ECB into dangerous political territory. (See Otmar Issing's 2022 "Sword of Damocles" for warnings on this subject, including political dangers.) The ECB rightly does not want to enter these waters.

To cure moral hazard, the nature of the procedure also needs to be public and transparent. The Securities Market program (SMP) interventions in 2010–2011 culminated in secret letters with conditionality requests sent in summer 2011 by the ECB to the Italian and Spanish prime ministers, signed by the ECB president and respective national central bank governors (see chapter 5). Such conditionality may have helped those ministers not to overuse the SMP in that particular crisis, but it is not the best way to craft a permanent program, whose limitations are there to precommit the ECB *not* to act, and to guide expectations of others so they *will* act, and act ahead of time. For good reasons, the SMP was scrapped when OMT was introduced.

In this vein, the TPI does include some general eligibility criteria, largely assessed by the European Commission. The criteria are:

1. "Compliance with the EU fiscal framework."
2. "Absence of severe macroeconomic imbalances," as measured by EU procedures.
3. "Fiscal sustainability: in ascertaining that the trajectory of public debt is sustainable, the Governing Council will take into account, where available, the debt sustainability analyses by the European Commission, the European Stability Mechanism, the International Monetary Fund and other institutions, together with the ECB's internal analysis."
4. "Sound and sustainable macroeconomic policies," as measured by compliance with the "commitments submitted in the recovery and resilience plans . . . and with the European Commission's country-specific recommendations."[17]

However, these eligibility criteria are less binding on ECB purchases, and less forceful as incentives for countries not to count on ECB rescue, than they may appear at first sight.

They are only to be taken into account as an "input" into the ECB's considerations, not binding limits.

On criterion 1, we just mentioned the defects of the new EU fiscal framework. Limits that are not likely to lead to a declaration of non-compliance and official sanction on their own are even more unlikely to constitute a measurable line that places a country off limits for ECB intervention. For official non-compliance, it is not sufficient that a country has been put by the EU Council into the so-called corrective arm of the excessive deficit procedure. The country must also be found not to have taken effective action to address its troubles. This finding is a political decision. It has been made only six times since 1999 (Redeker, 2022) and did not carry the consequence of barring ECB intervention.

Criterion 2, macroeconomic imbalances, and criterion 4, sound and sustainable macroeconomic policies, allow large room for interpretation and discretion by the European Commission. The Commission has approved, with a few concrete exceptions, all the recovery plans, and given them all the same grades. The Commission has been flexible on determining when milestones and targets were met for disbursements. Exceptions have been Hungary and Poland, which are not part of the euro area, for which the Commission used its power to force the member states to take anticorruption measures or to correct laws that limit the independence of judicial courts or judges. And that exception proves the rule that these are political decisions not purely technocratic measurements of debt sustainability.

Condition 3, a sustainable public debt trajectory, is just as nebulous as a matter of economics. Will such a determination be binding and effectively stop ECB loans to countries that cannot repay them? As the 2018–2020 Argentina-IMF loan saga shows, with the right assumptions and enough political will, a declaration by the institutions that debt is sustainable is not difficult to achieve, even when markets are plainly unwilling to sustain the same debt.[18]

Interest costs are a central part of debt sustainability. In addition to the overall level of interest rates, spreads matter. Any debt sustainability assessment must thus also make assumptions about the nature, volume, timeline, and impact on risk premia and yields of announced and future actions of the ECB. Debt might be assessed as sustainable only because the existence of TPI and possibly other tools has compressed yield spreads. If the ECB wishes to intervene only if debt is already sustainable, a logical conundrum results.

These are ongoing determinations. The ECB does not have to ask for a new analysis or blessing before buying bonds. Thus, so long as a government has managed to escape official violation of these fiscal and economic blessings, the ECB can buy bonds as it wishes unless other agencies act affirmatively in a way that stops ECB intervention after it has started.

In making such a declaration of unsustainable debt, multilateral institutions including the European Commission, the European Stability

Mechanism ESM, and the IMF would be taking steps that they know could trigger a sovereign funding crisis. With no fiscal backstop in place, these institutions will likely not be ready to manage the sovereign debt crisis with swift bridge loans and an orderly sovereign debt restructuring. A declaration of unsustainability could trigger a crisis, for which they will be blamed. These institutions have strong incentives to declare debt "sustainable," and thereby shift the burden of solving the problem to the ECB.

So the ECB will likely be forced to intervene. Suppose that a country's yield spreads rise because functional markets rightly worry about default risks. When the ECB realizes what bond market analysts had figured out, the ECB is supposed to stop intervening "based on an assessment that persistent tensions are due to country fundamentals."[19] But then of course, if the ECB pulls out, a crisis will erupt. Is it really imaginable for the ECB to declare, "No, we found out that it's really fundamentals, not 'dysfunction.' Go ahead and default"?

And of course, given past loosening of the rules, it does not take too cynical an observer to suspect that if spreads rise again in a still fragile system, the ECB will come up with a new program with even looser rules.

So the rules constraining the TPI would only work if they are clear enough to force such a declaration from unwilling institutions, or for outsiders to prove that a green light given by the international institutions is wrong, and for some force to constrain the ECB from loosening its programs once again. To say that this is unlikely is generous.

The fogginess of "sustainability" is understandable. It does not represent nefarious behavior, it just represents pretending to do the impossible. Economists can't agree whether any country's debt, from Japan to Argentina, is sustainable. Some economists think all government debt is sustainable, as the long-term interest rate is less than the GDP growth rate. Every country is solvent with enough austerity, and every country is insolvent with enough largesse. It is harder still to distinguish market dysfunction, illiquidity, or multiple equilibria from insolvency in real time.

In the kinder interpretation alluded to previously, EU fiscal rules and institutions may well be suited for one purpose, but unsuited for another. The new process underlying the complex new fiscal framework may help to put slow pressure on countries. But it is poorly suited to create a bright-line precommitment for the ECB to stop itself from offering help and thereby create ex-ante incentives for the member states not to get in trouble in the first place.

It is significant in this context how the ECB explains TPI. President Lagarde stated that TPI will be activated to "counter unwarranted, disorderly market dynamics that pose a serious threat to the transmission of monetary policy across the euro."[20] The ECB seems to also diagnose rising yield spreads in response to its higher policy rates as "fragmentation," and "market dysfunction" rather than straightforward default spreads, which respond rationally to lesser debt sustainability at higher interest rates (i.e., to weaker fundamentals).

This framing suggests that the ECB does not want to buy debt of insolvent sovereigns, does not want to sustain member states' fiscal policies, and wants to preserve the incentives that such a precommitment implies. After all, rising spreads due to rising default spreads would be just as much a headache for the ECB in trying to raise rates as market "dysfunction," so trying to mold incentives and limit future interventions is the only reason to go through the effort.

Yet this self-imposed restriction is likewise hardly credible. Objectively measuring market "dysfunction" is if anything more difficult than measuring fiscal sustainability. At least there is some notion of how one might define sustainability, reflected in the above criteria. But the ECB provides no information on how concretely it or anyone else has or could objectively assess whether market dysfunction causes the rise in spreads, rather than "fundamental" economic factors such as default risk. And the standard is high, as the point is to precommit against an intervention when ex post there will be strong pressure to intervene. Just how will the ECB limit itself from intervention, if spreads are actually due to "fundamentals?" What would the ECB do as spreads rocket higher and a rollover crisis looms?

We do not deny that multiple equilibria, illiquidity, "dysfunction," or "fragmentation" may at times be responsible for increasing spreads. We note only that the distinction between these concepts and fundamental risk premiums, judging from publicly available material, do not amount to a serious precommitment for the ECB not to act against fundamentally justified spreads. In turn, governments then have less incentive to enact politically difficult reforms, to make preparations for an orderly sovereign debt restructuring, to complete the architecture of the euro, or to restrain leveraged bond investors, in particular banks, from taking large sovereign risk. Interestingly, as the TPI was put in place, governments were quietly announcing that they were abandoning efforts to put in place a European Deposit Insurance.[21] In turn, without credible institutional reforms, it seems nearly impossible for the ECB not to act in the next turmoil.

TPI's disincentives, which create the very fragility that makes intervention more likely, go beyond the standard list. While an ESM program can require upfront debt restructuring, this will not be the case for TPI. Knowing that TPI is available, countries will have every reason to resist restructuring and conditionality. Italy already refused an ESM program, well before TPI. Restructuring, conditionality, and a fiscal rescue are likely to be slower or more contentious than even in the Greek case, now that everyone knows the ECB has a program as "flexible" as TPI waiting in the wings. Delay is of course great news for banks and short-term bondholders.

As we see it, then, while TPI helped the ECB to raise policy rates swiftly and substantially, it risks opening the door to essentially unlimited country-specific bond purchases and credit-spread control by the ECB.

TPI represents the epitome of our theme and concerns. There is little constraint tying the ECB to the mast to keep from intervening when voices throughout Europe are screaming to be bailed out. And knowing that, there is less incentive for anyone to put their houses in order. A central bank would like to say "just this once, to give you time to put your houses in order" to investors, banks, and countries. But without precommitments, without an acceptable alternative, without some credible structure by which next time does not look exactly like this time, we all know that the central bank will most likely make the same choice again. And each time becomes larger, and more likely a fiscal bailout rather than a justified reaction to true multiple equilibria, illiquidity, or dysfunction.

Thus, TPI points to the need to reform the underlying framework of sovereign bond buying, the need to reform the rest of the euro framework such that the ECB will not remain the only game in town facing larger and larger crises, and to consciously rebuild the long-term institutional structure of the euro rather than just patch away during crises.

10.2   Lack of Structural Reforms and Growth

In contrast to initial expectations, several of the twelve countries that joined the euro area at an early stage did not catch up toward, or even fell back relative to, the EU countries with the highest real GDP per capita. When compared with the United States, Italy, Spain, and even France fell significantly back in terms of real GDP per capita (see figure 10.1). Italy, tragically, has almost the same GDP per capita in 2023 as it had in 2000, showing no growth for a quarter century. Even the leading countries such as Germany have stagnated, losing ground rather than catching up to the United States.

In contrast, several eastern EU countries, which were not part of the euro area during its first decade, such as the Baltics and Slovenia, or which still have not yet joined, such as the Czech Republic, Hungary, Poland, and Romania, have been growing well in real terms, and they account for the reasonable performance of the EU average, although that average remains 40% below the U.S. value. Some of the latter growth is, of course, catch-up growth following the fall of the Iron Curtain.

Low growth, or even stagnation, is unfortunate, of course, and not just for the improvement in people's lives that a 40% rise in GDP to match the United States would mean. The debt-to-GDP ratio is easiest to fix by raising GDP.

Stagnation is also puzzling. The benefits of the single market should have supported growth and catching up throughout Europe. Europe should converge to the United States, not on average remain 40% below it.

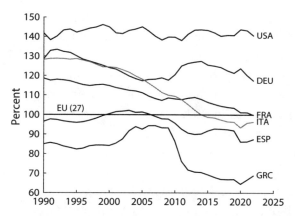

FIGURE 10.1. GDP per capita: percent of EU (27) total. International dollars at 2017 prices. *Source*: World Bank (2023), https://ourworldindata.org.

Long-term growth rests on microeconomic and structural policies and institutions, not monetary affairs. In the end, euro versus dollar is the same as meter versus yard. Member states still face large challenges, such as low innovation, low productivity and potential growth, and labor market and social program distortions, leading to high unemployment.

A common currency and a credible central bank that maintains price stability and avoids distorting incentives are important. They contribute a good deal to efficiency, and surely add a few percentage points to the level of GDP per capita in Europe. Without the euro and the ECB, things would have been even worse. The common market surely had a similar beneficial effect. That these wonderful innovations did not lead to greater convergence toward the United States shows how strong the adverse microeconomic and structural headwinds have been.

The World Bank's Worldwide Governance Indicators (WGI) dataset summarizes how companies, citizens, and experts view the quality of governance, including institutional quality, regulations, and rule of law. There is evidence that good institutional quality as measured by the WGI is an important determinant of longer-term economic performance of EU member states (see, for example, Masuch, Moshammer, and Pierluigi, 2017). None of the twelve countries that joined the euro at an early stage saw an improvement over 1998 values of institutional quality as measured by the average of WGI indicators for rule of law, regulatory quality, government effectiveness and control of corruption. Several saw a significant deterioration, among them Greece, Italy, Spain, Portugal, Austria, Germany, and the Netherlands, in ascending order of their scores in 2022. In contrast, several EU countries that adopted the euro more than a decade after its inception improved their institutional quality between 1998 and 2022. This has been the case for Slovakia (which joined in 2009), Estonia (2011), Latvia (2014), Lithuania (2015), and Croatia (2023). From the EU member states that are still outside the euro area, Romania and Czech Republic saw significant improvements.[22] Of course, improving institutional quality is part of the catch-up from communism unrelated to monetary affairs, and joining the EU requires and is a great force for such institutional improvement.

EU bodies are aware of the growth challenge and the resulting reform needs. The large joint borrowing program, Next Generation EU, launched during the pandemic, is in part one such response. It provides financial incentives to less productive and debt-heavy nations to make public investments and to kick-start reforms. If reform implementation is strong and the money is spent wisely, such investments can help to lift potential growth.

It is too early for a comprehensive assessment. However, some early signs are not promising. Next Generation EU spending was not primarily targeted on projects that raise long-term productivity. It was designed as much as Keynesian pump-priming with a productivity veneer. We mentioned already the Spanish pension reform, undertaken as part of the plan but in fact drastically worsening the structural deficit. A recent book-length evaluation by economists Tito Boeri and Roberto Perotti of the Italian plan (Boeri and Perotti, 2023) concludes that "It [Next Generation EU] allocates absurdly high amounts on useless or deleterious but 'easy' expenses like the Superbonus or 'fashionable' like digital in primary schools while neglecting expenses that are necessary for our society, starting with those to offer opportunities to young people in the urban suburbs. Almost all the major 'epochal' reforms, on which according to the governments the success of the Plan depended, are at a standstill, and many were abandoned before starting."[23] (The "superbonus" is a plan in Italy by which people can get 110% reimbursement for energy efficiency–related home repairs. Naturally, people padded their bills to get larger reimbursements.)

More generally, the consensus of growth economists and history suggests that private innovation rather than massive public investments using borrowed money—by countries already spending half of GDP and with debts of 100% of GDP—are the key to sparking stagnant long-run growth. Good public infrastructure is important, but it is the road, not the automobile.

10.3 Reform Paralysis

We have emphasized the long-term disincentives for banks, investors, and member state governments resulting from some of the ECB's balance sheet policies, as much as those interventions stopped crises in the short term. A final disincentive is the disincentive to reform. The expectation among officials and politicians that the ECB will deal with major future fiscal and financial problems, buying bonds, lending at favorable rates, and inventing new tools as needed, makes it harder for the euro-area policymakers to push through politically difficult but needed improvements of fiscal, financial, and economic institutions.

As we have emphasized, the ECB was forced to act due to key shortcomings of the EMU's institutional setup, and those remain today. The ECB will continue to be forced to act as long as those shortcomings are not addressed. Two are paramount: institutions to deal with sovereign debt crises, and a financial architecture in which sovereign debt troubles do not threaten systemic stability. Completing banking union is one prominent option for the latter issue.

Debt Crises

There still is no well-worked-out institutional structure comparable to corporate bankruptcy to deal with potential sovereign debt crisis, insolvency, rollover failure, or even the financial fallout of yield spreads rising on fear of such events, in a predictable way.

When a sovereign gets in trouble, what are the options? The ECB could always monetize debts, but that leads to obvious bad incentives, can lead to inflation, and can implement a fiscal transfer from the rest of the eurozone to the troubled country and its bondholders. We're trying to avoid that option.

The country could default and simply announce lower payments. Bond prices do whatever they want to do. That would require a second massive institutional reform, placing sovereign debt in hands that can bear default losses or wait through periods of mark-to-market losses, whether they are "fundamental" or due to multiple equilibria, liquidity, or even "dysfunction." That is, not highly leveraged banks and other financial institutions, with portfolios biased toward the country in question, whose failure raises fears of "systemic risk," as is now the case.

As we have emphasized, a middle way would be useful. There should be a common or intergovernmental *fiscal* institution to manage crises. That institution would have the power to provide temporary fiscal support, to force and manage debt default and restructuring, and to negotiate and impose conditionality in terms of policies that a country must follow to improve its fiscal situation as a condition of fiscal support. If nothing else, such an institution would make the option of its use more credible, and thus strengthen the ECB's ability not to intervene.

As we outlined in our brief history, such an institution was constructed after the Greek crisis in the form of the European Stability Mechanism (ESM) and used successfully in several subsequent stabilizations. The ECB developed a tool for temporary help as well, the Outright Monetary Transactions (OMT), which paired monetary sovereign debt purchases with an ESM program. But the ESM is less powerful than we would suggest. One would have hoped (as we did) that these institutions would be refined and strengthened.

Moreover, Italy refused ESM programs, and Spain only accepted a program with conditionality limited to financial-sector issues. Italy also categorically ruled out using ESM funds in multiple occasions.

Recently, Prime Minister Giorgia Meloni declared that Italy won't access ESM as long as she is prime minister.[24]

A first set of ESM reforms was agreed to in principle in a June 2019 Euro summit. But Italy blocked ratification of ESM reform, most recently in June 2023.[25] Italy was concerned that the reform, although minor, would not just make debt restructuring easier and more orderly, but also more likely. In the words of Banca d'Italia governor Ignazio Visco in 2019, "The small and uncertain benefits of a debt restructuring mechanism must be assessed in the face of the enormous risk that would be taken by introducing it: the mere announcement of such a measure could trigger a perverse spiral of insolvency expectations, likely to be self-fulfilling. We should all bear in mind the terrible consequences that followed the announcement of private sector involvement in the resolution of the Greek crisis after the Deauville meeting at the end of 2010."[26]

This is partly right. The existence of a restructuring possibility *would* make it more likely to be used. With unchanged national policies, it could lead to bond spreads rising in expectation of its use if the alternative option is perpetual ECB support. It could also lead to lower bond spreads if the alternative option is disorderly default. It would mean private-sector losses, as was the case of private sector involvement in Greece in 2012. But if restructuring is off the table, an ESM has no teeth to demand conditionality. And if private parties can never take any losses, if any such losses have "terrible consequences," then we are right back where we started: The ECB must always support sovereign debt and sovereign yield spreads with unlimited purchases using newly created money.

That is pretty much where we are. The ESM seems politically dead or dormant. Efforts to improve it are dead or dormant. Countries such as Italy won't take ESM money, and other governments and the ESM seem less and less able or willing to consider a program with conditionality or investor haircuts. The ECB's new TPI bond-buying framework doesn't include any ESM programs or conditionality.

The ECB will surely try to impose some limits on its bond buying, as it did before, once the disincentives of the current system become clear. However, without a powerful ESM or a similar alternative institution, the ECB will likely still feel that it is the only one that can act to maintain stressed countries' ability to borrow, and to rescue bondholders and banks. But then the ECB alone will have to negotiate fiscal and economic policies with the country in return for help, to initiate any sovereign debt restructuring, and to take responsibility for implied fiscal transfers and re-distributions. The ECB will take the blame for the recession typical of an adjustment period. It will be forced to make judgments on a country's economic and fiscal policies, and thereby on the quality of the country's political leadership. All these actions are political. They are the proper province of elected politicians, not independent central bank technocrats, and they are poison to continued support for an independent ECB.

Stalled Banking Union

As we have emphasized, the fact that banks and other highly leveraged financial institutions hold so much sovereign debt, especially of their own country, adds pressure on the ECB or fiscal authorities to bail out sovereign debt. Sovereign debt needs to be in hands that can bear risk—of eventual default and also of mark-to-market losses when prices decline—and enjoy the corresponding yields.

Banking union, which one would expect to be a natural part of economic union, would help a lot. Banks would diversify their assets. If a bank gets in trouble, recapitalization from international resources would be easier to accomplish. Union-wide resources would stand behind any deposit insurance and efforts to save banks. Deeper banking reforms to undo banks' continual fragility would help as well.

The objectives of the banking union effort were precisely to "sever the vicious link between bank and sovereign fragility," "the restoration of private liability in banking," and to "reinforce the basis for the single market in banking services" (Beck et al., 2022). These aims would be accomplished by establishing a single Europe-wide banking supervisor; by establishing a single, centralized, crisis management and deposit insurance framework; and by reducing concentrated sovereign exposure on bank balance sheets (Bénassy-Quéré et al., 2018).

Sadly, after a short burst of action in 2012–2014, banking union and effective bank regulatory reform remain stalled. Beck et al. (2022) summarize that the banking union is "far from complete. . . . This perpetuates the 'doom loop' between banks and sovereigns. . . . Despite the successful adoption of common rules and standards, pivotal responsibilities in bank crisis management still remain at national level."

The Single Supervisory Mechanism (SSM)[27] was established in November 2014 to create a more effective and harmonized supervisory framework. It delegated various prudential tasks to the European Central Bank (ECB), supported by National Competent Authorities (NCAs) from participating countries. However, the SSM is not entirely "single": While the ECB has overarching authority, national supervisors still report locally, often causing coordination challenges. The ECB oversees 110 significant banks through Joint Supervisory Teams with about 25% ECB staff and conducts on-site inspections with even fewer ECB personnel (around 10%). This dependence on local resources, combined with staffing shortfalls from the national competent authorities relative to their initial commitments, has impeded effective supervision, especially given the additional responsibilities assigned to the SSM in areas like operational resilience, digitalization, and AI.

Less significant institutions remain under national supervision, though in collaboration with the ECB. Cross-border financial integration faces significant regulatory restrictions. Cross-border capital waivers are prohibited, and no liquidity waivers have been granted due to resistance from the national competent authorities, which can use powers outside the prudential domain to block such moves. Similarly, the conversion of international subsidiaries into branches is rare in retail banking, due in part to local deposit insurance schemes and tax considerations, though some international wholesale banks have used this structure. This fragmentation limits the potential economies of scale of cross-border mergers.

International banks remain subject to multiple national regulators and supervisors, as well as the SSM. This can still lead to conflicts between the supervisors of the headquarters country (home) and those of the bank's subsidiaries (host). Home and host supervisors sometimes issue conflicting orders, require duplicate capital and liquidity, and make cross-border mergers inefficient. Host countries fear that home-country supervisors will prefer saving the parent bank to the detriment of foreign subsidiaries. Host countries impede inside-the-bank resource transfers in order to protect local depositors and boost local lending. Both home and host authorities may influence credit allocation of the banks toward their country.

These problems are not the fault of the officials in charge of the Single Supervisory Mechanism. They must apply the existing regulatory and institutional architecture, including the fact that in some cases, they add to rather than substitute for national regulation. But that architecture "is still not powerful enough to offset a national bias that dominates banking sector policy. Most member states still wish to maintain control over their banking systems, limit cross-border exposures to liquidity needs in times of crises, protect national or regional banks against foreign competitors, and leverage their domestic banking systems to facilitate government financing in times of stress" (Beck et al., 2022).

Little effective progress has been made on bank resolution and crisis management. The Bank Recovery and Resolution Directive was designed to make it easier to resolve or shut down failing banks and to impose losses on shareholders and uninsured creditors, rather than taxpayers (Lane, 2021). The Single Resolution Board (SRB) was operational on January 1, 2016.[28] Theoretically, the Board was tasked to decide whether to put a bank in resolution and which resolution tools to use, including financing through the Single Resolution Fund. In practice, this leg of the banking union operated only on paper. The SRB has been reluctant to intervene, leaving individual states responsible for bailing out, recapitalizing, merging, or liquidating their banks. The SRB has not considered middle-sized banks to meet the "public interest" criterion for resolution. The SRB may not be able to resolve very large banks with the resources at its disposal, €66 billion as of July 2022 and a maximum €68 billion from the potential ESM credit line.[29] Member states, afraid of imposing losses on or bailing in bondholders, which is required in order to use Single Resolution Fund financing, are all too happy to avoid European entanglements.

The basic principle that junior debt and shareholder equity take losses (bail-in) before calling on public funds has rarely been applied. A significant exception was Spain's Banco Popular rescue in 2016, which did apply the new Bank Recovery and Resolution Directive rule book. In most other cases, bail-in of uninsured creditors was fully or partly avoided, shifting burdens onto the government and thus taxpayers. Examples include Germany's regional banks NordLB and HSH, Italian banks Monte dei Paschi, Veneto Banca, and Banca Popolare di Vicenza, and the Cyprus Corporative Bank (see Garicano, 2020).

European Deposit Insurance has not seen the light of day. The European Commission made a legislative proposal in 2015 that "would reduce the vulnerability of national deposit guarantee schemes to large local shocks. . . . weakening the link between banks and their national sovereigns."[30] However, the resistance from members of the European Parliament, as well as some member states, ensured that this proposal was never considered in Parliament or at the European Council.

Absent European Deposit Insurance, national deposit guarantee schemes remain liable for banking rescues. The bank-sovereign doom loop remains: In the event of sovereign default or even price decline, banks become insolvent. Deposits are then guaranteed by the same national treasury that is suffering a sovereign debt crisis. And banks can become bigger than the national treasury.

Banks and their regulators likely expect that the ECB will step in to avoid a major financial crisis. In turn, the lack of effective deposit insurance in the event of sovereign debt trouble forces the ECB to intervene. Neither banks nor regulators expect the Single Resolution Mechanism and its Single Resolution Fund to handle the situation.

Exposure of banks to their own sovereign via government securities remains high. In some countries with debt-to-GDP ratios above 100%, sovereign exposures of the national banking systems are around

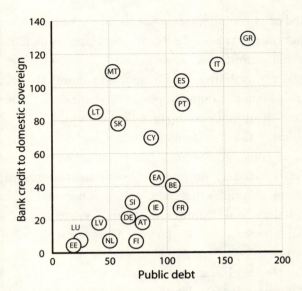

FIGURE 10.2. Bank exposure to the domestic sovereign via government securities versus public debt, Q4 2022. X-axis: percent of GDP. Y-axis: percent of bank CET1 capital. *Source*: Masuch et al. (2023).

100% of bank Common Equity Tier 1 (CET1) capital (see figure 10.2). Averages being averages, some banks are more exposed.

A Eurogroup meeting to set up a road map for a banking union tried to build a package reducing banks' sovereign exposures and introduce European Deposit Insurance. The effort was postponed indefinitely. The Eurogroup could only agree that "Subsequently, we will review the state of the Banking Union and identify possible further measures with regard to the other outstanding elements to strengthen and complete the Banking Union."[31] In sum, European Banking Union has stalled, and thus largely failed in its main objectives other than the nascent Single Supervisory Mechanism. The key factors contributing to the doom loop between banks and sovereigns remain in place: In most bank failures after those in Cyprus in 2013, taxpayers were again burdened and uninsured depositors were made whole.

The European banking market remains fragmented and national. Banks' intra-euro-area exposures actually declined in the decade after the crisis by 24% from 2008 levels. The percentage of euro-area cross-border loans decreased to reach 6% (Schmitz and Tirpák, 2017). A 2022 ECB report argues: "As further domestic and cross-border bank consolidation could help address structurally low profitability and fragmentation in retail credit markets, it should be considered to remove remaining regulatory obstacles."[32]

Stagnation of overall banking reform is a global problem. In the United States, simple reforms to stabilize the Treasury market had not been implemented for years, leading to hiccups in 2019 and such a large dislocation in March 2020 that the Federal Reserve began buying the majority of new Treasury issues (Duffie, 2023). A money market fund bailout, direct lending to state and local governments, and a "whatever it takes" commitment that corporate bond prices shall not fall followed. The Silicon Valley Bank and First Republic Bank failures followed runs that broke out because the banks had invested large uninsured deposits in long-term treasury securities. The latter unsurprisingly fell in value when interest rates rose to fight inflation. These failures showed a regulatory and supervisory system that was unable to manage the most basic risks imaginable. In the United Kingdom, a near-collapse of pension funds borrowing short and lending long treasury debt similarly surprised its central bank. In Switzerland, the failure of Credit Suisse showed that all the promises about orderly resolution, priority of claimants, convertible bonds, shareholder wipeouts, and living wills were empty (on all of these, see Cochrane and Seru, 2024).

Resistance to reform is not surprising. Higher equity to prevent crises and bail-ins and restructuring to address crises will never be popular with investors and financial institutions. Why should banks and investors abandon a system in which they make gains in good times and bear few losses in bad times? Why should banks support a European Deposit Insurance system or a regulatory reform that recognizes that government bonds bear default risk and requires them to issue capital to hold such assets? Deposit insurance will cost premiums, while ex-post bailouts by the state or ECB support are free to banks and their creditors and investors. Why should national banks give up the protection that national regulators provide, and why should national politicians and regulators give up the benefits of national banks whose credit they can direct and who provide willing customers for their national debts?

10.4   Balance Sheet and Market Footprint

While the ECB managed to almost fully unwind its large lending to banks between early 2022 and mid-2024, the ECB's bond portfolio has been declining only very gradually. Unwinding a large central bank balance sheet is hard. Stemming expectations of swift and largely unconstrained asset purchases in any market turmoil is harder.

The balance sheet blurs the line between fiscal and monetary policy. In a March 2, 2023 speech entitled "Quantitative Tightening: Rationale and Market Impact," ECB Board member Isabel Schnabel argued that "The size of our balance sheet should only be as large as necessary to ensure sufficient liquidity provision and effectively steer short-term interest rates towards levels that are consistent with price stability over the medium term."[33]

Balance Sheet and Monetary Policy

The original operating procedures of the ECB were designed to "make the policy stance effective while at the same time leaving a minimal imprint on the financial system" (Borio, 2023, p. 2). To accomplish this objective, the ECB was to set interest rates as follows, according to the ECB's own description:

Our primary monetary policy instrument is the set of ECB policy rates. The Governing Council of the ECB sets three rates:

1. The interest rate on the main refinancing operations. In these operations banks can borrow funds from the ECB against collateral on a weekly basis at a pre-determined interest rate.
2. The rate on the deposit facility, which banks may use to make overnight deposits at a pre-set rate lower than the main refinancing operations rate.

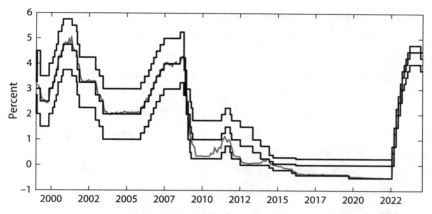

FIGURE 10.3. ECB policy rates. Lower line: Deposit Facility Rate. Middle line: Main Refinancing Operation (weekly loans). Upper line: Marginal Lending Facility (overnight). Gray line: Euro Overnight Index Average rate.

3. The rate on the marginal lending facility, which offers overnight credit to banks at a pre-set interest rate above the main refinancing operations rate.

The rate on the deposit facility and the rate on the marginal lending facility define a floor and a ceiling for the overnight interest rate at which banks lend to each other. This creates an interest rate corridor for money markets.[34]

This corridor system permits a certain variation in interest rates, reflecting market forces, but it also ensures that interest rates are broadly anchored.

With a small balance sheet and banks holding few low-interest deposits, market interest rates were driven primarily by the refinancing rate, as that was the more active margin. Figure 10.3 plots the ECB rates with the Euro Overnight Index Average (OEIR) rate.

The system's functioning started to change in autumn 2009. Desiring stimulus, the ECB started lending to banks at fixed rates with full allotment. It changed further with the start of Quantitative Easing under the Asset Purchase Program in October 2014. The expansion in reserves, which are much larger than reserve requirements, meant that the return on reserves must equal market rates for banks to hold them. (See table 3.1 and figure 3.2 for the expansion of reserves.) Market interest rates descended toward the ECB's deposit facility rate.[35] The corridor system, which was effectively a ceiling system, became a floor system. The relevant margin for a bank was no longer borrowing from the ECB to make a new loan or purchase a security, but lending abundant deposits to the ECB versus lending to private parties.

There are two important and separate elements of the current balance sheet and operating procedures: Abundant interest-paying reserves (bank deposits at the ECB) and full allotment lending to banks, against wide collateral. Abundant reserves can be supported by asset purchases alone, as they are in the United States, which has very little central bank lending.

Abundant Reserves. There are good arguments that, with the lessons of this experience in mind, a balance sheet that provides ample reserves with a deposit rate equal to market risk-free rates is overall a good thing from a monetary policy perspective. The economy can live the Friedman (1969) optimal quantity of money, awash in liquidity, wasting no time on cash management, and spared from creating run-prone private substitutes for interest-paying money. Money is oil in the car of the economy, and monetary oil is free to create. Don't try to slow a car by draining oil.

In this view, the QE era provided a decisive natural experiment on a long-standing and deep question of monetary theory: Can a regime with a fixed interest rate, no interest spread between money and bonds, and satiated in reserves persist without stoking inflation? Even Friedman, the inventor of the eponymous optimal quantity of money, did not argue for its implementation, especially via a fixed (zero) interest rate target and an endogenous supply of reserves. (Reserves are huge via asset purchases, and endogenous via full allotment ECB lending, which essentially implements a real bills doctrine.) Friedman, in keeping with standard monetary doctrine before 2008, thought that such a regime could not control the price level. He preached money supply control instead. Even admitting an interest rate target, standard doctrine held that reserves must be small, via zero interest on reserves or a substantial interest rate penalty. If the economy ever hit zero interest rates, this was feared to be a "liquidity trap," in which deflation would soon spiral out of control. Interest-paying reserves generate the same liquidity-trap mechanism.

A decade of ample reserves in the United States and Europe, and three decades in Japan, show that this analysis is false. The analysis was plausible. Before our central banks tried the experiment, nobody knew. But it turns out that inflation is surprisingly steady under the ample reserves regime, with central bankers reduced to worrying about decimal points (e.g., 1.7% versus 2% inflation), which their predecessors would have thought was close enough. Of all the alleged causes of the 2021 inflation surge, nobody has blamed ample reserves. Of all the alleged causes of inflation's easing, nobody has praised a return to scarce reserves because that has not happened. (See Cochrane, 2023a, and works cited therein on the view expressed in the last two paragraphs.)

To create ample reserves, however, the ECB must either purchase assets or lend to banks. The downsides of the ECB's ample reserves regime are largely concentrated on these operations.

Assets. Most obviously, as we have emphasized, large asset holdings put default risk on the central bank balance sheet, with important fiscal implications. In 2022, the Eurosystem's outright holdings of euro-area government bonds amounted to about one-third of all outstanding government bonds. Large asset holdings represent credit allocation to some borrowers over others, a form of fiscal policy. Large holdings of long-term assets mean that interest rate rises cause losses for the central bank. The latter two intersect: Interest rate rises that imperil asset issuers may cause default losses as well. Large purchases of long-term government bonds effectively shorten the maturity structure of government debt, meaning that costs of interest rate changes spread more quickly to government finances. Figure 10.4 tracks the ECB's increasing footprint in sovereign debt markets. Sooner or later, large asset purchases will attract political pressure to allocate credit toward favored regions or industries.

Loans to Banks. ECB lending to banks, in fixed-rate full-allotment loans and against a wide range of collateral, creates a different set of concerns.

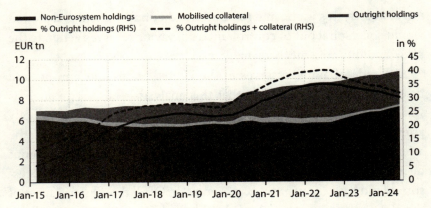

FIGURE 10.4. Eurosystem footprint in euro-area sovereign bond markets.
Source: Schnabel (2023). "Outright holdings" refers to European government
bonds held by the Eurosystem, adjusted by the amount of bonds loaned back to
the market via securities lending against cash. "Mobilized collateral" includes
European government bonds used as collateral for open market operations.
APP: Asset Purchase Program; PEPP: Pandemic Emergency Purchase Program.

Borrowing from the ECB has largely displaced the private unsecured inter-bank funding market (González-Páramo, 2011). A bank
that needs funds no longer borrows from another bank or financial
institution, but from the ECB instead. The ECB has used the term
"favorable" rates. This means that for many banks, such ECB loans are
cheaper than borrowing from the market. The shrinkage of the interbank market would also take time to reverse, as Borio (2023, p. 6)
points out: "The damage is long-lasting. If you don't use a muscle, it
atrophies. Desks are dismantled. Institutional memory withers."

Information provided by the unsecured interbank market has largely
disappeared. All banks face the same funding costs when borrowing
from the ECB, where riskier banks faced higher funding costs in private markets. These costs may have provided a useful market signal to
the bank and to bank supervisors.

However, this is a small addition to a longstanding problem of current banking practices and regulation. On the introduction of deposit
insurance, depositors no longer took any interest in bank risk, and
both the ability to attract deposits and the rates paid lost usefulness as

market signals. Widespread bailouts and extreme reluctance of regulators and the ECB to allow creditor losses further remove default risk from interest rates on loans to banks. The whole point of overnight borrowing, especially with collateral, is that counterparties pay little attention to risk because they can always exit the next day. Gorton and Metrick (2012) refer to debt, and especially collateralized overnight borrowing, as informationally insensitive. It is designed precisely *not* to require any risk assessment by lenders. Lehman Brothers was borrowing overnight right up to the day that it failed. We expect oversight, information production, and market prices revealing of information in prices of *equity* and subordinated bank bonds, not overnight lending rates. For that reason, among others, robust markets for bank stocks and bonds are vital. Strangely, central bank officials and regulators who bemoan the lack of market information in overnight lending rates often seem to distrust the information value of the market that is designed to trade on information: equities. Capital requirements reference the book value of equity, not market value, throwing out a valuable source of information about bank health.

The loosening of collateral requirements for ECB lending introduces important additional distortions. Collateral requirements were loosened in the financial and sovereign debt crises, as described previously, to encourage banks to borrow and invest in riskier assets. Like many programs, this collateral policy was initially understood as temporary, but it became permanent.

The looser collateral requirements mean that banks can use significant amounts of risky and non-marketable collateral to borrow from the ECB. Unlike private lenders, the lending rate does not depend on the collateral quality. The ECB ends up subsidizing riskier banks to invest in riskier securities or loans. This is exactly the ECB's intent in crisis times. But it is an undesirable market distortion in regular times. It is also another fiscal implication of monetary policy, especially given the reluctance of all European institutions to allow banks to fail.

When ECB Board member Isabel Schnabel explained and supported the new operational framework, she also was clear about some of the risks:

[The lower] the spread between the rate banks pay for borrowing reserves and the remuneration they receive when depositing these reserves back with the central bank . . . the greater the incentive for banks to obtain liquidity primarily through the central bank. But . . . discouraging banks from seeking market-based funding solutions may be undesirable as it risks weakening the resilience of the banking system and may go against the principle of an open market economy.

These risks are especially high when banks have access to longer-term refinancing operations and are permitted to pledge non-marketable assets as collateral.

Since excess reserves count towards the fulfilment of prudential liquidity ratios, the combination of a very low cost of carry and a broad collateral framework encourages banks to engage in excessive liquidity transformation, as they receive Level 1 high-quality liquid assets (HQLA) by pledging non-HQLA as collateral.

Buy a risky bond. Pledge it as collateral against a low-cost loan. Leave the money as deposits at the ECB, at an interest rate that almost covers the loan. Now count the deposits as HQLA. The appearance of "liquidity" is created at nearly zero cost.

In the first half of 2023, before banks began repaying their TLTRO loans, non-HQLA accounted for about 80% of collateral with the Eurosystem.[36]

Some of these unintended consequences could be remedied fairly simply. If the ECB wishes to continue to allow low-grade or non-marketable collateral, it can adjust the lending rate to reflect the collateral quality.

In sum, once again, "where we are" in the Eurosystem is a long way from where we started, including a large balance sheet, abundant reserves, liberalized lending, and different operating procedures. While abundant reserves and a corridor system for interest rate control are in principle a sound operating procedure, the specifics of the ECB's implementation creates unintended consequences: Deposit rates above (risk adjusted) market rates are a subsidy to banks, as other institutions cannot access them. Full-allotment loans at fixed rates and against weak (i.e., non-marketable) collateral subsidize weak banks and weak debt.

This change blurs the distinction between Emergency Liquidity Assistance lending and regular monetary policy operations. Both now allow weak collateral. Supervisors may have less leverage to strengthen weak banks.

Asset purchases to prop up market rates subsidize issuers and bondholders. Borrowing and then depositing at the ECB can be an arbitrage, or a way to synthesize illusory liquidity.

Most of these provisions were implemented as temporary expedients to support banks and banks' investments in crises or the zero-bound era. But they now have, or are expected to, become permanent parts of the ECB's toolkit.

In the rest of this book we have emphasized the obvious dangers of the ECB's large holdings of risky assets and the expectations that it will buy such assets or subsidize banks to do so in any period of market trouble. Here, we summarize a whole laundry list of additional concerns with the large balance sheet. Many of these are still debated, so we summarize arguments on both sides without taking a stand, but just to highlight issues that need attention.

10.5 The ECB and the Balance of Payments

The ECB continues to finance the balance of payments, via Target2 balances. Such financing otherwise would come from markets or from a crisis management institution such as the IMF or the ESM. Figure 10.5 shows the history of Target2 balances for selected countries.

As explained in section 3.7 of chapter 3, the rapid rise of Target2 balances to finance trade deficits and capital flows was an unintended consequence of the move to ample reserves and easier lending. We see that the balances were small before those policies took form in the early 2010s. Target2 balances increased in the debt crisis, and then improved somewhat. They improved even more in the four countries

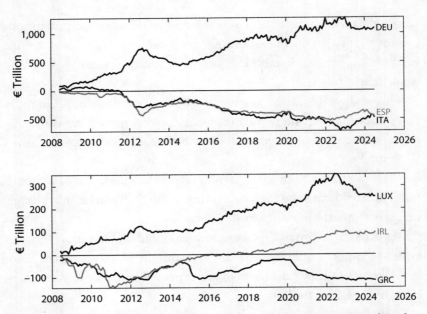

FIGURE 10.5. Target2 balances, end of month. *Source*: European Central Bank, "Data Categories," https://data.ecb.europa.eu/data/data-categories.

(see chapter 5) for which EU/IMF financial assistance and adjustment programs helped to address the underlying fiscal and financial problems and reverse the capital outflow. However, Target2 balances then steadily increased, as a result of large-scale asset purchase programs, ECB loans to banks at favorable conditions, and persistent trade deficits or capital outflows. Target2 debts decreased somewhat when the ECB withdrew the bulk of its large-scale lending to banks under its TLTRO programs in 2023. Germany and Luxembourg are the mirror image of Italy and Spain, accumulating Target2 credits.

Ireland's Target2 balances are smaller because its economy is smaller, but the pattern is interesting. Ireland also accumulated a large debt during its sovereign debt crisis, around 100% of annual GDP in late 2010. But Ireland then turned around and became a creditor, both as a result of solving its economic problems and as the rescue package substituted fiscal for monetary balance of payment support.

Eisenschmidt, Kedan, and Schmitz (2022) analyze carefully the source of Target2 balances:

Prior to the financial crisis, when liquidity conditions in the euro area were neutral and TARGET balances were small, very large flows in the other BoP [balance of payments] components—partly stemming from current account deficits, but mainly from private financial flows—were observed without notable changes in TARGET balances. . . .

During the sovereign debt crisis, a substantial part of the liquidity provided by the Eurosystem to banks in TARGET liability countries was used for external transactions related to the current account deficits and the collapse in private financial inflows, thereby leading to an increase in TARGET liabilities. Correspondingly, the euro area countries with the largest TARGET claims (Germany, Luxembourg and the Netherlands) received foreign inflows, while recording a surplus in the current account.

As of November 2024, Target2 balances remain large. The highest Target2 debts are recorded in Spain (€435 billion), Italy (€429 billion), France (€177 billion), and Greece (€106 billion), while large target claims are in Germany (€1,067 billion), Luxembourg (€238 billion), Ireland (€90 billion), and Belgium (€73 billion).

The ECB continues to play a large role in financing the balance of payments. In a currency union, direct bond buying has a balance of payments effect. When buying Italian bonds, the ECB provides euros that allow Italy to keep importing goods and that allow investors to (for instance) buy German rather than hold Italian securities. In a crisis, supporting the balance of payments is much of the point of the intervention, to avoid a "sudden stop." But crisis interventions tend to become permanent.

And here we are. This is obviously a situation that needs reconsideration and reform.

Some short-term ECB financing of balance of payment outflows can be helpful. The point of monetary policy and a central bank, after all, is that prices and wages are not completely flexible, nominal events spill to real events, and there are crises in which central bank liquidity is an important ingredient. When there is a temporary liquidity issue or a sharp downturn, having the central bank lend resources that allow a slower response is consistent with the rest of the philosophy of central banking.

However, the Target2 mechanism, largely an unintended consequence of operating procedures and operating on autopilot, is not well suited for temporary balance-of-payments support. As liquidity and lender of last resort functions are conscious operations using (hopefully) well-crafted institutions, so should be balance of payments support. And as central banks lend rather than send gifts, balance of payments support needs to unwind swiftly.

When a country suffers a debt or rollover crisis, as in the European sovereign debt crisis, reflecting poor fiscal and structural policies, fiscal transfers with conditionality also provide balance of payments support and do a better job of controlling incentives. They should take over as soon as they can.

As always, interventions that stop prices and interest from moving muffle the market signals that lead to economic equilibrium. For example, banks could in principle offer higher interest rates or reduce their risks to stop outflows. But they have a reduced incentive to do so, as they can borrow new money from the ECB at a lower rate than from the market. Some argue that it is the task of the ECB to always ensure a level playing field among euro-area banks, and different interest rates in different countries amount to "fragmentation." However, this view neglects the fact that higher rates paid by weaker banks or sovereigns are often a normal feature and a useful price signal, as one would expect from "an open market economy with free competition, favoring an efficient allocation of resources." The price of strawberries is not the same in every market from Finland to Sicily, and there is no reason that counterparty risks and thus interest rates should be the same either.

Persistent capital outflows and trade deficits, or a drying up of capital inflows and foreign investment, are either desirable features of dynamic economies, or they reflect persistent, country-specific weaknesses that require national fiscal, financial-sector, and structural policy interventions, not perpetual central bank support. Even when international pressure for policy reform in the form of conditionality, in exchange for temporary balance of payment support, is wise, that job is better suited to fiscal authorities, not the ECB.

To be clear, the ECB is quite properly involved in managing cross-border payments, and nothing in principle is wrong with the Target2 system. The problem is the accumulation of balances that provide permanent balance-of-payments financing in place of private capital markets.

Importantly, the ECB's involvement in financing the balance of payments of individual countries would remain, even in the hypothetical case without national central banks. In this case, the accounting system would no longer show Target2 loans from the ECB to national central banks and vice versa. However, the ECB could still replace private cross-border capital flows with its balance sheet, if it provides sufficient loans to banks at favorable conditions and/or helps to keep risk premia, and thus yields on bank bonds, interbank lending, or sovereign bonds, below the market yields that would result without such central bank interventions.

11

Reform Proposals

The main goal of the euro should remain that it is a stable common currency, facilitating European trade, markets, finance, and economic integration. We retain the philosophy that member states retain sovereignty over most fiscal and economic policies, rather than call for greater union. We suggest reforms consistent with that view.

The initial vision of an independent central bank, whose main mandate is price stability, with an effective separation between monetary and fiscal policy, is still the best way to accomplish this goal, along with fiscal and financial institutions that insulate against demands for monetary intervention. This was the fundamental philosophy of the Maastricht Treaty, and it is desirable in all standard views of monetary policy. The challenge is how to implement that institutional framework, given what we have learned from the sequence of crises and in light of the ad hoc expedients that have morphed into a new institutional framework in that time.

A comprehensive reform and redesign package is needed. Most elements interlock, each supporting the others. We outline our ideas in this chapter.

Underlying most reforms, the ECB must be unburdened from problems surrounding sovereign debt. Options for orderly sovereign default and debt restructuring need to be created. The sovereign-bank nexus needs to be resolved so that banks and financial systems do not continue as hostages against bond losses. Euro-area governments, individually and collectively, must take responsibility for national debt problems. We outline the structure of a European fiscal and political institution that can provide temporary fiscal assistance and impose conditionality to resolve debt crises.

A group of fourteen French and German economists (Bénassy-Quéré et al., 2018) argues for "creating the economic, legal and institutional underpinnings for orderly sovereign-debt restructuring of countries whose solvency cannot be restored through conditional crisis lending. First and foremost, this requires reducing the economic and financial disruptions from debt restructuring—by reducing the exposure of banks to individual sovereigns . . . and by creating better stabilisation tools and a euro area safe asset. . . . In addition, orderly and credible debt restructuring requires . . . ESM policies and procedures that provide an effective commitment not to bail out countries with unsustainable debts." Brunnermeier et al. (2016) call for the creation of a "European safe asset" from tranched portfolios of euro-area sovereign bonds.

Precommitments for the ECB *not* to act must also be strengthened, in part so that governments, banks, and investors do not just sit back and wait for the ECB to jump in and try to solve problems. The ECB should continue to provide adequate reserves, but any ECB purchases of sovereign debt to that effect should be sharply limited to keep default risk off its balance sheet, as we describe later in this chapter. Monetary policy loans to banks must be based on high-quality marketable collateral.

These reforms, taken together, would dramatically reduce the severity of debt crises, and likely their frequency as well. Restructuring initially might happen a bit more often, but restructuring would not create a crisis. The reforms would therefore reduce the demands on the ECB or fiscal authorities to jump in with rule-stretching interventions.

In past crises, the ECB and the euro-area member states felt strong pressure to act from fear of contagion, that any default or restructuring in a relatively small country such as Greece could lead to crises in other larger countries such as Italy or lead to a financial meltdown worse than 2008. But what is "contagion"? As we argued, if investors expect ECB or EU intervention to ensure that sovereign bonds never default, news that Greek bonds might be allowed to default would surely affect Italian or Spanish bonds. If some banks are loaded with Greek debt, then news that Greek bonds might be allowed to default would spread to trouble at those banks.

Once one states any sensible meaning of "contagion," one can see that our reform proposals, acting together, would reduce or eliminate it. With a credible and well-known resolution process and a European authority using it to offer temporary support subject to conditionality, nothing that happens in Greece needs to affect expectations about what will happen in Italy. Once a regime is in place, actions no longer redefine a new regime. With sovereign debt in hands that can bear price drops or restructuring losses, sovereign defaults no longer threaten systemic financial failures.

However, words like "contagion," "systemic risk," "dysfunction," "disorderly," and so forth are too often used and too seldom defined. They scare people, perhaps intentionally, rather than calm the waters of a crisis. They offer a false aura of technocratic understanding and control. We also advocate a conscious use of more transparent language. It is not a crisis if somebody, somewhere, loses some money.[1]

We close this chapter with some political-economy observations. A thoroughgoing reform is feasible, and now is the time to achieve it. The ECB may object to having a diminished role, but the diminished role will actually preserve the ECB's ability to fulfill its core mission. Reforms can take time, and one may argue for sequencing. But any delay allows time for renegotiation and for pieces to fail without their supporting parts. Conversely, each of our reforms helps on its own, makes the others work better, and increases incentives for authorities to pursue the others, so sequencing and delay are not even theoretically valuable. We favor quick and unified action.

11.1   A European Fiscal Institution

One can imagine two extreme visions for a currency union. In one, national governments can default just as companies do. In the other, fiscal rules are so stringent and well enforced by internal or external pressures that no country ever gets in trouble.

We think that a middle road is more practical. Pretending to take one extreme, as the initial design of the euro did, is likely to lead quickly to exception after exception. On this middle road, default, haircuts, and restructuring can happen, in a well-organized structure and without bank failure or systemic financial failure. Fiscal rules and institutions motivate member states to better fiscal and structural policies. But there is also a strong European *fiscal* and, yes, political institution that offers temporary financial and balance-of-payments support in crisis, with conditionality. This institution can purchase national sovereign bonds, issuing its own debt in exchange, and it can provide guarantees to the ECB. Any ECB involvement can then be highly limited and temporary to smooth over genuine market disruption.

Why? Sovereign default, like corporate bankruptcy, is never clear cut. There is a muddy middle ground between repay and default, between insolvency and illiquidity. Bankruptcy typically involves reorganization, not liquidation. Similarly, a government having trouble rolling over its debt or selling new debt may well recover if debt holders wait a while and take some small losses, and if new funds can support the government while it puts reforms in place. Moreover, forcing all claims to wait stops a run, in which investors and depositors try to grab assets or get paid first while they can.

Temporary financing as provided by the IMF or the ESM is analogous to debtor-in-possession financing in corporate bankruptcy, which allows firms to continue operating while bankruptcy arrangements and a reorganization are worked out. IMF rescue packages involve similar (hopefully) temporary senior financing arrangements; new borrowing supports operations and is paid back before old claims.

Here especially, it is better to have institutions, with procedures, pre-committments, and hard limitations on what they will not do worked out ahead of time rather than make it up and negotiate who will lose what with interested parties in the heat of crisis. Bankruptcy follows seniority rules among claimants.

One might so far think that temporary help could come from fiscal or monetary sources, and the crisis-management institution could be a central bank, as central banks often host financial regulators that resolve banks. There are, however, important practical reasons why a independent and limited central bank of a currency union such as the ECB should not be in charge of sovereign rescue. Some of this "temporary" financing ends up being permanent, especially if the effort fails. It also amounts to fiscal transfers from the rest of the EU to the country in trouble and its bondholders. Diagnosing and addressing the structural and fiscal causes of debt troubles, deciding the criteria for help or its denial, deciding what politically painful steps a country must take to obtain help, enforcing and (inevitably) renegotiating those steps, deciding how much debt restructuring takes place and who takes losses, and offering the resources of other member states' taxpayers are all fiscal and political decisions.

An institution regularly making such decisions—not just once in an extreme, unforeseeable crisis—should *not* enjoy far-reaching independence but rather the mandate and accountability that only the participation and assent of elected representatives confers. If the central bank starts making such political decisions, it cannot remain independent for long. Contrariwise, fear of being blamed for making deeply political decisions may bias the central bank toward bailing everyone out, never forcefully demanding conditionality, and never abandoning an aid program.

Thus, a common euro-area fiscal and political institution, with the necessary tools, powers, and sufficient capital provided by member states, and with the participation of political leaders, should be fully in charge of crisis management. This institution could be a much enhanced and revitalized version of the European Stability Machanism (ESM). It could also be a new institution, constructed with the lessons of the ESM in view. It could be enshrined in the Treaty or constructed by intergovernmental arrangement, as is the ESM. It could have more or less responsibility for union-level fiscal policy more generally, while still functioning as a sovereign debt crisis management mechanism. On one hand, it can be useful for the crisis management institution to also be the institution that monitors and enforces debt and deficit limits. That way, the institution knows countries' finances in great detail. On the other hand, such a joint institution may hesitate to enforce deficit or economic policy conditionality for fear of making a crisis worse. If the institution is structured like the ESM, with representatives such as euro-area finance ministers giving approval, it must be able to make swift decisions with qualified majority, not requiring unanimity.

For brevity and with all these possibilities in mind, we will call it a European Fiscal Institution, and we invent a new acronym for it: EFI.

Once European banking union and coordinated European bank regulation have been established, the EFI could also be involved in the financing of any government-based recapitalization of large pan-European banks, after sufficient creditor bail-ins. Government-financed recapitalizations, as happened in 2007–2008 and afterward, are contentious, and we do not take sides on that debate here. We just point out that if such policies are going to be pursued for large pan-European banks, a European fiscal and political institution is needed, and the EFI is a logical choice.

How much fiscal help should the institution offer, and what should the nature of that help be? What rules and procedures should be set up ahead of time to guide and limit the institution's activities? What is its mandate? It's really up to member states and voters to decide how much fiscal integration they desire at this point. We suggest rules consistent with the founding philosophy of the EU, which maintains national fiscal sovereignty and frowns on fiscal transfers, especially for countries that have overborrowed and enacted poor economic policies.

The EFI, like the ESM, admittedly violates the strict interpretation of the no-bailout philosophy of the euro's founding. But it should follow a philosophy of "as little bail-out as possible." It should not fund perpetual deficits. If the EU is going to issue common debt to finance regular spending of member states, including infrastructure or climate initiatives or social spending, such activities need to be separate from crisis financing. The institution must be able to say no at some point. All insurance invites moral hazard, and the EFI's mandate and operations should be designed to contain that moral hazard toward governments and bondholders as much as possible.

The standard rules should apply: only help a solvent government, diagnose why markets worry about solvency, insist on a reform program to restore solvency, monitor compliance, and so forth. The EFI rules should insist that loans are loans and actually repaid, not slowly becoming gifts over time via gradual extension of maturities, Official Sector Involvement, reductions in interest rates, and so forth. Those rules exist for a purpose, not for their own sake, so that governments feel the incentive to fix their fiscal situations and avoid crises in the first place rather than rely too much on repeated emergency funding. The fiscal institution must be able to stop what has happened to the ECB, a slide toward ever-increasing support for member-state debts in each event, as some member states become more fragile each time.

Thus, assistance will require the establishment and assessment of criteria for eligibility and the definition, negotiation, imposition, and monitoring of conditionality that includes fiscal and microeconomic reforms. A powerful common fiscal institution that does regular country surveillance, has access to all necessary country information, assesses and monitors program conditionality, and is committed to pay attention is important for this effort to work. It is also important that such new monies are actually spent in growth-enhancing activities, and not mainly to make existing bondholders whole or to continue the sorts of ineffective spending that got countries in to trouble in the first place. Fiscal and balance-of-payments adjustments should be quick, and EFI support temporary.

Just what the beneficiary state will do with temporary fiscal assistance bears close attention and monitoring. In our view, spending should be quick and narrowly focused on the most vulnerable and on avoiding widespread business failure, as well as keeping the narrowest of financial commitments that avoid a financial crisis. Subsidies should be cut quickly. Time to adjust often means time to renegotiate. While productivity-enhancing public investments are in principle a good idea, governments in fiscal trouble don't have a good history of making public investments that actually raise productivity in the horizon of a few years. Spending for Keynesian fiscal stimulus is likely to be unwise. Stimulus, general social spending, and infrastructure can quickly turn into perpetual subsidies preserving inefficient activities. The point is for the government to make the necessary reforms and adjustments as quickly as possible. The EFI is there to stop the debt crisis, not to delay economic and financial adjustment. Covid-era fiscal transfers did not by and large hew to these principles, and the IMF has moved to greater emphasis on climate, social spending, and inequality reduction in the policies that it requires for support. However, these are political decisions of what the EU taxpayer is willing to support. This consideration is the reason that the EFI must be politically accountable and not pretend to technocratic independence.

In the likely case the stressed member state is assessed as solvent, perhaps with reforms, but markets are not convinced and still charge high risk premiums, legacy debt's higher risk premia must not spill over to the yields on new borrowing. New EFI loans must not bail out existing debt. The EFI should thus provide any new loans or purchase bonds with seniority in any eventual haircut or restructuring. As precedent, T-Bills issued in the Greek crisis were exempted from the debt restructuring and haircuts in Greece in 2012. The package should also typically include restructuring or "bail-in" as early as possible, before principal on short-term debt must be paid, denying bailout to existing debt holders. Moral hazard does not just lie with governments that borrow too much, but also with the bondholders that lend them too much while expecting a bailout. The EFI should have the power to require prolongation of maturities of outstanding government debt, for example, or rolling over legacy debt to new long-term debt with a low coupon.

It's always important to distinguish whether the country or its creditors are being helped. Rescue packages tend to confuse this issue. For helping the country, the key issue is to give it access to *new* financing while debt problems are worked out, *not* to prop up the prices of legacy debt, and thus the wealth of legacy bondholders. Here, the introduction of an EFI with crisis-management powers intersects with removing sovereign risk from the banking system or other institutions viewed as too "systemically important" to bear losses.

Buying legacy debt, if done at all, should be done only at large discounts. Doing so helps to protect the balance sheet and credibility of the EFI and to strengthen incentives of all parties involved. This is diametrically different from what central bank asset purchase programs, including the SMP in 2010–2011 and the TPI today, normally aim at, namely, pushing up existing bond prices so as to lower yields on both outstanding and new debt. The ECB has different aims and views, expressed as protecting "monetary policy transmission," and addressing "dysfunctional" markets for existing long-term debt, and under the shadow of an unreformed sovereign-bank nexus. The ECB is not well placed to deliver successful fiscal crisis management.

If the adjustment program is successful, the EFI could give some of the profits it makes on having bought legacy debt at low prices back to the stressed country, thereby supporting incentives for strong implementation of the adjustment policies. Allowing legacy bond prices to fall and then to rise if the adjustment is successful also gives debt holders an incentive to stay invested or indeed offer more support. By contrast, propping up legacy bond prices gives their holders an incentive to sell as quickly as possible while the price support is in place. It also encourages them to press for public support. Price supports seem to put out the fire, but in fact they fan the flames. Your fire sale is my buying opportunity. More generally, the habit of central banks to prop up prices in times of turmoil front-runs the pools of capital that can provide liquidity in times of stress, thereby drying up those pools and making the financial system more fragile.

One should never make threats that one cannot or will not make good on. If the country refuses conditionality, the EFI should be prepared to reduce or stop its fiscal support, rely on greater restructuring of existing debt, and allow the country to face a rapid fiscal and balance-of-payments adjustment. If government and bondholders refuse restructuring, it is not credible to then offer only disorderly default. A quick but orderly default needs to be a viable possibility.

Where is all this money to come from? To be credible, the EFI needs firepower sufficient to rescue the largest state in the union, if need be, and people must know it has that firepower. Any limit is sure to be tested. At a minimum, if limits are politically necessary, they should be larger. Ex-ante contributions in the form of capital are not likely to be large enough. The EFI should be able to request funds from member states, which includes requiring them to borrow to provide funds. Alternatively, or as well, the EFI should be able to issue bonds, joint liabilities of the member states or liabilities of the EU that come with EU taxing power—Eurobonds. The EFI could even issue Eurobonds, with the understanding that it has thereby mutualized the default risk and the mandate to do so. We describe Eurobonds next, and we advocate that the ECB can buy Eurobonds. In this way, the ECB can contribute to crisis management, but without taking on the stressed country's default risk or making the intensely political decisions that crisis management entails.

A central bank, in charge of monetary policy, has an advantage as crisis-quelling lender of last resort. If a central bank wants to declare that it will do "whatever it takes" to stop nominal default by printing money, there is indeed no limit to what it can do. But a currency union without fiscal union cannot rely on that power. The EFI must *not* have the authority to create euros or to monetize its debts with direct sales to the ECB at non-market prices. It must be limited to deploying fiscal transfers or selling debt that carries the clear fiscal backing of the member states. The EFI cannot have such an unlimited capacity, but it should not have preannounced limits. The EFI must at least have a flexible capacity to ask member states for more help if the crisis demands it. Limits have been useful to get countries to participate, but a successful crisis management institution must be able to credibly threaten to do "whatever it takes" if the situation demonstrably demands more.

11.2 European Bonds

Financial market innovation, including various flavors of Eurobond, have been widely suggested. They can help to improve monetary policy and avoid unintended monetary-fiscal interactions. Eventually focusing or limiting ECB asset purchases to such bonds, in place of individual issues of sovereign debt, is one of those improvements.

One flavor of Eurobond is simply an institution that issues bonds backed by a diversified portfolio of euro-area sovereign debt. That can be a private institution such as a floating-value fund. Such bonds would already be useful as an easy way for small and less sophisticated banks to diversify sovereign debt portfolios. More deeply, they would allow Europeans to hold diversified risky sovereign debt directly and more easily rather than through a fragile and leveraged banking system. If individual Europeans as well as long-run institutions like insurance and pension funds could easily access such funds, banks could more easily get out (or be forced out) of the business of holding sovereign debt, especially concentrated sovereign debt, and restructuring or mark-to-market price declines would cease to threaten financial stability. Other funds could focus on high-yield debt for those with a greater appetite for risk.

Stronger concepts of Eurobonds are claims on the collective rather than individual fiscal surpluses of the union. Such bonds are backed by EU tax revenues or by collective pledges of member states to back the bonds with a high priority. They also include legal guarantees of repayment of both principal and interest. Such Eurobonds can include bonds issued by supranational European authorities, such as the EU Commission, the European Stability Mechanism or a new European Fiscal Institution. Eurobonds could also be claims issued against a diversified portfolio of sovereign debt, but with an additional explicit credit guarantee from the EU or member states collectively. They could be formed out of tranches of a portfolio of sovereign debt, with only the safest (most senior) tranche guaranteed. However, simplicity and wide appeal are important, such that Eurobonds have a deep and liquid market, less prone to "dysfunction," whether real or perceived.

When Eurobonds are created and have developed a sufficiently liquid market, the ECB could move its asset purchases to Eurobonds and eventually limit its asset purchases to such bonds. In turn, such ECB purchases would help to create a liquid market, as central banks have done since the 1600s.

If the ECB were to gradually move to holding Eurobonds as an asset, that would go a long way toward precommitting against ECB intervention in member-state sovereign debt, it would mitigate sovereign risks threatening European inflation; and it would mitigate the incentive for countries to count on a specific bailout. If the Eurobonds are not guaranteed by the EU or member states, the ECB would still hold some default risk. But such risk would be limited if the ECB held only the most senior tranche. If Eurobonds collect sovereign debts, a capital-key-weighted, guaranteed portfolio is ideal for the ECB. But perfection need not stand in the way of improvement.

We have called euros issued by the ECB "Eurobonds" somewhat informally, as they are in the end backed by collective fiscal surpluses. But they actually are not Eurobonds, in that they carry no legal guarantee of interest or principal repayment, the ECB has no solid legal basis to demand recapitalization from collective member states, they are limited in maturity, and only banks can hold them. A central bank can inflate away its obligations. Eurobond issuers such as the EFI cannot.

We have discussed extensively the longer-term risks of current practices and expectations: they discourage fiscal responsibility from member states and risk management from bondholders and regulators. They enable disproportionate support to more indebted nations. They limit the incentives for EU policymakers to make necessary institutional reforms. Additionally, they strain the credibility, political neutrality, and independence of the ECB. Purchases are perceived by many people to contribute to financing government deficits in a way that contravenes the EU's treaty provisions against monetary financing. (This is not our view, however.)

And the ECB may need to impose conditionality in return for its rescues, telling countries what taxes, spending, and microeconomic reforms it must follow—all highly political actions. Restricting the ECB's bond purchases to securities issued by European authorities, with the explicit fiscal backing of EU or member-state fiscal resources, addresses these concerns effectively.

With a EFI in place to take care of crises and a financial system immunized against sovereign default, the ECB no longer needs to feel that it is the only game in town to support individual sovereigns. The ECB could still provide support in a deep crisis of specific member states, but only indirectly via purchasing (ideally short-term) bonds issued by the new EFI, and if it receives guarantees from member states that protect it against losses related to materialisation of default and interest rate risks on new bond holdings. Such guarantees would protect the capital of the ECB, and importantly, avoid creating additional fiscal risks by providing windfall gains to private investors holding outstanding bonds.

The ECB could then keep the quantitative easing and yield curve management tool of bond purchases, if it wishes to do so, by buying Eurobonds or lending to banks against Eurobond collateral. It thereby could address monetary transmission through long-term interest rates and by maintaining a liquid and well-functioning market for long-term debt. Likewise, purchases to provide (more) reserves, such as in the context of a structural portfolio, are ideally made with Eurobonds.

However, the ECB will lose the power to intervene in particular sovereign debt markets, even if there genuinely is "illiquidity," "market dysfunction," "fragmentation," or other market ills, and somehow rising yields in a particular country's sovereign debt markets impair the "transmission" of monetary policy.

However, remember the context: There is also an EFI to handle sovereign debt problems, which can include market disruption. Europe has also solved the nexus of sovereign debt and financial stability, so if "transmission" really means to "keep banks afloat," the ECB no longer need worry about that. Again, the pieces fit together.

So, in that context, is interference in markets for outstanding individual-country sovereign debt really a necessary part of monetary policy? Recall that, in the conventional view of monetary policy, the central bank sets the short-term rate of interest, but the central bank does not manage or interfere in stock and bond markets at all. Trying to influence long-term yields was only introduced at, and due to, the zero bound, and whether it did any good overall is still contentious. The view that any central bank's mandate, which includes tools as well as objectives, includes detailed supervision and micromanagement of all asset markets, including sovereign debt, corporate debt, and perhaps next equities, is fairly radical. Indeed, one might object even to Eurobond purchases that are made with an eye toward managing the Eurobond yield curve.

Our view is no. The European Central Bank should not intervene, sovereign debt markets should be left alone, especially with an alternative more appropriate institution in place to handle underlying fiscal problems, with banks removed from the line of fire, and given our skepticism over how objectively verifiable the remaining stories of "dysfunction," as opposed to "fundamentals" are, and how easy it is to cloak quasi-fiscal sovereign debt support in those stories. In our proposal, the ECB forswears such interventions.

The pieces of the puzzle fit together. Eurobonds, a European Fiscal Institution, banking reform, and restrictions on ECB intervention are each helpful alone, but each supports the functioning and incentive to pursue the others. For example, while an EFI has not been implemented, credible limits on ECB interventions give governments the incentive to face rather than postpone the hard choices between default, cross-country transfers, and conditional programs, without the hope that monetary policy will buy them time.

There is currently no permanent joint Eurobond issuance program in place. In the interim, the ECB could return to buying sovereign debt only in proportion to capital key.

11.3 ECB Lending: Banks and Target2

We do not object to the basics of the ECB's new operating procedures: ample reserves that pay interest, full-allocation lending to banks against collateral, interest rate control through a corridor system enforced by relatively tight lower and upper bounds. Others wish to return to scarce reserves, no interest on reserves, and limited lending. In this case, reserves would be a much smaller part of bank assets, and interbank lending or money markets would be a much more important part of bank funding. We do not rehash the pros and cons here. In our reform program, either operating procedures would work.

However, borrowing from the ECB went too far. Banks were able to post low-quality, non-marketable collateral, which amounted to a subsidy for banks.

The answer is straightforward. Except in a severe, systemic, Europe-wide crisis, the ECB should no longer provide large-scale subsidized loans to banks. Outside a major systemic banking crisis, the ECB should no longer accept non-marketable or low-quality debt as collateral for monetary policy operations. These could only be used for Emergency Liquidity Assistance.

Bank reforms dovetail with this ECB reform. Euro-area banks should have sufficient capital buffers, liquidity, and strong risk management, such that they that can finance riskier lending via the inter-bank and repo markets or by issuing equity and bank bonds. It is not inconsistent with a corridor system that funding from the ECB at the upper corridor risk-free rate must have risk-free collateral (and perhaps limited to banks with an excellent risk profile), while higher rates prevail in private markets, which take riskier collateral. Yes, the cost of capital will be higher for riskier investments, as it should be. Only when those funding markets are genuinely inoperative in a major crisis should the ECB lend at low rates against weaker collateral. And afterward, this time, bank regulation should address the inadequate capital and long-term financing plus regulatory errors that caused such a crisis so it doesn't happen again and again.

Similarly, the Eurosystem must gradually reduce the stock of Target2 loans from the ECB to national central banks, and ensure that the combination of the Target2 system and ECB operating procedures do not again inadvertently and indirectly end up permanently financing large amounts of net imports or net private capital outflows. Temporary Target2 loans are a natural function of the ECB in managing the European payment system, but trade financing and private capital flows should soon be settled by the exchange of securities. One mechanism to achieve this would be a gradual increase in the interest rate that the debtor's central banks has to pay on its Target2 liabilities to the ECB. The interest rate could also increase with the size and duration of the Target2 balances. The resulting ECB profits would be redistributed to national central banks according to the capital key.

11.4 Restructuring

An orderly sovereign debt restructuring, rather than chaotic default or euro exit, which includes default, needs to be a realistic option. By and large, countries in trouble should reform in order to fully repay their debts. Frequent default makes it hard to borrow in the first place. But, as formalized in Lucas-Stokey state-contingent defaults, very rarely burdening investors rather than imposing crushing tax rates or truly economy-destroying spending cuts is an appropriate policy. Prompt restructuring or creditor bail-ins should be part of EFI crisis management, as discussed earlier in this chapter. If European taxpayers are going to pitch in, so should bondholders. A deeper restructuring, an orderly default, needs to remain a viable plan B in case the country does not accept conditionality or later abandons it.

The essence of the currency union is that member states abandon the option to inflate away debt, which is a default in real terms. There must be a mechanism, then, by which a government in sufficient fiscal trouble can default in nominal terms and bondholders bear losses. Default or restructuring must be orderly without creating economic and political chaos. Sovereign debt must become like corporate debt. The alternatives, unlimited transfers or monetization, could eventually tear the union apart. High sovereign yields of countries that appear likely to default or to default too often are important market signals for the country to improve its finances. Yes, it would be nice if countries obeyed debt and deficit rules and never got in trouble. But never is a long time. The main lesson of the sovereign debt crisis is that even a rare danger needs a plan. Even a supposedly unsinkable ship needs lifeboats. Not surprisingly, then, several economists developed proposals for a sovereign debt default mechanism in the euro area. (See, for example, Gianviti et al., 2010, and Bénassy-Quéré et al., 2018.)

Again, the pieces interlock. For restructuring to be credible, debt must be held by investors who can bear losses in return for the higher yields that they reap when losses do not materialize. Highly leveraged, systemically important banks are obviously poor candidates to hold large portfolios of risky sovereign debt, especially in undiversified concentrated form. Banking reform and restructuring reform go hand in hand. Again, though, rather than each piece having to wait for the others, they form mutually beneficial reform incentives. If restructuring and default are on the table, bank risk managers and bank regulators cannot go on pretending that sovereign debt is risk free.

It is unwise to try to invent orderly restructuring on the fly in the middle of a crisis. This was also the lesson of the 2008 financial crisis. It is much better for markets, bondholders, and financial regulators to understand the regime, the nature of the losses that they will occasionally bear, which categories of debt are paid in what order, and what rights each has in the event of trouble. Such a predictable regime discourages discretion and politics from decisions over who suffers billions of losses. And it blunts the incentive for banks and other private institutions to be, or appear to be, the most systemically dangerous, and thus most in need of protection. And it allows prompt restructuring, cutting short the efforts of claimants to run and get their money out while they can.

Restructuring must be a preplanned, structured, and transparent process. Corporate bankruptcy follows such a process. IMF rescue plans are more discretionary, but over time they developed into a somewhat predictable regime. It must be clear who is in charge and what their powers are, and that must be an existing institution, not something like an ad hoc meeting of finance ministers. A reformed and strengthened ESM or a new EFI is our answer. Plans for upfront debt restructuring should be developed and published by the EFI. The options include debt write-downs, restructuring (exchange of short-term debt for low-interest, longer-maturity debt or debt with contingent payments). Such options need to be spelled out and operationalized ahead of time.

In the European case, a single sovereign bankruptcy mechanism may be superior. A single mechanism would better define the rules and may avoid some of the known pitfalls of the current market-based approach. Not all debt is bonded debt; not all bonded debt instruments have the same terms; seniority structure is unclear; and debt is issued under different legal umbrellas, giving different rights to bondholders. Such a change might require a treaty change, however, as well as supporting legislation.

Most crises come when short-term debt must be rolled over, not when the country is unable to pay coupons on long-term debt, or tries to borrow and is unable to do so. A forced maturity extension or rollover into long-term debt is one way to address the crisis. Yes, it is a mark-to-market loss for bondholders, but it helps to avoid the element of runs that many crises involve.

Long-term debt can also be restructured into debt that requires lower interest payments or lower short-term payments balanced by higher long-term payments. The back-loaded interest rates can be quite good, and if the plan succeeds, bondholders eventually end up making money. Restructuring can include something like equity securities, such as GDP-linked bonds and something like capital calls. "Default" is not as simple as lenders not getting their money back! In many ways, in a successful restructuring that includes default, lenders invest a bit of their wealth in the reform rather than trying to run away with other people's money.

Restructuring must happen swiftly. Muddling through and fully paying back debt that matures in the meantime with financial assistance funds, as happened in Greece from spring 2010 until March 2012, let those short-term debt holders off the hook, concentrating losses on everyone else. In turn, expectation that short-term debt holders will be able to get out leads to an incentive to issue, buy, and hold short-term debt.

Moreover, uncertainty makes crises worse. In a long period in which people are uncertain how and when a crisis will be solved—with orderly default inside the union, with an exit, and the chaotic defaults that redenomination implies, or muddling through with large increases of income and wealth taxes—they will try to sell immediately and they will try to get assets out of the country, and they will stop investing in the country.

A successful reform program must also change expectations, and to do that adopt a more concrete and realistic language in describing policy. Sovereign restructuring has been considered anathema, with a vague but widely accepted assertion that it would be an unthinkable economic calamity for anyone to suffer a write-down of bond values. ECB monetary or EU fiscal support for repaying outstanding debt in place of restructuring is described as "rescuing" the country and its citizens. It primarily rescues creditors. Creditors have been too successful in threatening everyone else with calamity and misdirecting the perception of who benefits from support.

Some economists (e.g., Tabellini, 2018) fear that taking steps to make sovereign debt restructuring easier would increase the likelihood of it happening. That would increase debt financing costs, increase market volatility as the probability of restructuring comes and goes, and hence make a debt crisis more likely. This concern is certainly true, relative to a world in which a fiscal or monetary bailout will always come to repay debt or even to quash rising sovereign spreads. But that world is no longer tenable. It is certainly true, relative to a world in which fiscal rules and fear of costs of disorderly default drive governments to be so responsible that they never get even close to trouble. But that illusion fell apart in the sovereign debt crisis. It is certainly true that in the midst of a crisis, announcing that bondholders, who expected fiscal or monetary rescue, may have to bear unspecified haircuts at some unspecified time in the future will induce them to run even faster. But that does not apply to a long-anticipated and well-considered institutional reform. And the restructuring mechanism comes with the introduction of the EFI for temporary support and banking reform, not all by itself. Moreover, a credible option of orderly debt restructuring inside the euro area would decrease the probability of disorderly default, a country leaving the euro, or chaotic interventions. This is a major benefit.

11.5 Sovereign Debt

Reforms to the structure of sovereign debt would substantially alleviate crises and improve markets.

First, long-term government debt is broadly preferable to short-term debt. When a government issues short-term debt, which it then must roll over, it opens itself up to several dangers. If interest rates rise, the government must pay higher interest costs on the debt. General interest rates may rise, and the government's interest rates or spread may rise even more. If people get worried about default, they demand a higher rate to roll over debt, and that higher rate raises interest costs, and pushes the government closer to default. Dysfunction or other market hiccups other than default premiums could start the process. Even if this feedback loop does not go all the way to the economic theorists' multiple equilibrium, it amplifies any crisis. The rollover may simply fail, with investors refusing to buy new bonds. A government financed by short-term debt, whose corresponding asset is decades of eventual fiscal surpluses, is very much like a bank financing illiquid risky assets with deposits and short-term debt, which is open to a run-like failure.

Long-term debt alleviates all of these problems. When a government issues long-term debt, its interest payments are locked in. Spreads may rise and markets may malfunction, but interest rate changes have no significant effect on the government's interest costs. Only new borrowing is affected. Without rollover, there can be no rollover crisis. Governments may still have trouble with new borrowing and be forced to adjust fiscal policies quickly. Governments may suffer a crisis, threatening default or restructuring when big principal payments become due. But that could be alleviated by issuing interest-only debt, with no principal, or perpetuities.

Why do governments issue short-term debt at all, then? Because it's often cheaper. Long-term debt buys a lot of insurance, and its higher yield is the insurance premium. Not buying insurance is cheaper, until the house burns down. The effect can be substantial. If the long rate is 2% and the short rate is 1%, borrowing long doubles interest costs, as long as short rates stay low. Moreover, locking in interest costs loses the option to benefit if interest rates decline, as they did throughout the 2010s.

The current regime provides disincentives to issue long-term debt. Why pay a premium to lock in debt costs and prevent a run if the ECB, EU, or other member states will come to the rescue? Indeed, by exposing themselves to runs, countries make it more likely that they will be rescued.

Thus, a European Financial Institution, or whatever EU institutions will manage sovereign crises and implement debt and deficit rules, should require that countries fund themselves primarily with long-term debt. The *maturity structure* of debt is as important to debt sustainability as its *quantity*. Sustainability means the ability to repay, but it also means the ability to avoid debt crises along the way. Currently, crisis interventions largely let short-term debt get repaid and long-term debt get resolved. That should be turned around; short-term debt should bear the brunt of prompt restructuring, to remove the incentive for investors to buy it.

Additional refinements would help. Long-term floating-rate debt is at least better than short-term debt in that it does not explicitly have to be rolled over. It is easier to pause payments on long-term debt, which is precisely why ready-to-run investors prefer short-term debt. Long-term debt that pays a variable rate tied to the ECB policy rate or other rates independent of country risks can protect the government against a doom loop or issue-specific dysfunction, while allowing rises and falls in general European rates to flow through. Indexed debt allows the government and bondholders to protect against unexpected inflation and deflation. GDP-linked debt is an ever-popular idea among economists to create an equity-like government security, in which the government is protected against economic downturns by sharing in the bounty of good times. It automatically restructures itself in recessions. Governments that wish to protect themselves from interest rate rises but benefit from interest rate declines can easily issue variable-rate debt with a cap on the interest rate. Governments can protect themselves against a wide variety of risks via interest rate swaps.

None of this is difficult financial engineering, and most of these securities have existed for decades in private debt markets. The EU has a role to play, potentially through the new EFI, however. It is easier to issue standardized securities in a thick market than to hope for individual countries each to reinvent the wheel.

Diversified portfolios of eurozone sovereign debt would be quite useful for individuals, institutions, and banks. Eurobonds backed by individual sovereign bonds or mutual funds could serve that purpose.

Sovereign debt is different from private debt in that sovereign debt does not include collateral, or other assets or income streams that creditors can seize in bankruptcy. That need not be the case. Many debts historically were funded by specific revenue streams, not general obligations. Much U.S. municipal debt is still so backed. That protection goes both ways: If a specific tax stream fails, the bonds can default without dragging down the entire issuing entity. Conversely, bondholders can often seize the specific stream—tolls on a bridge, say—if the city as a whole goes bankrupt. When it is admitted that sovereigns can default, bond investors may start to demand better protection against default in these ways, or by demanding the right to seize assets.

The European system of sovereign debts evolved with sovereigns that issued their own currency and would thereby usually avoid explicit default. The precommitment not to inflate under the common currency naturally changes the desirable structure of debt from that previous regime. By presuming that sovereign debt can never default under a common currency, the EU inadvertently squashed this natural institutional evolution.

11.6 Breaking the Sovereign-Bank Nexus

Fear that banks and other financial institutions might fail, or just lose enough that they contract credit, has been a constant impetus for quick bailouts, fear of restructuring, squashing yield spreads, and forsaking previous efforts to commit against intervention. In turn, the expectation of intervention leads banks and regulators to choose fragile but profitable operations. It's essential to cure banks as hostages.

We emphasize two central steps here. First, bank exposure to concentrated sovereign risk must be reduced. Second, the Single Resolution Board should be reformed to reduce sovereigns' exposure to banks. These are elements of the long-languishing need to establish a banking union, comparable to the common market in other goods and services. Garicano (2020) discusses the issues in more detail.

Sovereign Debt Exposure

One can start with the simplest reform of all: Recognize throughout banking regulation, accounting, and ECB procedures that sovereign debt is risky, just like corporate debt. A monetary union without fiscal union requires the possibility of sovereign default. Amazingly, after all we have been through, sovereign debt still carries no risk weight in financial regulation and incurs no capital requirement in banking regulation.

If individual bonds carry zero risk weight, that means that concentrated positions in one country's sovereign debt are counted as having no more risk—zero—than a diversified portfolio of sovereign debts. Consequently, banks have an obvious incentive to load up on sovereign debt, rather than equivalent corporate debt or household and corporate lending, and to load up on the sovereign debt of one country, either to chase yields or to please regulators.

If regulations introduced risk weights, which trigger capital and liquidity requirements, and required more capital and liquidity for less diversified portfolios, that step alone would reduce bank demand for sovereign debt. It also would force bank risk managers and regulators to demand diversified portfolios of sovereign debt.

Obviously, one wants higher risk weights for riskier debt. Regulators are loath to use market prices (yield spreads) to measure risk. One might introduce risk weights based on the credit ratings of sovereign bonds. However, credit ratings in the past have often reacted too late, but then too sharply. Many of the assets that failed spectacularly in 2008 had good credit ratings right up to the moment of default.

More deeply, it would seem simple for regulators to notice portfolios of concentrated sovereign exposures and tell banks to do something about it. But it would also seem simple for regulators to notice portfolios with large interest rate exposure and do something about that. The Silicon Valley Bank failure does not boost confidence.

Véron (2017) presents a detailed proposal for Sovereign Concentration Charges Regulation as new EU legislation. Véron proposes zero risk weight for sovereign exposures up to 33% of Tier 1 capital, and increasing risk weights for exposures beyond this limit, rising steeply for holdings above 100% of Tier 1 capital. He proposes a multiplicative "sovereign concentration charge" for overly concentrated portfolios.

Large European banks operate with about 17% Tier 1 capital to risk weighted assets. Total assets are about three times risk weighted assets, however, so banks operate with about 6% Tier 1 capital to total assets. Therefore, Véron's capital charge would apply when a bank holds sovereign debt above 2% of its assets. To a bank, this may appear a stringent requirement. But it forces us to face reality. Even small concentrated sovereign debt investments put banks' capital at risk. A bank with 6% capital to total assets and 6% of its assets invested in a sovereign's debt would be wiped out by default. Under Véron's proposal, a bank with 6% capital and 2% in a single sovereign would get a strong signal not to increase this concentration risk further.

To the inevitable howls of complaint from banks, we counter, What's so terrible about equity? A capital requirement does not say that "you may not hold more than 33% of Tier 1 capital of sovereign debt." It says, "Hold all the sovereign debt you want, but you must fund large sovereign debt investments in part by issuing equity or retaining earnings, not by borrowing money and forcing us to bail you out if the risk goes bad. And more so for risky, high-yield debt." The underlying principle, again, is that sovereign debt must be held in a form and by institutions that can bear default and mark-to-market losses. Equity financing can. Short-term debt financing cannot. Banks that hold large sovereign debt portfolios funded with equity pose no risk to the financial system, though their shareholders may argue otherwise.

Banks in general are overleveraged, and overdependent on government support in bad times. The regulatory juggernaut that attempts to control risks is creaky. Supervisors are slow to react to bank troubles, and bail-ins by uninsured depositors and other creditors too rare and too late. Supervisors often do not declare banks "failing or likely to fail" before most of the liabilities that could be bailed in have flown out.

A move to much more equity and long-term debt financing for risky bank investments would solve many of these problems. But less ambitious reforms can also help. As with other grander schemes, we limit ourselves here to the smallest necessary changes.

The possibility that different countries face different risk weights is also politically contentions. Several European countries do not accept in principle any proposal that discriminates between different countries' debt. They claim that it would lead to market "fragmentation," a term also used by the ECB to describe differences in yields, and another example of how obfuscatory language has permeated discussion of euro affairs. In reality, countries worry, correctly in the short term, that without the ability to sell debt to their own banks at zero risk weight, and without the implicit subsidy that bailouts and spread-compressing purchases add, markets for risky debt would be smaller and countries' financing costs higher.

Garicano (2020) suggests that risk supervision should start based on a European "Safe Portfolio." Banks' capital charges would then rise according to how far their sovereign portfolio deviates from that diversified safe portfolio. The Safe Portfolio could be modeled after the ECB's capital contribution key. Garicano suggests that in calculating the safe portfolio, future cash flows should be discounted at the risk free rate (e.g., the OIS rate). Otherwise, when a country's risk premium rises, its bond prices fall, and banks could be forced to buy more of their bonds. Alternatively, a bit less precisely but more transparently, bonds could be included at their face value or historical cost rather than their market value.

This proposal has the advantage of reducing exposure to the domestic sovereign, while maintaining overall demand for sovereign issuances from lower-rated countries. It would force diversification. It would not imply any ex-ante discrimination between different countries' debt, such as based on ratings. It would also facilitate the path toward a European safe asset.

To avoid banks making diversified but highly leveraged sovereign debt investments, there should naturally also be limits or capital charges on the overall position and interest-rate risk of sovereign bonds.

There are more detailed proposals, including by Brunnermeier et al. (2016), who propose that banks' sovereign bond holdings should consist of the senior tranche of a well-diversified portfolio of sovereign debts. This proposal would create a Europe-wide "safe asset" by virtue of its seniority and diversification.

Who will buy and hold sovereign debt, if not banks? This question gets to the heart of member states' concerns over risk weights, banking union, and other measures designed to get concentrated sovereign debt off banks' balance sheets. The general answer: Sovereign debt should be held by people and financial institutions that can bear to suffer losses in default or restructuring, can bear to suffer mark-to-market losses if yields rise temporarily, can bear occasional bouts of illiquidity or market dysfunction without needing instant ECB intervention, and are ready to earn the nice yields that banks currently earn in return. There are plenty of such institutions and potential institutions. People can hold diversified portfolios of sovereign debt through mutual funds and exchange-traded funds. Pension funds, insurance companies, sovereign wealth funds, and similar international investors have a long-term horizon, are not leveraged, and do not cause financial crises when they lose some asset value or must wait a few days to sell. Banks should lend to people and businesses, not funnel deposits to sovereign debt markets. Europe is surprisingly undeveloped financially in this regard. Individuals can easily hold mutual funds that hold sovereign debt, and by doing so they would earn a lot more interest than in bank accounts. In the end, people hold sovereign debt and its risks in one way or another. The only question is through which intermediaries, and the cost of that intermediation process.

The goal is clear and simple. Banks and other institutions, which the ECB and EU officials regard as systemically important and unable to bear losses, must not have large or concentrated positions in sovereign debt. That goal can be achieved by a variety of means, of which we outline only a few. Detailed regulatory proposals to reach that end face political opposition and practical challenges. But that practical elaboration and discussion needs to happen, and a sustainable system needs to be created.

Banking Union

Completing a banking union, as Europe has completed the single market in most other areas, would be a central step to eliminating the sovereign-bank nexus. Several concrete steps could get that process moving again.

First, the Public Interest Assessment applied by the Single Resolution Board (SRB) to determine when the European Resolution framework should apply, must be clarified to cover all European financial institutions requiring substantial funds for resolution. Current standards for banks to be in the European public's interest are too stringent. The assessment should be clarified and broadened to cover all banks operating in more than one member state and all Single Supervisory Mechanism (SSM)-supervised banks.

Second, the SRB needs adequate funds and recourse to additional funds if needed. Midsized banks that rely on depositor funding could be helped by providing the SRB with coordination powers over national Deposit Guarantee Schemes (DGS).

Third, to ensure the SRB has sufficient funds to resolve banks and national DGSs and regulators cooperate, European Deposit Insurance should be implemented. This scheme would consist of national deposit guarantee schemes and a European central fund. The contributions to this fund would be risk-based to ensure fairness, address moral hazard, and avoid regulatory arbitrage. A strict rule needs to ensure that deposit guarantee funds must be used only to protect insured deposits, and only after bail-in of shareholders, bondholders, and other non-insured creditors has been applied. Regulators and central bankers are always tempted to extend deposit insurance ex post. The extension of deposit insurance to all uninsured deposits in the SIlicon Valley and First Republic runs is a recent example of this temptation.

11.7 Emergency Liquidity Assistance and Money Creation

Emergency Liquidity Assistance (ELA) is the Eurosystem's lender of last resort program for banks.[2] It aims to "provide central bank money to solvent financial institutions that are facing temporary liquidity problems, outside of normal Eurosystem monetary policy operations." ELA is conducted by the national central banks but provides fresh new euros. The ECB explains:

ELA occurs when a Eurosystem national central bank (hereinafter an "NCB") provides:

a. central bank money and/or
b. any other assistance that may lead to an increase in central bank money to a financial institution or a group of financial institutions facing liquidity problems.[3]

Emergency Liquidity Assistance should become an ECB task and no longer remain a national task. This change would allow the Governing Council of the ECB to develop a single and clear procedure for the whole euro area. It would answer the question of how ELA is provided to multinational European banks. The ECB is also better positioned to insist that banks that need ELA face consistent incentives to quickly take action, such as by issuing new shares, selling assets, cutting dividends to increase capital buffers, or imposing other conditions to ensure that ELA loans remain temporary and are swiftly repaid. Finally, the Governing Council of the ECB needs to be in charge of money creation.

National central banks also retain the power to create new money to purchase assets, so long as the purchases are "non-monetary" "national" tasks; that is, not intended to change the Euosystem's monetary policy. The Governing Council of the ECB can reject such actions only by a two-thirds majority. But printing money to buy assets has monetary effects, no matter the intent.

One can understand why this right was retained during the formation of the euro. Countries joining the euro likely wished to maintain flexibility in view of the natural uncertainty about the functioning of the new currency, to preserve some of their legacy operations, and to smooth the transition from a national to a single monetary policy. They did not want to instantly transfer all their legacy assets to the new central ECB. But arrangements to handle legacy assets and a transition are not ideal 25 years later. Likewise, one can understand that member states had a preference for maintaining their own national central banks rather than closing up shop and sending all operations to the single ECB, in parallel to their desire to maintain national-level banking regulation. They may have wished to retain some powers, such as to make national lender of last resort loans to domestic banks, to buy securities, and to create profits that are remitted to national treasuries.

One can also understand that such a structure was not highly objectionable in the era before a large-scale financial crisis, a large sovereign debt crisis, the move to ample reserves and full-allocation lending, and large sovereign debt purchases.

Some reform efforts have occurred, notably the agreement between the national central banks and the ECB on net financial assets (ANFA).[4] This agreement defines an overall limit to the total amount of money creation by an national central banks relating to national, non-monetary policy tasks.

Clearly, it is time to revisit the relation between national central banks and the ECB.

One option would be to merge the national central banks into a new, single ECB with a single, large balance sheet. The national central banks would play a role similar to the one of U.S. regional Federal Reserve banks. But this step is not necessary. It would also be a complex and politically risky operation that might require a treaty change.

The main objective of a new agreement between the ECB (in a narrow sense) and the national central banks should be to ensure that new money creation can happen only in relation to monetary-policy decisions or ECB-decided Emergency Liquidity Assistance and thus it is an exclusive competence of the Governing Council of the ECB. "New" allows the maintenance of a fixed, small amount per NCB, largely reflecting legacy assets. NCBs would continue to perform the decentralized implementation of monetary operations, but they would not conduct substantial "non-monetary" transactions as "national tasks" financed by new euros.

Ideally, foreign reserves and gold and the related revaluation accounts would be redefined as being related to monetary policy. They would be kept on national central bank balance sheets, and realized profits and losses would continue to accrue to the respective NCB and be rebated to the national treasuries. But monetary policy operations are decided by the Governing Council of the ECB, not the national central bank. When a national central bank desires to purchase an asset rather than creating new euros, it should borrow the euros from the central ECB. It can accrue a temporary Target2 balance for that purpose.

However, in line with our reform of Target2 balances, it must swiftly sell another asset to reduce its Target2 balance.

National fiscal tasks should be the province of national fiscal, not monetary, institutions. The other existing "non-monetary" balance-sheet items of NCBs would be shifted to these institutions. As we propose the creation of a European fiscal institution to take on fiscal tasks now implicit in ECB actions, countries could establish national fiscal institutions that take on the buying and selling of financial assets, but without the ability to create new euros. Alternatively, these can simply be functions of the existing fiscal institution, the national treasury.

These reforms would mitigate the current blurred separation between the single monetary policy and "national tasks" and thus the possibility that national central banks can finance "national tasks" with money creation. This reform would ensure that significant money creation can happen only in relation to the single monetary policy and is an exclusive competence of the Governing Council of the ECB.

11.8 Monetary Policy

This is a book about fiscal/monetary interactions, so we have avoided the many questions surrounding the conduct of monetary policy. They are important but separate issues.

A few issues of monetary policy interact with our central focus, however. As mentioned previously, the ECB explains its announcement of sovereign debt purchases under TPI, designed to reduce spreads on long-term sovereign debt, as necessary to address "fragmentation" or "dysfunction" in markets, and thereby to preserve "monetary policy transmission" toward the single goal of price stability. Earlier large-scale QE purchases were undertaken to lower the spread between long- and short-term bonds. Previously, we were a bit critical of these justifications, but here let us take them at face value.

However, even if such actions are taken with the purest of monetary policy motives, they still have fiscal policy and moral hazard consequences. Buying lots of sovereign debt and reducing its spreads cannot avoid fiscal consequences. And, as long as such programs and motives are in place, given the impossibility of distinguishing "dysfunc-tioning" markets from fundamental forces in real time, they will lead to interventions that subsidize sovereign debt and bond investors.

So, how necessary are these elements of purely *monetary* policy? In the beginning, the ECB, like other central banks, also limited itself to a single tool—the short-term interest rate—and let other markets do what they may. Is it really necessary, in order for a central bank to influence the price level, to monitor and frequently intervene in long-term debt markets, moving toward direct control of several long-term and risky interest rates, not just the overnight risk-free rate? Are mar-kets so perpetually fragile and dysfunctional that a permanent central bank intervention program must wait in the wings? If so, what are the structural reasons for such dysfunction? Should they not instead be understood and fixed?

Even if a particular market, such as the high-risk sovereign debt mar-ket, is "dysfunctional," how does that impede "transmission" of mone-tary policy? What is the channel from the ECB's lending and borrowing rate to saving and investment decisions in the private euro-area econ-omy, and then to inflation, that runs through the spread in secondary market for, say, long-term Italian bonds over German bonds? Indeed, in the event that motivated TPI, the ECB raised rates and wished long rates to rise. But Italian rates were rising *more* than the ECB wished. Is that not even more effective "transmission" of the ECB's desire to soften the economy, rather than too little?

Some observers think that the ECB and other central banks should swiftly stop QE asset purchases and yield-curve management, regard-ing these as measures restricted to a return of zero bound and deflation threats. Others go further, suggesting that once the crisis was over, addi-tional stimulus at the zero bound was and is unneccessary, and the ECB should have stopped worrying about inflation a few decimal points below 2%. Among others, Hall and Kudlyak (2024) estimate that the slow decline of unemployment in the 2010s reflected simply a slow decline of natural unemployment due to the search-and-matching nature of the labor market. With stable inflation within a few decimal points of the target, they note, it is an inevitable implication that the output and employment gap were near zero the whole time. (Stable π_t and $\pi_t = \beta E_t \pi_{t+1} + \kappa x_t$ implies $x_t = 0$.) In this view, central banks could well permanently forswear asset purchases and yield curve management as part of monetary policy. Cochrane (2023a) argues that inflation is stable at the zero bound in modern theory. The history of inflation at the zero bound around the world, especially Japan, confirms that theory. No deflation spiral ever broke out. In this view, the great fear of deflation was misplaced. Massive QE that did not bring inflation back to target also suggests that QE is ineffective. Trillions of euros, and we're arguing about basis points?

Monetary policy, like bailouts and many other policies, tends to enshrine whatever expedients were tried in the last tumult as holy writ, so long as the outcome was not evidently disastrous. While this is a natural habit for institutions under constant political criticism, it is not a habit that we external analysts should indulge in as often as we do. Sometimes a reconsideration should find that expedients of the last crisis were ineffective. Or, as we argue throughout this book, they created bad long-term incentives.

A return to using only the short-term rate as policy instrument, forswearing attempts to directly influence long-term and risky asset prices by purchases, would have a great benefit in committing to a separation between monetary and fiscal policies.

Despite our evident doubts, we leave these as questions needing discussion. If the ECB is going to regularly diagnose bond market "fragmentation" and then intervene to produce asset prices it likes via large-scale asset purchases, then monetary policy will have important fiscal and incentive spillovers that will be much harder to contain. Our main point is to point out these costs of such interventions. Both the necessity for this kind of policy and its costs bear much more skeptical analysis than they get today.

11.9 Political Feasibility

Which reforms should come first? With multiple reforms, some more contentious than others, the question of sequencing always comes up.

As we have explained, the reforms work as a package. In our view, an attempt to plan a protracted sequencing seems unwise. Getting sovereign debt out of banks allows authorities to restructure sovereign debt; allowing the restructuring of sovereign debt wakes up regulators and risk managers to get sovereign debt out of banks; and so forth. Each reform helps on its own, however, and does not require the others for it to help. So there is neither any reason to delay reform until the whole package can be implemented, nor reason to intentionally delay any element of the package. Moreover, each reform increases the incentive to adopt the others, so they build on each other politically as well as economically. Delay and sequencing, while frequent playthings of economic reformers, also neglect a central political reality: Any delay is a chance for renegotiation.

However, a fully functional reform of the euro requires the implementation of all the reforms we propose here. They should be understood as a package, not a shopping list of alternatives. Selling them as a package that should be implemented simultaneously, even if some end up taking a bit longer than others, offers the best chance of success.

In our view as non-lawyers, our core proposals do not require a change in the Maastricht Treaty. They therefore can be implemented swiftly and without the political headache of Treaty changes.

A larger discussion is taking place over Treaty changes that shift sovereignty over important economic policies, public spending, and taxation from national governments and parliaments to the EU government and parliament, along with changes to the structure of the EU and its parliament to render them more responsive and effective. Some proposals argue for permanent cross-border fiscal risk sharing and include substantially greater taxes imposed by the EU to finance EU-level spending and to repay European bonds. Our reforms would easily be integrated into such a program. But such programs require important changes to the Maastricht Treaty and the entire foundational structure of the EU and EMU.

Such Treaty changes are contentious, to say the least. Europe is, as we write, hardly in the spirit of greater integration that prevailed in the 1990s, nor are those who complain to revert about "Brussels" yet in a spirit to constructively reform and expand EU authority rather than simply reverting to greater national authority.

Europe cannot afford to wait to fix the euro for a program of deeper integration and reform, meanwhile pretending and muddling through. The next crisis may well arrive before a comprehensive Treaty change can be effected.

In the other direction, some readers may criticize our reforms as being too ambitious, and point to political constraints. They may regard the current arrangements as second-best or third-best, given those constraints. Some may say that we are where we are. Some may argue that the ECB is effectively the only feasible common *fiscal* institution, able to swiftly issue common euro debt (in form of interest-paying bank reserves), as well as money. It is the only one that can promptly and effectively buy sovereign debt and support banks, thereby helping member states to finance potential urgent European priorities (yesterday Covid, tomorrow perhaps national defense). Others may argue that some member states will never accept a change in banking regulation that reduces the influence of national authorities over their banks, nor will they accept sovereign debt restructuring in a large country. And of course many banks, bond investors, and other private parties benefit from the current system—at least until it blows up.

We do not deny that reforms may be politically difficult. But it is nihilistic to say that we cannot even think about reforms, in spite of the problems of the current system, because powerful interests may oppose them. Obviously, if we had found an easier set of reforms that would actually work, we would have advocated them. So the alternative is to do nothing and wait for the ultimate crisis, in which the system crashes.

Right now, the public and most commenters do not seem to understand just how unsustainable the present course is. Our intended audience is them, and perhaps you. It does no good to just try to whisper into the ears of politicians or bureaucrats. Our job as economists is to inform the public, as well as politicians and policy makers, that the current situation is not sustainable, that large economic and social costs will eventually result without decisive institutional reforms today, and to describe simple, achievable, and effective reforms. Economists should ignore the temptation to disregard unpleasant elephants in the room, constrain their proposals to patches that they know will not work, based on an armchair view of current political realities, or to try to appeal to political constituencies.

Once the public and commentators, as well as fellow economists, officials, and policymakers understand just how unsustainable the present track is, and that a simple set of reforms can fix them, they will demand change. What was previously politically unfeasible can quickly become politically unstoppable. If nobody ever describes the promised land, but only argues over whether we should turn right or left at the next bush in the desert, we will surely never get there. The euro and European union were politically difficult to achieve. They happened only because people articulated a vision long before it was politically feasible. Moreover, economists are typically poor judges of what is and is not politically feasible, and crafting minor reforms that reflect our ideas of political feasibility would truly be a waste of time. Our hope is that our analysis helps to clarify these risks, contribute to the public debate, and set necessary reforms in motion.

Some may argue that the risks we are trying to avoid are only theoretical, not a realistic description of what can happen. That optimism forgets just how painful the past crises were, how theoretical and improbable they seemed, and how they reflected much smaller built-up stresses of the system at the time. The Greek and other sovereign debt crises were deep and painful. Much of their severity resulted from the simple lacunae: insufficient incentives for fiscal responsibility, expectations that sovereign default would somehow always be prevented, banks loaded with sovereign debt, no resolution mechanism, and more. All of the stresses or risks are larger today.

Some argue that far-reaching institutional reform is only possible in a crisis. Jean Monnet (2022) coined the famous statement that "Europe will be forged in crises, and will be the sum of the solutions adopted for those crises" ("L'Europe se fera dans les crises et elle sera la somme des solutions apportées à ces crises").

However, not every crisis will result in an improved institutional structure, a deeper and better functioning Europe and EMU, or more public support for European integration. Guiso, Sapienza, and Zingales (2016) write:

> So far history seems to have vindicated Monnet's theory. Before the 2010 European Sovereign Crisis, nobody would have anticipated a common supervision of the European banking sector any time soon. Since November 2014 this has become a reality. Yet, was this move triggered by a rising consensus towards more integration or was it forced down the throat of reluctant voters? Answering this question is crucial to the future of the euro and of Europe in general. If integration increases the demand for further integration, political integration is just a question of when, not if. In contrast, if integration forces further integration against voters' will, the integration process is more at risk. As all chain reactions, there is the risk of a meltdown. . . . Europe seems trapped: there is no desire to go backward, no interest in going forward, but it is economically unsustainable to stay still.

Our historical analysis points to an opposite force: Yes, crises breed institutional changes, and those changes can overcome previous political and institutional barriers. But changes adopted in a crisis are often the opposite of reform. They get us through the crisis but they form a poor basis for long-run institutions. That is the current situation. Larger and less constrained monetary and fiscal interventions have been the products of crises. But without reforms they sow the seeds of worse crises ahead.

We now need the kind of reform that changes the rules of the game, an institutional reform to align long-term incentives, not the kind of quick institutional innovation that addresses a crisis. This kind of reform happens in the calm after a crisis.

The euro itself was put together in the second half of the 1990s, a time of quiet growth in Europe, not during the turmoil of the 1970s and 1980s. The U.S. Fed was founded in 1913, in response to the crisis of 1907 but not in the midst of that crisis. The current bank regulations, like them or hate them, were implemented in the years after the 2008 crisis and reversed many of the expedients of that crisis.

As the saying goes, nobody worries about moral hazard in a crisis. Our reforms are precisely the kind that are *not* and should not be implemented in the crisis. Thus, if we wait for the next crisis, our reforms are the type that can be put in only afterward. Perhaps a next, huge crisis is what it will take to focus Europe's attention. But we hope not, as the next crisis will likely be larger than the last.

We have stayed away from politics, but this last political fear is real. Popular and political support for the EU seems not as strong as it once was. Faith in technocratic elites is not as strong as it once was. Repeated bailouts and interventions, far beyond the original conception of the euro and described in acronym-laden and abstruse language, needed or not, correct or not, continue to undermine popular and hence political support for the euro. Clarity and limited purposes can build support for this vital project.

The euro was founded as a set of *institutions* comprising both formal rules and informal norms. Management of the euro was almost a machine, following a predictable course. In the press of unexpected events, leaders made consequential decisions that far exceeded anything contemplated by the euro's institutions. That is natural; but the habit persisted. The euro is now guided by *decisions*. Even when run by the wisest leaders, a regime of decisions will not work as well as a regime of institutions. Will the ECB stifle the next breakout of a sovereign spread? Will member states or the ECB save a big bank? Which bondholders will get rescued and which will not? It's anybody's guess. Will member states get their debt under control? People, businesses, governments, bureaucrats, and regulators all structure their affairs based on such guesses, and to attract the ECB's favor. As time goes on without major reforms, people inevitably will figure out that pressuring the ECB to make momentous decisions in their favor is a good investment. Fundamentally, our proposals amount to rebuilding a euro based on durable institutions, which lead to predictable behavior.

Crises lead to innovative expedients. After a crisis, any political body must decide whether to enshrine the actions of the crisis as wise innovations, ready to be repeated; as horrible mistakes to be avoided; or as understandable stopgaps, but stopgaps that show the need for institutional reform so they won't have to be repeated. In our view, Europe seems to be following the first path, where the third is the right one.

The time for reforming the euro is now. EU institutions and member states should not wait for the next crisis. Doing so will only increase the associated costs and pain. However, if the political will fails, we at least hope that our analysis will serve to guide the reforms that all will see are urgently needed after the next crisis.

NOTES

Preface

1. Collections at https://www.johnhcochrane.com/news-op-eds-overview/europe and https://johnhcochrane.blogspot.com/search/label/European%20Debt%20Crisis.

2. https://euronomics.princeton.edu.

3. https://www.ineteconomics.org.

Chapter 1. Introduction and Overview

1. For an overview from the perspective of Eurosystem experts (whose views do not necessarily reflect those of the Executive Board or the Governing Council of the ECB), see Masuch et al. (2018).

2. See, for instance, Garicano, Lelarge, and Van Reenen (2016) for an analysis of size-dependent regulations on firm size and productivity distribution.

Chapter 2. Key Economic Ideas

1. See among many others, Sargent and Wallace (1981), Leeper (1991), Sims (1994), Woodford (1994), Cochrane (2023b), and Bassetto and Miller (2022).

2. See, among many examples, Sims (1997), Sims (1999), Detken, Gaspar, and Winkler (2004), Debrun et al. (2021), and Del Negro and Sims (2015).

3. *ECB Monthly Bulletin*, June 2010, https://www.ecb.europa.eu/pub/pdf/other/mb201006_focus01.en.pdf.

4. See the speech by Isabel Schnabel, "The Eurosystem's Operational Framework," March 14, 2024, https://www.ecb.europa.eu/press/key/date/2024/html/ecb.sp240314~8b609de772.en.html.

5. See also Barro and Gordon (1983); Rogoff (1985); Persson and Tabellini (1993); Walsh (1995) and Woodford (2003).

6. See, among others, Calvo (1988); Cole and Kehoe (2000); Aguiar and Gopinath (2006) and Arellano (2008).

7. See Barro and Gordon (1983); Rogoff (1985); Alesina and Summers (1993); Walsh (1995).

Chapter 3. The Design of the Economic and Monetary Union

1. https://eur-lex.europa.eu/LexUriServ/LexUriServ.do?uri=CELEX%3A12008E123%3 AEN%3AHTML.

2. https://eur-lex.europa.eu/legal-content/EN/TXT/?uri=CELEX%3A12016E127.

3. ECB Press Release, "A Stability-Oriented Monetary Policy Strategy for the ESCB, 13 October 1998," https://www.ecb.europa.eu/press/pr/date/1998/html/pr981013_1.en .html.

4. https://www.ecb.europa.eu/press/pr/date/2003/html/pr030508_2.en.html.

5. Wim Duisenberg, "EMU—How to Grasp the Opportunities and Avoid the Risks," 22 January 1998, https://www.ecb.europa.eu/press/key/date/1998/html/sp980122.en .html.

6. https://www.ecb.europa.eu/ecb/climate/our-climate-and-nature-plan/html/index.en .html.

7. https://www.ecb.europa.eu/home/search/review/html/ecb.strategyreview_monpol _strategy_overview.en.html.

8. https://www.ecb.europa.eu/press/pr/date/2020/html/ecb.pr200318_1~3949d6f266 .en.html.

9. Source: https://data.ecb.europa.eu/publications/ecbeurosystem-policy-and-exchange -rates/3030616.

10. https://www.federalreserve.gov/monetarypolicy/files/fomc20100805memo02.pdf.

11. https://eur-lex.europa.eu/legal-content/EN/TXT/?uri=CELEX%3A12016E127.

12. https://www.consilium.europa.eu/en/european-council/role-nominations-appoint ment/, also Article 283 of the Treaty on the Functioning of the European Union, https:// eur-lex.europa.eu/legal-content/en/TXT/?uri=CELEX:12016E283.

13. Article 11 of the Protocol on the Statute of the European System of Central Banks.

14. Deutsche Bundesbank, Monthly Report, March 2016, https://www.bundesbank .de/resource/blob/626154/6b755a17608bfc01399b87cb9c50dba2/mL/2016-03-role-data .pdf.

15. See ECB explainer: "What Are Net Financial Assets (NFA)?," February 24, 2023, https://www.ecb.europa.eu/ecb/educational/explainers/tell-me-more/html/anfa_qa.en .html.

16. European Central Bank, *Convergence Report*, June 2022, https://www.ecb.europa.eu /press/other/convergence/html/ecb.cr202206 e0fe4e1874.en.html.

17. See the ECB, "What Are Target2 Balances?," https://www.ecb.europa.eu/ecb-and-you /explainers/tell-me-more/html/target2_balances.EX.html.

18. https://data.ecb.europa.eu/publications/ecbeurosystem-policy-and-exchange-rates/3 030621.

Chapter 4. Prelude to Financial Crisis

1. Council Regulations, No 1055/2005 and No 1056/2005, amending Regulations 1466/97 and 1467/97, respectively, https://eur-lex.europa.eu/legal-content/EN/TXT/HTML

/?uri=CELEX:32005R1055. See Morris, Ongena, and Schuknecht (2006) for an in-depth discussion.

2. "The Reform of the Stability and Growth Pact," *ECB Monthly Bulletin*, August 2005, https://www.ecb.europa.eu/pub/pdf/mobu/mb200508en.pdf.

3. "The Changes to the Stability and Growth Pact," *Deutsche Bundesbank Monthly Report*, April 2005, https://www.bundesbank.de/resource/blob/706528/f741454b9a581fdef80f847 a169ca888/mL/2005-04-changes-stability-data.pdf.

4. See Breakdown of Eurosystem Aggregate Balance Sheet, https://data.ecb.europa.eu /publications/money-credit-and-banking/3031819. A historical data source with slightly different aggregates is given in the *ECB Monthy Bulletin*, Statistical Annex, Aggregate Balance Sheet of Area MFIs, Eurosystem, column 7, "Holdings of Securities . . . , General Government," https://www.ecb.europa.eu/pub/economic-bulletin/mb/html/index.en.html.

5. See Chen, Milesi-Ferretti, and Tressel, 2012, figure 1.

6. https://www.ecb.europa.eu/press/key/date/2005/html/sp051121.en.html.

7. https://www.wsj.com/articles/SB118670471880693703.

8. Jean-Claude Trichet, "Introductory Statement," September 6, 2007.

9. "France, Germany Clash on Financial Rescue," Reuters, October 2, 2008.

10. *New York Times*, October 6, 2009, https://www.nytimes.com/2008/10/05/business /worldbusiness/05iht-hypo.4.16708030.html.

11. See Bindseil et al. (2017), section 3 and figure 3.

12. See Runkel (2022b), figure 1.

13. https://www.ecb.europa.eu/press/pr/date/2009/html/pr090507_2.en.html.

14. See the consolidated balance sheet of euro-area MFIs, https://data.ecb.europa.eu /publications/money-credit-and-banking/3031820.

Chapter 5. The Sovereign Debt Crisis

1. "Ich sage auch mit Blick auf einzelne Länder mit sehr hohen Defiziten: Jeder einzelne Mitgliedstaat ist verantwortlich für gesunde öffentliche Finanzen." https://dserver.bundestag .de/btp/17/17012.pdf.

2. https://www.consilium.europa.eu/media/21428/20100211-statement-by-the-heads-of -state-or-government-of-the-european-union-on-greece-en.pdf.

3. https://www.ecb.europa.eu/press/key/date/2010/html/sp100211.de.html.

4. https://www.telegraph.co.uk/finance/financialcrisis/7608361/Germany-warns-of-Leh man-crisis-if-Greece-defaults.html.

5. https://www.consilium.europa.eu/uedocs/cms_data/docs/pressdata/en/ec/113686 .pdf.

6. European Central Bank, Aggregate balance sheet of euro-area MFIs excluding the Eurosystem, https://data.ecb.europa.eu/publications/money-credit-and-banking/3031821.

7. International Monetary Fund (2017), figure 17.

8. Franco-German Declaration, Deauville, October 18, 2010, https://www.eu.dk/~ /media/files/eu/franco_german_declaration.ashx?la=da.

9. https://www.nytimes.com/2010/10/19/world/europe/19iht-summit.html.

10. https://www.reuters.com/article/uk-france-germany/eu-countries-to-cut-budgets-or -face-sanctions-idUKTRE69H46520101018.

11. https://www.ft.com/content/56984290-df96-11df-bed9-00144feabdc0.

12. Peter Spiegel, "How the Euro Was Saved," *Financial Times*, May 11, 2014. https://www .ft.com/content/f6f4d6b4-ca2e-11e3-ac05-00144feabdc0.

13. See also https://www.imf.org/en/Publications/CR/Issues/2017/02/07/Greece-Ex -Post-Evaluation-of-Exceptional-Access-Under-the-2012-Extended-Arrangement-Press-44 636.

14. Peter Spiegel, "Inside Europe's Plan Z," *Financial Times*, May 11, 2014. https://www.ft .com/content/0ac1306e-d508-11e3-9187-00144feabdc0.

15. International Monetary Fund (2013), 8.

16. https://www.imf.org/external/np/pp/eng/2013/042613.pdf.

17. https://www.imf.org/external/pubs/ft/scr/2013/cr13156.pdf.

18. https://www.ecb.europa.eu/press/pr/date/2015/html/pr150204.en.html.

19. Mario Draghi. Letter to Mr Marco Zanni and Mr Marco Valli, 2015, https://www.ecb .europa.eu/pub/pdf/other/150918letter_vallizanni.en.pdf.

20. https://www.bloomberg.com/news/articles/2015-07-19/greece-s-real-crisis-deadline -arrives-with-ecb-debt-to-pay.

21. https://www.consilium.europa.eu/en/policies/financial-assistance-eurozone-membe rs/greece-programme.

22. https://www.imf.org/en/Publications/CR/Issues/2017/07/20/Greece-Request-for -Stand-By-Arrangement-Press-Release-Staff-Report-and-Statement-by-the-45110.

23. In 2015, the ECB published the full text of the secret letter: https://www.ecb.europa .eu/press/html/irish-letters.en.html.

24. European Banking Authority, "2010 Stress Tests," https://www.eba.europa.eu/risk -and-data-analysis/risk-analysis/eu-wide-stress-testing/eu-wide-stress-testing-2010.

25. https://fred.stlouisfed.org/series/IRLTLT01PTM156N.

26. Spain: Memorandum of Understanding on Financial-Sector Policy Conditional- ity, July 20, 2012, https://ec.europa.eu/economy_finance/eu_borrower/mou/2012-07-20 -spain-mou_en.pdf.

27. See https://fred.stlouisfed.org/series/INTGSTITM193N.

28. Patrick Wintour and Larry Elliott, "G20 Leaders Press Italy to Accept IMF Checks on Cuts Program," *The Guardian*, November 4, 2011, https://www.theguardian.com/world /2011/nov/04/g20-italy-imf-checks-cuts.

29. https://www.reuters.com/article/us-italy-monti-reforms-factbox-idUSBRE8B90ZA 20121210.

30. See International Monetary Fund (2014a), box 1.

31. https://www.ecb.europa.eu/press/pr/date/2013/html/pr130321.en.html.

32. https://economy-finance.ec.europa.eu/publications/ex-post-evaluation-economic-ad justment-program-cyprus-2013-2016_en.

33. https://www.nytimes.com/2013/08/22/world/europe/russians-still-ride-high-in-cy prus-after-bailout.html.

34. European Central Bank, "ECB Decides on Measures to Address Severe Tensions in Financial Markets," May 10, 2010, https://www.ecb.europa.eu/press/pr/date/2010/html /pr100510.de.html.

35. Jean-Claude Trichet, "Central Banking in Uncertain Times: Conviction and Responsibility," European Central Bank, https://www.ecb.europa.eu/press/key/date/2010/html /sp100827.en.html.

36. European Central Bank, "ECB Decides on Measures to Address Severe Tensions in Financial Markets."

37. The letters were later published on the ECB website; see https://www.ecb.europa .eu/ecb/access_to_documents/document/pa_document/shared/data/ecb.dr.par2021_000 1lettertoItalianPrimeMinister.en.pdf and https://www.ecb.europa.eu/ecb/access_to_docu ments/document/correspondence/shared/data/ecb.dr.cor20110805Zapatero.en.pdf.

38. https://www.ecb.europa.eu/stats/policy_and_exchange_rates/key_ecb_interest_rates /html/index.en.html.

39. https://www.ecb.europa.eu/press/pr/date/2011/html/pr111208_1.en.html.

40. Peter Eavis, "Forget Zou Bisou Bisou, the Sarkozy Trade. Is the Hot French Export." *New York Times*, March 28, 2012, https://archive.nytimes.com/dealbook.nytimes.com/2012 /03/28/forget-zou-bisou-bisou-the-sarkozy-trade-is-the-hot-french-export/.

41. Speech by Mario Draghi, president of the European Central Bank at the Global Investment Conference in London, July 26, 2012, https://www.ecb.europa.eu/press/key/date /2012/html/sp120726.en.html.

42. Mario Draghi, "The Euro, Monetary Policy, and Reforms," speech given on May 6, 2013.

43. European Central Bank, "Technical Features of Outright Monetary Transactions," September 6, 2012, https://www.ecb.europa.eu/press/pr/date/2012/html/pr120906_1.en .html.

Chapter 6. Institutional Reforms

1. Speech by Mario Draghi, president of the European Central Bank at the Global Investment Conference in London, July 26, 2012, https://www.ecb.europa.eu/press/key/date /2012/html/sp120726.en.html.

2. Euro Area Summit Statement, June 29, 2012, https://www.bankingsupervision.europa .eu/about/milestones/shared/pdf/2012-06-29_euro_area_summit_statement_en.pdf.

3. Guy Chazan, "Wolfgang Schäuble Warns of Debt-Driven Global Financial Crisis," *Financial Times*, October 8, 2017, https://www.ft.com/content/9de0533c-aab8-11e7-93c5-6483 14d2c72c.

4. https://commission.europa.eu/system/files/2019-09/2019-09-10-assessment-of-eu -fiscal-rules_en.pdf.

5. https://www.esm.europa.eu/sites/default/files/2016_02_01_efsf_faq_archived.pdf.

6. https://www.esm.europa.eu/about-us.

7. https://www.esm.europa.eu/sites/default/files/20180530esmfactsheet.pdf.

8. http://www.consilium.europa.eu/media/21548/20141020-banking_union_-_relevant _ec_conclusions.pdf.

9. https://finance.ec.europa.eu/banking/banking-union/european-deposit-insurance-sch eme_en.

10. https://www.bankingsupervision.europa.eu/ecb/pub/pdf/aggregatereportonthecom prehensiveassessment201410.en.pdf.

11. Euro Area Summit Statement, June 29, 2012, https://www.consilium.europa.eu/media /21400/20120629-euro-area-summit-statement-en.pdf.

Chapter 7. The Zero Bound

1. https://www.ecb.europa.eu/stats/policy_and_exchange_rates/key_ecb_interest_rates /html/index.en.html.

2. https://www.ecb.europa.eu/mopo/implement/app/html/index.en.html.

3. https://curia.europa.eu/juris/document/document.jsf?docid=208741&doclang=EN.

4. https://www.ecb.europa.eu/press/key/date/2013/html/sp130506.en.html.

5. https://www.ecb.europa.eu/press/pressconf/2019/html/ecb.is190307~de1fdbd0b0.en .html.

6. Christine Lagarde, "The Monetary Policy Strategy Review: Some Preliminary Considerations," speech at the ECB and Its Watchers XXI Conference, Frankfurt am Main, September 30, 2020, https://www.ecb.europa.eu/press/key/date/2020/html/ecb.sp200930 ~169abb1202.en.html.

Chapter 8. The Pandemic

1. "ECB Announces €750 Billion Pandemic Emergency Purchase Program (PEPP)," press release, March 18, 2020, https://www.ecb.europa.eu/press/pr/date/2020/html/ecb .pr200318_1 3949d6f266.en.html.

2. Christine Lagarde and Luis de Guindos, Introductory Statement, Press Conference, March 12, 2020, https://www.ecb.europa.eu/press/pressconf/2020/html/ecb.is200312~f85 7a21b6c.en.html.

3. European Central Bank, Press conference, March 12, 2020, https://www.ecb.europa .eu/press/press_conference/monetary-policy-statement/2020/html/ecb.is200312~f857a2 1b6c.en.html.

4. https://www.ecb.europa.eu/press/key/date/2013/html/sp130506.en.html.

5. "ECB Announces €750 Billion Pandemic Emergency Purchase Program."

6. https://x.com/Lagarde/status/1240414918966480896.

7. https://eur-lex.europa.eu/legal-content/EN/TXT/?uri=CELEX:32020D0440.

8. "ECB Announces €750 Billion Pandemic Emergency Purchase Program."

9. https://eur-lex.europa.eu/legal-content/EN/TXT/?uri=CELEX:32020D0440.

10. https://www.euronews.com/next/2022/12/29/italy-esm.

11. This was agreed to in principle by the European Council on July 21, 2020.

12. See https://commission.europa.eu/business-economy-euro/economic-recovery/rec overy-and-resilience-facility_en for a map of all the funds and their distribution.

13. See the investor relations page of the European Commission, https://commission.euro pa.eu/strategy-and-policy/eu-budget/eu-borrower-investor-relations/nextgenerationeu_en.

Chapter 9. Inflation, War, and Tightening

1. https://www.ecb.europa.eu/press/pr/date/2021/html/ecb.pr210708~dc78cc4b0d.en.html.

2. https://www.federalreserve.gov/newsevents/pressreleases/monetary20200827a.htm.

3. "Monetary Policy Decisions," press release, March 10, 2022, https://www.ecb.europa.eu/press/pr/date/2022/html/ecb.mp220310~2d19f8ba60.en.html.

4. European Central Bank, "Monetary Policy Decisions," press release, April 14, 2022, https://www.ecb.europa.eu/press/pr/date/2022/html/ecb.mp220414 d1b76520c6.en.html.

5. "Christine Lagarde: 'I Should Have Been Bolder,' " *Financial Times*, October 27, 2023, https://www.ft.com/content/c916c994-492c-4639-84ae-4a6dc2cb7426.

6. "Monetary Policy Decisions."

7. "Monetary Policy Decisions."

8. "Monetary Policy Decisions," press release, June 9, 2022, https://www.ecb.europa.eu/press/pr/date/2022/html/ecb.mp220609~122666c272.en.html.

9. See the last three charts in Philip R. Lane, "Debate on 'Is the Inflation Surge over and What Are the Lessons for Monetary Policy?,' " ECB Watchers Conference, 2024, https://www.ecb.europa.eu/press/key/date/2024/html/ecb.sp240320_1~35a0100f88.en.pdf.

10. Mark Gertler's Macroeconomics 2 slides have an excellent presentation of this issue: https://wp.nyu.edu/markgertler/macro-theory-2-slides/.

11. https://www.washingtonpost.com/opinions/2021/05/24/inflation-risk-is-real/.

12. Mario Draghi and Emmanuel Macron, "The EU's Fiscal Rules Must Be Reformed," *Financial Times*, December 23 2021.

13. https://www.reuters.com/markets/europe/german-finance-minister-expects-higher-debt-burden-no-tax-rises-2022-11-28/.

14. See European Central Bank, "The Transmission Protection Instrument," press release, July 21, 2022, https://www.ecb.europa.eu/press/pr/date/2022/html/ecb.pr220721~973e6e7273.en.html.

15. Isabel Schnabel, "Is Monetary Policy Dominated by Fiscal Policy?," speech at a conference organized by Stiftung Geld und Währung to mark twenty-five years of the euro, Frankfurt, June 7, 2024, https://www.ecb.europa.eu/press/key/date/2024/html/ecb.sp240607~c6ae070dc0.en.html.

16. "Statement after the Ad hoc Meeting of the ECB Governing Council," press release, June 15, 2022, https://www.ecb.europa.eu/press/pr/date/2022/html/ecb.pr220615~2aa3900e0a.en.htm.

17. See "Italian Economy Italian Debt Market Flashes Warning as Draghi Government Teeters," *Financial Times*, July 15, 2022, https://www.ft.com/content/f01e3706-515c-4cb9-91e6-d53739767926.

Chapter 10. The Unsustainable Present

1. Benoît Cœuré, "Central Banking, Insurance and Incentives," December 6, 2012, https://www.ecb.europa.eu/press/key/date/2012/html/sp121206_1.en.html; and "Heterogeneity and the ECB's Monetary Policy," March 29, 2019, https://www.ecb.europa.eu/press/key/date/2019/html/ecb.sp190329~da3110cea9.en.html.

290 NOTES TO CHAPTER 10

2. Isabel Schnabel, "The Benefits and Costs of Asset Purchases," May 28, 2024, https://www.ecb.europa.eu/press/key/date/2024/html/ecb.sp240528 a4f151497d.en.html.

3. All values given here are for 2023. Source: https://www.ecb.europa.eu/stats/macro economic_and_sectoral/government_finance/html/index.en.html.

4. "EU Gives Budget Leeway to France 'Because it Is France'—Juncker," Reuters, May 31, 2016, https://www.reuters.com/article/idUSKCN0YM1MZ/.

5. Source: Eurostat, https://ec.europa.eu/eurostat/databrowser/view/tec00115/default/line?lang=en.

6. https://data.ecb.europa.eu/publications/macroeconomic-and-sectoral-statistics/3030 642.

7. https://ec.europa.eu/eurostat/statistics-explained/index.php?title=Pensions_in_na tional_accounts_-_statistics&oldid=514007.

8. See https://ec.europa.eu/eurostat/databrowser/view/tps00199/default/table?lang= en (last updated March 9, 2024).

9. https://ec.europa.eu/commission/presscorner/detail/en/qanda_20_24.

10. https://commission.europa.eu/news/focus-reducing-eus-dependence-imported-fossil -fuels-2022-04-20_en.

11. The new fiscal rules consist of two regulations and one directive. Regulation (EU) 2024/1263 introduces the new fiscal surveillance framework, Regulation 2024/1264 reforms the excessive deficit procedure within the Stability and Growth Pact, and Directive 2024/1265 establishes the new fiscal framework of Member States.

12. Regulation (EU) 2024/1263 of the European Parliament, article 6(a), https://eur-lex .europa.eu/eli/reg/2024/1263/oj.

13. Regulation (EU) 2024/1263 of the European Parliament, article 7.1(a).

14. Regulation (EU) 2024/1263 of the European Parliament, article 8.

15. See "2024 Ageing Report," Economic and Budgetary Projections for the EU Member States (2022–2070)," Directorate-General for Economic and Financial Affairs, Institutional Paper 279, April 18, 2024.

16. https://www.euifis.eu.

17. European Central Bank, press release on the TPI, July 21, 2022, https://www.ecb .europa.eu/press/pr/date/2022/html/ecb.pr220721~973e6e7273.en.html.

18. See "IMF Executive Board Approves US 50 Billion Stand-by Arrangement for Argentina," press release, June 20, 2018, https://www.imf.org/en/News/Articles/2018/06/20 /pr18245-argentina-imf-executive-board-approves-us50-billion-stand-by-arrangement.

19. "The Transmission Protection Instrument," press release, July 21, 2022, https://www .ecb.europa.eu/press/pr/date/2022/html/ecb.pr220721~973e6e7273.en.html.

20. Christine Lagarde and Luis de Guindos, "Monetary Policy Statement (with Q&A)," July 21, 2022, https://www.ecb.europa.eu/press/pressconf/2022/html/ecb.is220721~51ef 267c68.en.html. See also "Statement after the Ad hoc Meeting of the ECB Governing Council," press release, June 15, 2022, https://www.ecb.europa.eu/press/pr/date/2022/html/ecb.pr22 0615~2aa3900e0a.en.htm.

21. Eurogroup Statement on the Future of the Banking Union of June 16, 2022, https://www.consilium.europa.eu/en/press/press-releases/2022/06/16/eurogroup-statement-on -the-future-of-the-banking-union-of-16-june-2022/.

22. See also "The Euro Area Needs Better Structural Policies to Support Income, Employment and Fairness," *ECB Blog*, October 11, 2023, https://www.ecb.europa.eu/press/blog/date/2023/html/ecb.blog231011~b743839ce4.en.html.

23. From the book description, https://amzn.eu/d/cBaQUan.

24. https://www.ansa.it/english/news/politics/2023/03/15/italy-wont-access-esm-as-long-as-im-pm-meloni_aa0faefc-2bdc-4c12-979c-b5b2337b5836.html.

25. See Euroactiv, "Reluctant Italy Postpones Eurozone Bailout Fund's Ratification," June 27, 2023, https://www.euractiv.com/section/politics/news/reluctant-italy-postpones-eurozone-bailout-funds-ratification.

26. https://www.bancaditalia.it/pubblicazioni/interventi-governatore/integov2019/Visco_OMFIF_15112019.pdf.

27. https://www.bankingsupervision.europa.eu/about/thessm/html/index.en.html.

28. https://www.bankingsupervision.europa.eu/about/milestones/html/index.en.html.

29. https://www.srb.europa.eu/en/single-resolution-fund; https://www.esm.europa.eu/content/how-much-could-esm-lend-single-resolution-fund.

30. https://finance.ec.europa.eu/banking/banking-union/european-deposit-insurance-scheme_en.

31. "Eurogroup Statement on the Future of the Banking Union of 16 June 2022."

32. https://www.ecb.europa.eu/pub/fie/html/ecb.fie202204~4c4f5f572f.en.html#toc3.

33. https://www.ecb.europa.eu/press/key/date/2023/html/ecb.sp230302~41273ad467.en.html.

34. https://www.ecb.europa.eu/mopo/decisions/html/index.en.html.

35. See Isabel Schnabel speech, March 23, 2023, https://www.ecb.europa.eu/press/key/date/2023/html/ecb.sp230327_1~fe4adb3e9b.en.html#footnote.2. Figure 10.3 is adapted from that speech.

36. Speech by Isabel Schnabel, "The Eurosystem's Operational Framework," March 14, 2024, https://www.ecb.europa.eu/press/key/date/2024/html/ecb.sp240314~8b609de772.en.html.

Chapter 11. Reform Proposals

1. For a contemporaneous perspective, see Cochrane (2010).

2. https://www.ecb.europa.eu/mopo/ela/html/index.en.html.

3. https://www.ecb.europa.eu/pub/pdf/other/ecb.agreementemergencyliquidityassistance202012~ba7c45c170.en.pdf?dca797da3212289956ac24df607eb168.

4. Agreement between the National Central Banks and the ECB from December 2002 on Net Financial Assets (ANFA), https://eur-lex.europa.eu/legal-content/EN/TXT/PDF/?uri=IMMC:AGR/2022/12191.

BIBLIOGRAPHY

Admati, Anat, and Martin Hellwig. 2024. *The Bankers' New Clothes: What's Wrong with Banking and What to Do about It*. New and expanded ed. Princeton, NJ: Princeton University Press.

Aguiar, Mark, and Manuel Amador. 2021. *The Economics of Sovereign Debt and Default*. Princeton, NJ: Princeton University Press.

Aguiar, Mark, Manuel Amador, Emmanuel Farhi, and Gita Gopinath. 2015. "Coordination and Crisis in Monetary Unions." *Quarterly Journal of Economics* 130(4): 1727–1779.

Aguiar, Mark, and Gita Gopinath. 2006. "Defaultable Debt, Interest Rates and the Current Account." *Journal of International Economics* 69(1): 64–83.

Alesina, Alberto, and Lawrence H. Summers. 1993. "Central Bank Independence and Macroeconomic Performance: Some Comparative Evidence." *Journal of Money, Credit and Banking* 25(2): 151–162.

Andruszkiewicz, Oskar, Juliette Mathis, Charu Wilkinson, Michalis Vassiliadis, Peppas Konstantinos, and George Gatopoulos. 2020. *Study on the Financial Sector in Greece during the Economic Adjustment Programmes: 2010–2018*. Luxembourg: Publications Office of the European Union. https://data.europa.eu/doi/10.2765/403158.

Arce, Óscar, Matteo Ciccarelli, Antoine Kornprobst, and Carlos Montes-Galdón. 2024. "What Caused the Euro Area Post-pandemic Inflation?" ECB Occasional Paper 2024 /343. https://www.ecb.europa.eu/pub/pdf/scpops/ecb.op343~ab3e870d21.en.pdf?b3 433d7c62e5071efb6ad0d82f6626bd.

Arellano, Cristina. 2008. "Default Risk and Income Fluctuations in Emerging Economies." *American Economic Review* 98(3): 690–712.

Bagehot, Walter. 1873. *Lombard Street: A Description of the Money Market*. London: Henry S. King.

Balke, Nathan S., and Carlos E. Zarazaga. 2024. "Quantifying Fiscal Policy's Role in U.S. Inflation." Maniscript. https://bpb-us-w2.wpmucdn.com/people.smu.edu/dist/a/1609 /files/2024/04/Quantifying_Fiscal_Contribution_to_US_Inflation_3_2024-81aa51c1 758669d0.pdf.

Barro, Robert J. 1979. "On the Determination of the Public Debt." *Journal of Political Economy* 87(5, Part 1): 940–971.

Barro, Robert J., and Francesco Bianchi. 2023. "Fiscal Influences on Inflation in OECD Countries, 2020–2023." NBER Working paper 31838.

Barro, Robert J., and David B. Gordon. 1983. "Rules, Discretion and Reputation in a Model of Monetary Policy." *Journal of Monetary Economics* 12(1): 101–121.

Bassetto, Marco, and David S. Miller. 2022. "A Monetary-Fiscal Theory of Sudden Inflations." Federal Reserve Bank of Minneapolis staff report, No. 641.

Battistini, Niccolò, Marco Pagano, and Saverio Simonelli. 2014. "Systemic Risk, Sovereign Yields and Bank Exposures in the Euro Crisis." *Economic Policy* 29(78): 203–251. https://doi.org/10.1111/1468-0327.12029.

Baudino, Patrizia, Mariano Herrera, and Fernando Restoy. 2023. "The 2008–14 Banking Crisis in Spain." FSI Crisis Management Series No. 4. https://elischolar.library.yale.edu/ypfs-documents2/2333.

Beck, Thorsten, Jan Pieter Krahnen, Philippe J. Martin, Franz C. Mayer, Jean Pisani-Ferry, Tobias Tröger, Beatrice Weder, Nicolas Véron, and Jeromin Zettelmeyer. 2022. *Completing Europe's Banking Union: Economic Requirements and Legal Conditions*. Bruegel, https://www.bruegel.org/policy-brief/completing-europes-banking-union-economic-requirements-and-legal-conditions-0.

Bénassy-Quéré, Agnès, Markus Brunnermeier, Henrik Enderlein, Emmanuel Farhi, Marcel Fratzscher, Clemens Fuest, Florence Pisani, Pierre-Olivier Gourinchas, Philippe Martin, Jean Pisani-Ferry, Hélène Rey, Isabel Schnabel, Nicolas Veron, Beatrice Weder di Mauro, and Jeromin Zettelmeyer. 2018. "Reconciling Risk Sharing with Market Discipline: A Constructive Approach to Euro Area Reform." CEPR Policy Insight No. 91. https://cepr.org/publications/policy-insight-91-reconciling-risk-sharing-market-discipline-constructive-approach.

Bernanke, Ben. 1983. "Nonmonetary Effects of the Financial Crisis in the Propagation of the Great Depression." *American Economic Review* 73(3): 257–276.

Bernanke, Ben, Mark Gertler, and Simon Gilchrist. 1996. "The Financial Accelerator and the Flight to Quality." *Review of Economics and Statistics* 78(1): 1–15.

Bernanke, Ben, and Harold James. 1991. "The Gold Standard, Deflation, and Financial Crisis in the Great Depression: An International Comparison." In *Financial Markets and Financial Crises*, edited by R. Glenn Hubbard, 33–68. Chicago: University of Chicago Press.

Bianchi, Francesco, Renato Faccini, and Leonardo Melosi. 2023. "A Fiscal Theory of Persistent Inflation." *Quarterly Journal of Economics* 138(4): 2127–2179.

Bindseil, Ulrich, Marco Corsi, Benjamin Sahel, and Ad Visser. 2017. "The Eurosystem Collateral Framework Explained." ECB Occasional Paper Series, No. 189. https://www.ecb.europa.eu/pub/pdf/scpops/ecb.op189.en.pdf?d1d191fa1ab6d2ed2be2ac739e65b609.

Blanchard, Olivier. 2007. "Adjustment within the Euro: The Difficult Case of Portugal." *Portuguese Economic Journal* 6(1): 1–21.

Boeri, Tito, and Roberto Perotti. 2023. *PNRR: La Grande Abbuffata*. Milan: Feltrinelli.

Bordo, Michael D., and Lars Jonung, 2000, *Lessons for EMU from the History of Monetary Unions*. London: Institute of Economic Affairs.

Bordo, MIchael D., Lars Jonung, and Agnieszka Markiewicz. 2013, "A Fiscal Union for the Euro: Some Lessons from History." *CESIfo Economic Studies* 59(3): 449–488. https://doi.org/10.1093/cesifo/ift001.

Borio, Claudio. 2023. "Getting Up from the Floor." Bank for International Settlements Working Paper No. 1100. https://www.bis.org/publ/work1100.htm.

Brunnermeier, Markus K. 2015. "Financial Dominance." Paolo Baffi Lecture, Banca d'Italia. https://www.bancaditalia.it/pubblicazioni/lezioni-baffi/pblecture-12/index.html.

Brunnermeier, Markus K., Luis Garicano, Philip R. Lane, Marco Pagano, Ricardo Reis, Tano Santos, David Thesmar, Stijn Van Nieuwerburgh, and Dimitri Vayanos. 2016. "The Sovereign-Bank Diabolic Loop and ESBies." *American Economic Review* 106(5): 508–512.

Brunnermeier, Markus K., Harold James, and Jean-Pierre Landau. 2016. *The Euro and the Battle of Ideas*. Princeton, NJ: Princeton University Press.

Calvo, Guillermo A. 1988. "Servicing the Public Debt: The Role of Expectations." *American Economic Review* 78(4): 647–661.

Chahad, Mohammed, Anna-Camilla Hofmann-Drahonsky, Baptiste Meunier, Adrian Page, and Marcel Tirpák. 2022. "What Explains Recent Errors in the Inflation Projections of

Eurosystem and ECB Staff?" *Economic Bulletin*, Issue 3. https://www.ecb.europa.eu/pub /economic-bulletin/html/eb202203.en.html.

Challe, Edouard, Jose Ignacio Lopez, and Eric Mengus. 2019. "Institutional Quality and Capital Inflows: Theory and Evidence." *Journal of International Money and Finance* 96: 168–191.

Chang, Michele. 2006. "Reforming the Stability and Growth Pact: Size and Influence in EMU Policymaking." *European Integration* 28(1): 107–120.

Chari, Varadarajan V., and Patrick J. Kehoe. 2007. "On the Need for Fiscal Constraints in a Monetary Union." *Journal of Monetary Economics* 54(8): 2399–2408.

Checherita-Westphal, Cristina, Anna Rogantini Picco, Sebastian Schmidt, and Jean-David Sigaux. 2024. "Monetary and Fiscal Policy Interactions: Risks to Price Stability in Times of High Government Debt." ECB Discussion Papers, no. 26. https://www.ecb.europa.eu /press/research-publications/discussion-papers/html/index.en.html.

Chen, Ruo, Gian M. Milesi-Ferretti, and Thierry Tressel. 2012. "External Imbalances in the Euro Area." International Monetary Fund Working Paper WP/12/236. https://www.imf .org/en/Publications/WP/Issues/2016/12/31/External-Imbalances-in-the-Euro-Area -40027.

Cochrane, John H. 2010. "'Contagion' and Other Euro Myths." *Wall Street Journal*, December 2. https://www.wsj.com/articles/SB10001424052748704594804575648692103838612.

———. 2014. "Toward a Run-Free Financial System." In *Across the Great Divide: New Perspectives on the Financial Crisis*, edited by Martin Neil Baily and John B. Taylor, 197–249. Stanford, CA: Hoover Institution Press. https://www.johnhcochrane.com/research-all /toward-a-run-free-financial-system.

———. 2023a. "Expectations and the Neutrality of Interest Rates." *Review of Economic Dynamics* 53: 194–223.

———. 2023b. *The Fiscal Theory of the Price Level*. Princeton, NJ: Princeton University Press.

———. 2024. "Fiscal Narratives for US Inflation." Manuscript https://www.johnhcochrane .com/research-all/sims-comment.

Cochrane, John H., and Amit Seru. 2024. "Ending Bailouts, at Last." *Journal of Law, Economics and Policy* 19: 169–193.

Cæuré, Benooit. 2019. "Heterogeneity and the ECB's Monetary Policy." Speech, Paris, March 29, 2019. https://www.ecb.europa.eu/press/key/date/2019/html/ecb.sp190329 ~da3110cea9.en.html.

Cole, Harold L., and Timothy J. Kehoe. 2000. "Self-Fulfilling Debt Crises." *Review of Economic Studies* 67(1): 91–116.

Constâncio, Vitor. 2018. "Completing the Odyssean Journey of the European Monetary Union." In *The Future of Central Banking: Festschrift in Honour of Vítor Constâncio*, 191–213. Frankfurt am Main: European Central Bank. https://www.ecb.europa.eu/pub/pdf /other/ecb.futurecentralbankingcolloquiumconstancio201812.en.pdf.

Corsetti, Giancarlo, Lars P. Feld, Philip R. Lane, Lucrezia Reichlin, Hélène Rey, Dimitri Vayanos, and Beatrice Weder di Mauro. 2015. *A New Start for the Eurozone: Dealing with Debt*. London: Centre for Economic Policy Research. https://www.movimentoeuropeo .it/images/ceps_monitoring-the-eurozone.pdf.

Costain, James S., Galo Nuño, and Carlos Thomas. 2022. "The Term Structure of Interest Rates in a Heterogeneous Monetary Union." Banco de Espana Working Paper.

Cuñat, Vicente, and Luis Garicano. 2010. "¿Concedieron las cajas "buenas" créditos "malos"? Gobierno corporativo, capital humano y carteras de créditos." In *La crisis de la economía española: Análisis económico de la gran recesión*, edited by Javier Diaz-Gimenez Samuel Bentolila, Michele Boldrin and Juan J. Dolado, 351–398. Madrid: FEDEA Annual Policy Conference. https://crisis09.fedea.net/crisis.php.

da Costa, José Miguel Cardoso, and Nuno Silva. 2023. "A Novel Decomposition of National Central Banks' Profits in the Euro Area: Application to the Case of Banco de Portugal." *Economic Bulletin and Financial Stability Report Articles and Banco de Portugal Economic Studies.* https://www.bportugal.pt/en/paper/novel-decomposition-national-central-banks-profits-euro-area-application-case-banco-de.

Darvas, Zsolt, Lennard Welslau, and Jeromin Zettelmeyer. 2024. "The Implications of the European Union's New Fiscal Rules." Bruegel Policy Brief no. 10. Brussels: Bruegel. https://www.bruegel.org/system/files/2024-07/PB%2010%202024.pdf.

De Grauwe, Paul, and Yuemei Ji. 2013. "Self-Fulfilling Crises in the Eurozone: An Empirical Test." *Journal of International Money and Finance* 34: 15–36.

Debrun, Xavier, Klaus Masuch, Isabel Vansteenkiste, Marien Ferdinandusse, Leopold von Thadden, Sebastian Hauptmeier, Mario Alloza, Krzysztof Bańkowski, João Domingues Semeano, Jens Eisenschmidt, et al. 2021. "Monetary-Fiscal Policy Interactions in the Euro Area." ECB Occasional Paper. https://www.ecb.europa.eu/pub/pdf/scpops/ecb.op273~fae24ce432.en.pdf?3c28f10d4f90b8363f32d117cbca3380.

Del Negro, Marco, and Christopher A. Sims. 2015. "When Does a Central Bank's Balance Sheet Require Fiscal Support?" *Journal of Monetary Economics* 73: 1–19. https://www.sciencedirect.com/science/article/pii/S0304393215000604.

Detken, Carsten, Vitor Gaspar, and Bernhard Winkler. 2004. "On Prosperity and Posterity: The Need for Fiscal Discipline in a Monetary Union." SSRN Working Paper. http://dx.doi.org/10.2139/ssrn.617813.

Diamond, Douglas W. and Philip H. Dybvig. 1983. "Bank Runs, Deposit Insurance, and Liquidity." *Journal of Political Economy* 91(3): 401–419.

Draghi, Mario. 2013. "The Euro, Monetary Policy and Reforms." Speech, Rome, May 6, 2013. https://www.ecb.europa.eu/press/key/date/2013/html/sp130506.en.html.

———. 2024. "The Future of European Competitiveness: A Competitiveness Strategy for Europe." Brussels: European Commission, September 9. https://commission.europa.eu/topics/strengthening-european-competitiveness/eu-competitiveness-looking-ahead_en.

Duffie, Darrell. 2011. *How Big Banks Fail and What to Do about It.* Princeton, NJ: Princeton University Press.

———. 2023. "Structural Changes in Financial Markets and the Conduct of Monetary Policy." Jackson Hole Symposium. https://www.kansascityfed.org/documents/10211/Jackson_Hole_Symposium_4-25-24.pdf#page=103.

Eaton, Jonathan, and Mark Gersovitz. 1981. "Debt with Potential Repudiation: Theoretical and Empirical Analysis." *Review of Economic Studies* 48(2): 289–309.

Eisenschmidt, Jens, Danielle Kedan, and Martin Schmitz. 2022. "Euro Area Monetary Policy and TARGET Balances: A Trilogy." ECB Working Paper 2750. https://www.ecb.europa.eu/pub/pdf/scpwps/ecb.wp2750~6e6363c570.en.pdf.

European Central Bank. 2003a. "The Outcome of the ECB's Evaluation of Its Monetary Policy Strategy." *ECB Monthly Bulletin.* https://www.ecb.europa.eu/pub/pdf/mobu/mb200306en.pdf.

———. 2003b. "The Relationship between Monetary Policy and Fiscal Policies in the Euro Area." *ECB Monthly Bulletin.* https://www.ecb.europa.eu/pub/pdf/mobu/mb200302en.pdf.

———. 2011. "Institutional Provisions." https://www.ecb.europa.eu/pub/pdf/other/ecbinstitutionalprovisions2011en.pdf.

———. 2012. "A Fiscal Compact for a Stronger Economic and Monetary Union." *ECB Monthly Bulletin.* https://www.ecb.europa.eu/pub/pdf/other/art1_mb201205en_pp79-94en.pdf.

Farhi, Emmanuel, and Jean Tirole. 2012. "Collective Moral Hazard, Maturity Mismatch, and Systemic Bailouts." *American Economic Review* 102(1): 60–93.

Fernández-Villaverde, Jesús, Luis Garicano, and Tano Santos. 2013. "Political Credit Cycles: The Case of the Eurozone." *Journal of Economic Perspectives* 27(3): 145–166.

Friedman, Milton. 1969. "The Optimum Quantity of Money." In *The Optimum Quantity of Money and Other Essays*, 1–50. Chicago: Aldine.

Friedman, Milton, and Anna J. Schwartz. 1963. *A Monetary History of the United States, 1867–1960*. Princeton, NJ: Princeton University Press.

Garicano, Luis. 2020. "Two Proposals to Resurrect the Banking Union: The Safe Portfolio Approach and SRB." CEPR Policy Insight no. 108. https://cepr.org/system/files/publication-files/103124-policy_insight_108_two_proposals_to_resurrect_the_banking_union_the_safe_portfolio_approach_and_srb_.pdf.

Garicano, Luis, Claire Lelarge, and John Van Reenen. 2016. "Firm Size Distortions and the Productivity Distribution: Evidence from France." *American Economic Review* 106(11): 3439–3479.

Gianviti, Francois, Jürgen von Hagen, Anne O Krueger, Jean Pisani-Ferry, and André Sapir. 2010. *A European Mechanism for Sovereign Debt Crisis Resolution: A Proposal*. Vol. 9. Brussels: Bruegel.

González-Páramo, José Manuel. 2011. "The ECB's Monetary Policy during the Crisis." Closing Speech at the Tenth Economic Policy Conference, Málaga, Spain. https://www.ecb.europa.eu/press/key/date/2011/html/sp111021_1.en.html.

Gopinath, Gita, Şebnem Kalemli-Özcan, Loukas Karabarbounis, and Carolina Villegas-Sanchez. 2017. "Capital Allocation and Productivity in South Europe." *Quarterly Journal of Economics* 132(4): 1915–1967.

Gorton, Gary, and Andrew Metrick. 2012. "Securitized Banking and the Run on Repo." *Journal of Financial Economics* 104: 425–451.

Gros, Daniel, and Thomas Mayer. 2012. "Liquidity in Times of Crisis: Even the ESM Needs It." CEPS Policy Brief No. 265. https://www.ceps.eu/ceps-publications/liquidity-times-crisis-even-esm-needs-it/.

Guiso, Luigi, Paola Sapienza, and Luigi Zingales. 2016. "Monnet's Error?" *Economic Policy* 31(86): 247–297. https://doi.org/10.1093/epolic/eiw003.

Hall, George, and Thomas J. Sargent. 2014. "Fiscal Discrimination in Three Wars." *Journal of Monetary Economics* 61: 148–166.

Hall, George J., and Thomas J. Sargent. 2021. "Debt and Taxes in Eight US Wars and Two Insurrections." In *The Handbook of Historical Economics*, edited by Alberto Bisin and Giovanni Federico, 825–880. San Diego, CA: Academic Press.

Hall, George J., and Thomas J. Sargent. 2022. "Three World Wars: Fiscal–Monetary Consequences." *Proceedings of the National Academy of Sciences* 119: 1–12. https://doi.org/10.1073/pnas.2200349119.

Hall, Robert E., and Marianna Kudlyak. 2024. "Unemployment and Inflation Dynamics in the Monetary Policy Armamentarium." Hoover Institution Economics Working Paper 24105. https://www.hoover.org/sites/default/files/research/docs/24105-Hall-Kudlyak.pdf.

Hardouvelis, Gikas A., and Dimitri Vayanos. 2023. *The Greek Economic Crisis and the Banks*. London: Hellenic Observatory, London School of Economics and Political Science.

Hilscher, Jens, Alon Raviv, and Ricardo Reis. 2024. "How Likely Is an Inflation Disaster?" CEPR Discussion Paper No. DP17224.

Holmstrom, Bengt. 1982. "Moral Hazard in Teams." *Bell Journal of Economics* 133(2): 324–340.

International Monetary Fund. 2010. "Ireland: Request for an Extended Arrangement-Staff Report." IMF Country Report No. 10/366. https://www.imf.org/external/pubs/ft/scr/2010/cr10366.pdf.

———. 2013. "Greece: Ex-Post Evaluation of Exceptional Access under the 2010 Stand-By Arrangement." IMF Country Report No. 13/156. https://www.imf.org/external/pubs/ft/scr/2013/cr13156.pdf.

———. 2014a. *Cyprus: Staff Report for the 2014 Article IV Consultation*. October 22, 2014. https://www.imf.org/en/Publications/CR/Issues/2016/12/31/Cyprus-Staff-Report-for-the-2014-Article-IV-Consultation-42406.

———. 2014b. "Spain: Financial Sector Reform—Final Progress Report." IMF Country Report No. 14/59. https://www.imf.org/external/pubs/ft/scr/2014/cr1459.pdf.

———. 2017. "Greece—Ex-Post Evaluation of Exceptional Access under the 2012 Extended Arrangement." IMF Country Report No. 17/44. https://www.imf.org/en/Publications/CR/Issues/2017/02/07/Greece-Ex-Post-Evaluation-of-Exceptional-Access-Under-the-2012-Extended-Arrangement-Press-44636.

Issing, Otmar. 2015. "Completing the Unfinished House: Towards a Genuine Economic and Monetary Union?" CFS Working Paper Series No. 521. https://gfk-cfs.de/media/CFS_WP_521.pdf.

———. 2022. "A Sword of Damocles Hangs over Monetary Union." *The International Economy* 36(3): 58–63.

Jiang, Erica Xuewei, Gregor Matvos, Tomasz Piskorski, and Amit Seru. 2020. "Which Banks Are (Over) Levered? Insights from Shadow Banks and Uninsured Leverage." SSRN Working Paper 3584191. http://dx.doi.org/10.2139/ssrn.3584191.

Kapp, Daniel. 2012. "The Optimal Size of the European Stability Mechanism: A Cost-Benefit Analysis." De Nederlandsche Bank Working Paper No. 349. https://www.dnb.nl/en/publications/research-publications/working-paper-2012/349-the-optimal-size-of-the-european-stability-mechanism-a-cost-benefit-analysis/.

Kehoe, Timothy J., and Juan Pablo Nicolini. 2021. *A Monetary and Fiscal History of Latin America, 1960–2017*. Minneapolis: University of Minnesota Press. https://manifold.bfi.uchicago.edu/projects/monetary-fiscal-history-latin-america-1960-2017.

Kydland, Finn E., and Edward C. Prescott. 1977. "Rules Rather than Discretion: The Inconsistency of Optimal Plans." *Journal of Political Economy* 85(3): 473–491.

Lane, Philip R. 2021. "The Resilience of the Euro." *Journal of Economic Perspectives* 35(2): 3–22. https://www.aeaweb.org/articles?id=10.1257/jep.35.2.3.

Lastra, Rosa María. 2015. *International Financial and Monetary Law*. Oxford: Oxford University Press.

Leeper, Eric M. 1991. "Equilibria under 'Active' and 'Passive' Monetary and Fiscal Policies." *Journal of Monetary Economics* 27(1): 129–147.

Levy, Mickey D. 2024. "The Fed: Bad Forecasts and Misguided Monetary Policy." In *Getting Monetary Policy Back on Track*, edited by Michael D. Bordo, John H. Cochrane, and John Taylor, 261–290. Stanford, CA: Hoover Institution Press.

Lienemeyer, Max, Clemens Kerle, and Helena Malikova. 2014. "The New State Aid Banking Communication: The Beginning of the Bail-in-Era Will Ensure a Level Playing Field of Enhanced Burden-Sharing." *European State Aid Law Quarterly* 13(2): 277–288.

Lucas, Robert E., and Nancy L. Stokey. 1983. "Optimal Fiscal and Monetary Policy in an Economy without Capital." *Journal of Monetary Economics* 12(1): 55–93.

Maragopoulos, Nikos. 2021. "Removing the Regulatory Barriers to Cross-Border Banking." European Banking Institute Working Paper Series No. 85. https://papers.ssrn.com/sol3/papers.cfm?abstract_id=3792857.

Masuch, Klaus, Robert Anderton, Ralph Setzer, and Nicholai Benalal. 2018. "Structural Policies in the Euro Area." ECB Occasional Paper No. 210. https://www.ecb.europa.eu/pub/pdf/scpops/ecb.op210.en.pdf?3db9355b1d1599799aa0e475e5624651.

Masuch, Klaus, Wolfgang Modery, Ralph Setzer, and Nico Zorell. 2023. "The Euro Area Needs Better Structural Policies to Support Income, Employment and Fairness." *ECB Blog*, October 11. https://www.ecb.europa.eu/press/blog/date/2023/html/ecb.blog231011~b743839ce4.en.html.

Masuch, Klaus, Edmund Moshammer, and Beatrice Pierluigi. 2017. "Institutions, Public Debt and Growth in Europe." *Public Sector Economics* 41(2): 159–205.

McQuinn, Kieran, and Maria Woods 2012. "Modelling the Corporate Deposits of Irish Financial Institutions: 2009–2010." *Central Bank of Ireland Research Technical Papers* 2: 1–26.

Mody, Ashoka. 2018. *EuroTragedy: A Drama in Nine Acts*. Oxford: Oxford University Press.

Morris, Richard, Hedwig Ongena, and Ludger Schuknecht. 2006. "The Reform and Implementation of the Stability and Growth Pact." ECB Occasional Paper No. 47. https://www.ecb.europa.eu/pub/pdf/scpops/ecbocp47.pdf.

Peltzman, Sam. 1975. "The Effects of Automobile Safety Regulation." *Journal of Political Economy* 83(4): 677–725.

Persson, Torstenn, and Guido Tabellini. 1993. "Designing Institutions for Monetary Stability." *Carnegie-Rochester Conference Series on Public Policy* 39: 53–84.

Redeker, Nils. 2022. "Wielding the Big Gun—What the ECB's New Bond Purchasing Program Means for EU Governance." Hertie School Policy Brief. https://www.delorscentre.eu/en/publications/detail/publication/transmission-protection-instrument.

Reis, Ricardo. 2013. "The Portuguese Slump and Crash and the Euro Crisis." *Brookings Papers on Economic Activity*, Spring, 143–210. https://www.brookings.edu/wp-content/uploads/2016/07/2013a_reis.pdf.

Rochet, Jean-Charles, and Xavier Vives. 2004. "Coordination Failures and the Lender of Last Resort: Was Bagehot Right After All?" *Journal of the European Economic Association* 2(6): 1116–1147.

Rogoff, Kenneth. 1985. "The Optimal Degree of Commitment to an Intermediate Monetary Target." *Quarterly Journal of Economics* 100(4): 1169–1189.

Rostagno, Massimo, Carlo Altavilla, Giacomo Carboni, Wolfgang Lemke, Roberto Motto, Arthur Saint Guilhem, and Jonathan Yiangou. 2021. *Monetary Policy in Times of Crisis: A Tale of Two Decades of the European Central Bank*. Oxford: Oxford University Press.

Runkel, Corey. 2022a. "European Central Bank: Fine-Tuning Operations." *Journal of Financial Crises* 4(3): 787–816.

———. 2022b. "European Central Bank: Term Refinancing Operations." *Journal of Financial Crises* 4(3): 817–843.

Sargent, Thomas J. 2012. "Nobel Lecture: United States Then, Europe Now." *Journal of Political Economy* 120(1): 1–40.

Sargent, Thomas J., and François R. Velde. 1995. "Macroeconomic Features of the French Revolution." *Journal of Political Economy* 103(3): 474–518.

Sargent, Thomas J., and Neil Wallace. 1981. "Some Unpleasant Monetarist Arithmetic." *Federal Reserve Bank of Minneapolis Quarterly Review* 5(3): 1–17.

Schmidt, Sebastian. 2024 "Monetary–Fiscal Policy Interactions When Price Stability Occasionally Takes a Back Seat." ECB Working Paper No. 2889. https://doi.org/10.2866/71347.

Schmitt-Grohé, Stephanie, and Martín Uribe. 2004. "Optimal Fiscal and Monetary Policy under Sticky Prices." *Journal of Economic Theory* 114: 198–230.

Schmitz, Martin, and Marcel Tirpák. 2017. "Cross-Border Banking in the Euro Area since the Crisis: What Is Driving the Great Retrenchment?" *Special Features B, Financial Stability Review*, November.

Schnabel, Isabel. 2023. "Quantitative Tightening: Rationale and Market Impact." Speech by Isabel Schnabel, Member of the Executive Board of the ECB, at the Money Market Contact Group Meeting. https://www.ecb.europa.eu/press/key/date/2023/html/ecb.sp230302~41273ad467.en.html.

Schuberth, Helene. 2024. "The European Union's New Risk-Based Framework for Fiscal Rules—Overly Complex, Opaque and Self-Defeating." *Institute for New Economic Thinking Blog*. https://www.ineteconomics.org/perspectives/blog/fiscal-reform-in-the-eu-a-dangerous-new-framework#.

Sims, Christopher A. 1994. "A Simple Model for Study of the Determination of the Price Level and the Interaction of Monetary and Fiscal Policy." *Economic Theory* 4: 381–399.

———. 1997. "Fiscal Foundations of Price Stability in Open Economies." SSNR Working Paper No. 75357. http://dx.doi.org/10.2139/ssrn.75357.

———. 1999. "The Precarious Fiscal Foundations of EMU." *De Economist* 147: 415–436. https://link.springer.com/article/10.1023/A:1003819626903.

Sinn, Hans-Werner. 2014. *The Euro Trap: On Bursting Bubbles, Budgets, and Beliefs*. Oxford: Oxford University Press.

———. 2018. "The ECB's Fiscal Policy." *International Tax and Public Finance* 25: 1404–1433. https://doi.org/10.1007/s10797-018-9501-8.

Smets, Frank, and Raf Wouters. 2024. "Fiscal Backing, Inflation and US Business Cycles." Preliminary manuscript. https://www.frbsf.org/wp-content/uploads/01-Smets_Fiscal-Backing-rv.pdf.

Tabellini, Guido. 2018. "Risk Sharing and Market Discipline: Finding the Right Mix." VoxEU, July 16. https://cepr.org/voxeu/columns/risk-sharing-and-market-discipline-finding-right-mix.

Tooze, Adam. 2018. *Crashed: How a Decade of Financial Crises Changed the World*. New York: Penguin.

Trichet, Jean-Claude, 2010. "Central Banking in Uncertain Times: Conviction and Responsibility." Speech by Jean-Claude Trichet, President of the ECB, Jackson Hole, Wyoming, August 27. https://www.ecb.europa.eu/press/key/date/2010/html/sp100827.en.html.

Véron, Nicolas. 2017. *Sovereign Concentration Charges: A New Regime for Banks' Sovereign Exposures*. Brussels: European Parliament.

Walsh, Carl E. 1995. "Optimal Contracts for Central Bankers." *American Economic Review* 85(1): 150–167.

Whelan, Karl. 2012. "ELA, Promissory Notes and All That: The Fiscal Costs of Anglo Irish Bank." *Economic and Social Review* 43(4): 653–673.

Woodford, Michael. 1994. "Monetary Policy and Price Level Determinacy in a Cash-in-Advance Economy." *Economic Theory* 4: 345–380.

———. 2003. *Interest and Prices*. Princeton, NJ: Princeton University Press.

Xanthoulis, Napoleon. 2019. "Single Resolution Fund and Emergency Liquidity Assistance: Status Quo and Reform Perspectives on Emergency Financial Support in the Banking Union." In *The European Banking Union and the Role of Law*, edited by Gianni Lo Schiavo, 273–294. Cheltenham, UK: Edward Elgar.

Zettelmeyer, Jeromin, Christoph Trebesch, and Mitu Gulati. 2014. "The Greek Debt Restructuring: An Autopsy." *Economic Policy* 28(75): 513–563. https://doi.org/10.1111/1468-0327.12014.

INDEX

Note: Page numbers in *italics* indicate tables and figures.

adjustment programs. *See* EU/IMF adjustment programs

Asset Purchase Programs (APP), 76, 152; pandemic response in, 160; Quantitative Easing and, 152; rising inflation and, 173, 176

asset purchases by a central bank, 37; in global financial crisis, 48; threat of systemic runs and, 47

asset purchases by ECB, 20–21; expected future purchases, 21; implying transfers between countries, 21; inflation and, 21–23, 151–154; in proportion to sizes of member states, 24; sharing losses in any restructuring, 26; sterilized, 24, 135–136; through two types of programs, 23–25. *See also* Quantitative Easing (QE)

asset sales by ECB, 21–22, 23

Bagehot's rules, 48, 213

balance of payments, 84–91, 239–243; country fundamentals and, 85–86; cross-border credit flows and, 86–91; ECB's large role in financing, 241–243; ECB's large-scale loans to banks and, 105; ECB's loans to Greek banks and, 110; without nominal devaluation, 84–85

balance sheet of ECB, 73, 75, 75–78, 76, 232–239; interest rate policy and, 27–28; protecting the value of, 26–27; securities purchases behind rise in, 75, 76; small from 1999 through 2008, 2

balance sheet of Eurosystem, consolidated, 73, 74; declining from 2012 to 2014, 5; default risks of member states in, 12; increase by 2023 in securities held, 7

balance sheet of U.S. Federal Reserve, 77

bank failures: ECB interventions based on fear of, 25; in United States, 44, 231; unthinkable at the founding, 91–92

banking crises, 20; cycle of, 42–43; global financial crisis and, 99–102; sovereign debt crisis and, 105; summary of current situation, 49

banking regulation: abject failure of, 118; crisis support and, 48; cycle of risk and, 42–43; in design of Economic and Monetary Union, 54; historically a task of central banks, 42; ignoring possibility of sovereign default, 98; national, 78, 101–102; slowly moving to greater equity, 45, 49; sovereign risk and, 11; threat of systemic runs and, 47

banking union, 149–150; stalled, 226–232

bank reform, 12–13; as global problem, 231–232; incomplete banking union and, 149–150; issuing equity and long-term debt, 43. *See also* sovereign-bank nexus

bank runs, 43–45; on repurchase agreements in 2008, 45; sovereign debt crisis and, 106; uninsured deposits in United States and, 44, 231. *See also* systemic bank runs

banks: endangered under 2012 Long-Term Refinancing, 138–139; equity as risk buffer for, 44–45, 47–48, 49; exposed to Greek debt, 117; increased borrowing from ECB, 4; international, 150, 227–228; recapitalization of, 44, 48; sovereign debt holdings of, 11; sovereign exposures of, 229–230, 230; vicious circle between

301